The Wonders of Daily Drawing

The Wonders of Daily Drawing, 1st Edition

 Published by GoArchitect, LLC, Loma Linda, California

GoArchitect titles may be purchased in bulk for education, business, fund-raising, or sales promotional use. For more information, email sales@GoArchitect.com

HARDCOVER ISBN: 978-1-7329451-9-7
SOFTCOVER ISBN: 978-1-7352590-0-0
E-BOOK ISBN: 978-1-7352590-1-7

For more information visit GoArchitect.com

Contents

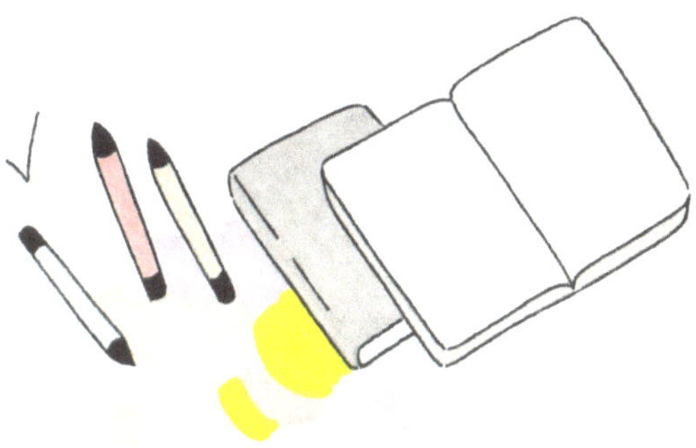

Introduction

Hello, I'm Julia and I have drawn every day for three years. Each day I capture my life in a Drawing Journal. This practice has made my daily routine much more interesting and colorful. In The Wonders of Daily Drawing I will tell you about this experience and show you how to keep your own Drawing Journal.

A Drawing Journal is about inspiration hidden in the beauty of our environment. It's a personal diary where you capture your impressions by drawing, writing, and other visual mediums.

A Drawing Journal helps bring inspiration to your daily routine, develop drawing skills, and increase mindfulness. It also helps to capture important moments and remember them for a long time. The process of drawing gives the opportunity to relax and meditate; a place away from all troubles and routine.

This guide is created for people who feel a lack of creativity and want to add a piece of art to their daily life.

It doesn't matter what level of experience in drawing you have, if you desire to create. With some practice and attention anyone can capture the beauty of a day.

With its many benefits, keeping a Drawing Journal can still be quite challenging. I've created exercises and step-by-step instructions in this book so you can develop daily drawing habits and learn to overcome roadblocks that might appear on your way.

My Drawing Journal has grown from a one-time impression of one day into a significant project that, in turn, has led to a positive life change. I hope that with the help of this book you will also foster your own daily drawing practice with newfound joy and appreciation for each day.

CHAPTER I

Where it all began

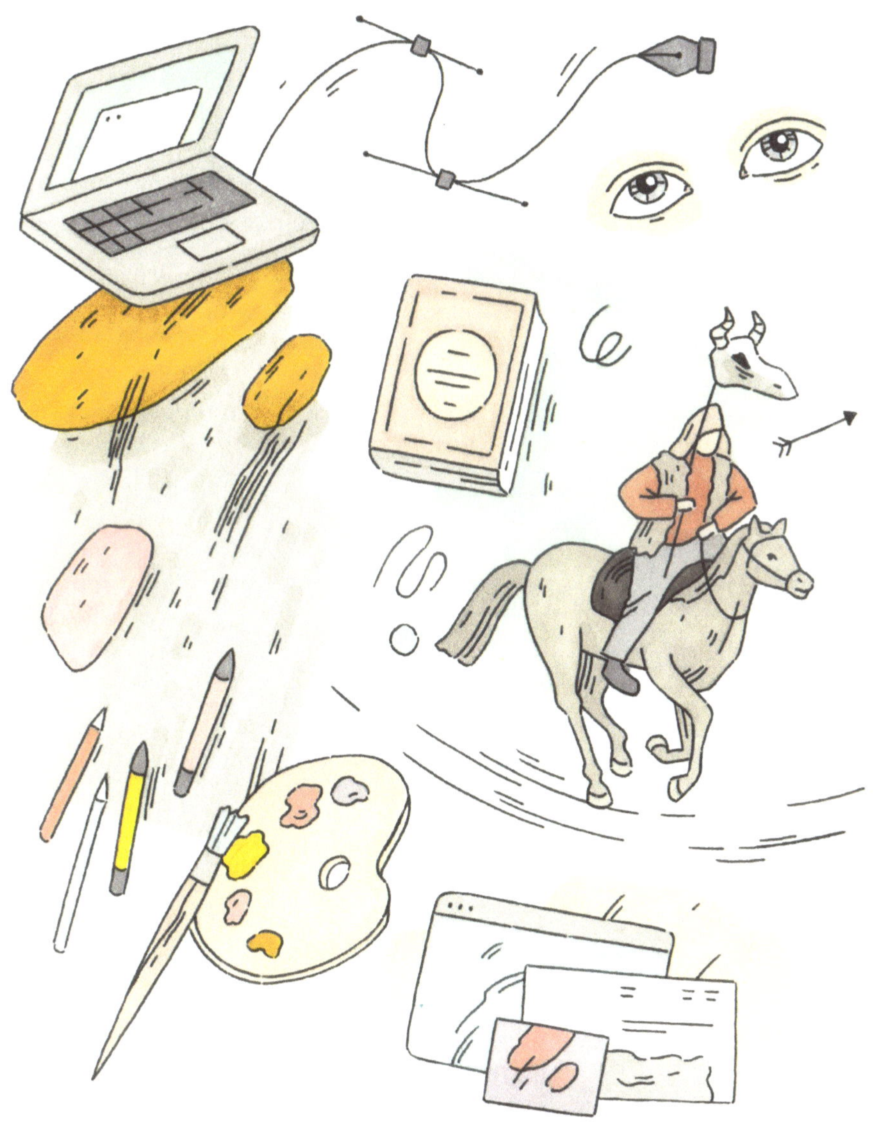

I have been drawing since childhood and have always been looking for new ways to create. For a long time I explored different techniques and tried diverse art directions. I could make an acrylic painting on canvas and on the next day cut elements from a magazine to make a collage.

Later I learned to use computer programs and started creating digital art. Eventually, I became a web designer and illustrator, where I have the opportunity to create alot of visual content — illustrations, websites, landing pages, and articles.

Through all of this, however interesting and beautiful digital art could be, drawing offline, using paper and different physical mediums always outweighed my desire to draw digitally.

For a few years, my sketchbooks had only random doodles and sketches. I started my Drawing Journal by accident and eventually it transformed into one of the biggest projects of my life.

The idea to draw my life every day came to me suddenly. I was reading The History of the Russian State by Boris Akunin when I noticed that besides interesting narration and facts, there were illustrations of ancient tribes. I was especially fascinated by the illustration of Huns riding horses to conquer all who came in their way.

Later that night I couldn't fall asleep, my mind kept running through all the things I had learned. In a spurt of creativity, I decided I wanted to illustrate my memories from the day. I sprang out of bed and in the middle of the night started drawing what I had seen in my sketchbook.

This simple event was the starting point of my journey. I went from one day to two and before I knew it, I was hooked. It was hard to understand why I hadn't started it earlier.

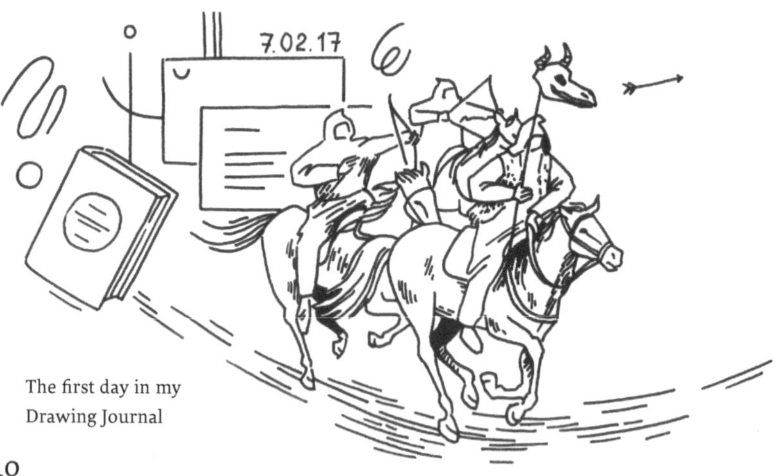

The first day in my Drawing Journal

After just a few days, I began to notice unexpectedly inspiring things in my daily routine. With time, each captured day grew and took up more space because it became easier for me to fill the page with interesting moments.

For example, I noticed how beautiful marble patterns in the Moscow subway are; they are abstract masterpieces with perfect composition and coloring. I even noticed how intricate and dynamic freshly boiled pasta is when you pull it from a pan and put it on a plate.

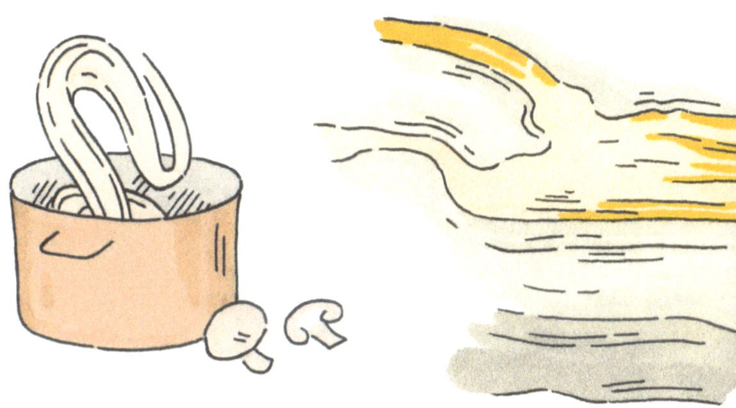

Look at everything from a different perspective, searching to see interesting and captivating things opens new possibilities.

Before long I had decided that I want to continue my Drawing Journal for at least one year. I was enjoying this process so much that without any hesitations I continued to keep my Drawing Journal and I've been doing it ever since.

CHAPTER II

What a Drawing Journal will bring into your life

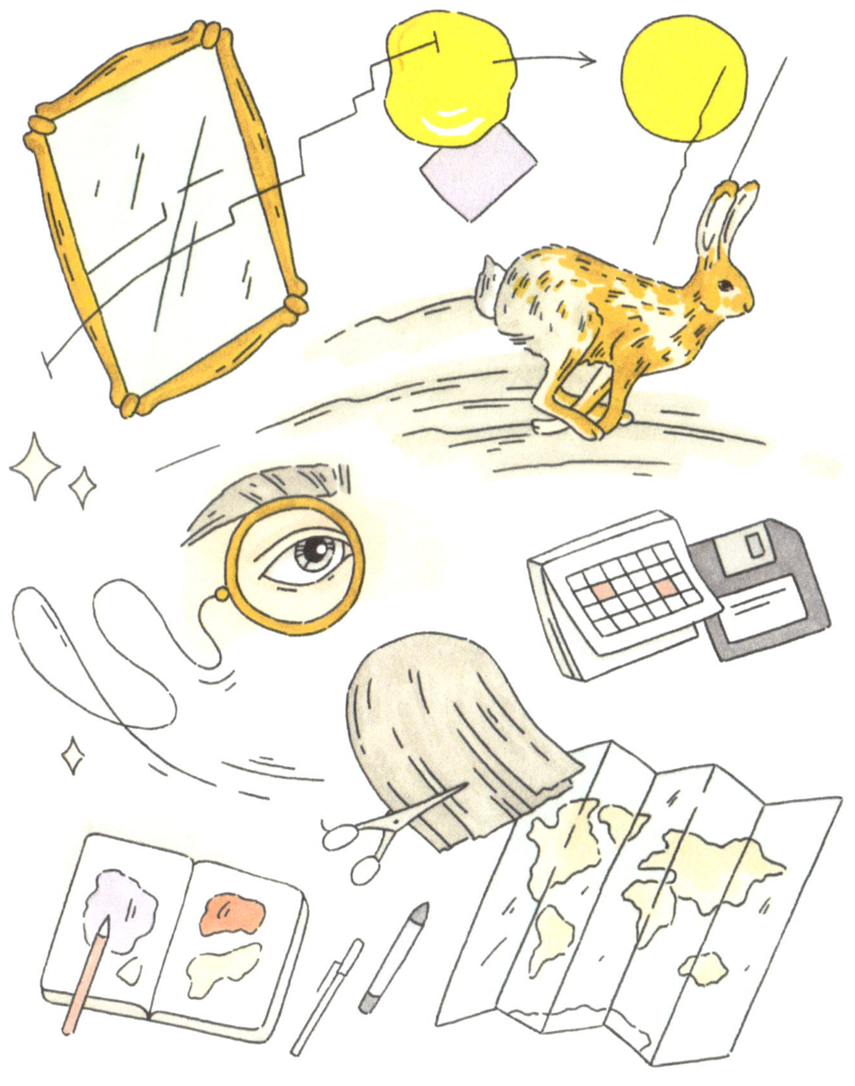

When my project started I could not imagine where it would take me. Over time, I realized how it changed my life and helped me grow emotionally, mentally and professionally.

You reflect on your life

Thinking about moments to draw and reflecting on past days helps you to better understand your accomplishments, successes and failures. You see your life from a distance and it becomes easier to spot areas for improvement. Whatever good or bad times you have, it is important to remember them. Eventually, it helps you grow, especially when you manage to deal with your problems.

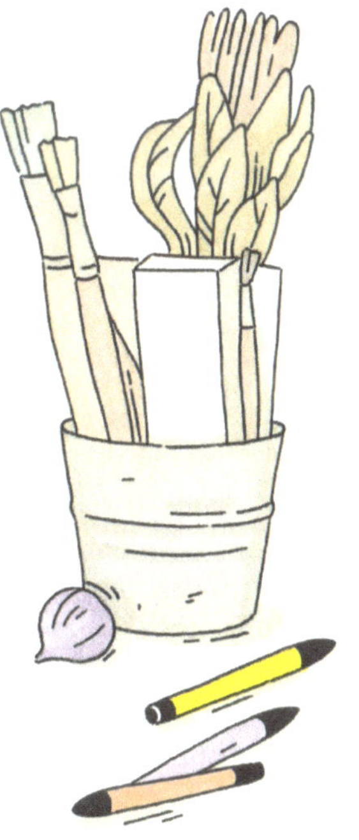

You draw better and faster

This one is easy. The longer you practice something – the better you become at it. In the beginning, it's hard to even imagine what you will be able to do.

When I look at the first few months of my Drawing Journal, I see how my skills have improved during this project.

- Drawing compositions become more balanced and the relationships between objects in a drawing become more understandable.
- Lines become better – circles become more circular, straight lines become straighter.
- Mistakes happen less often as drawings become neater.
- Imagination develops which helps to illustrate ideas and create metaphors.
- Memory becomes sharper– it's easier to remember how an object looked and capture it in a drawing.
- Your individual drawing style develops and becomes clearer.
- Drawing speed grows dramatically.

February 2017. The first days of my Drawing Journal

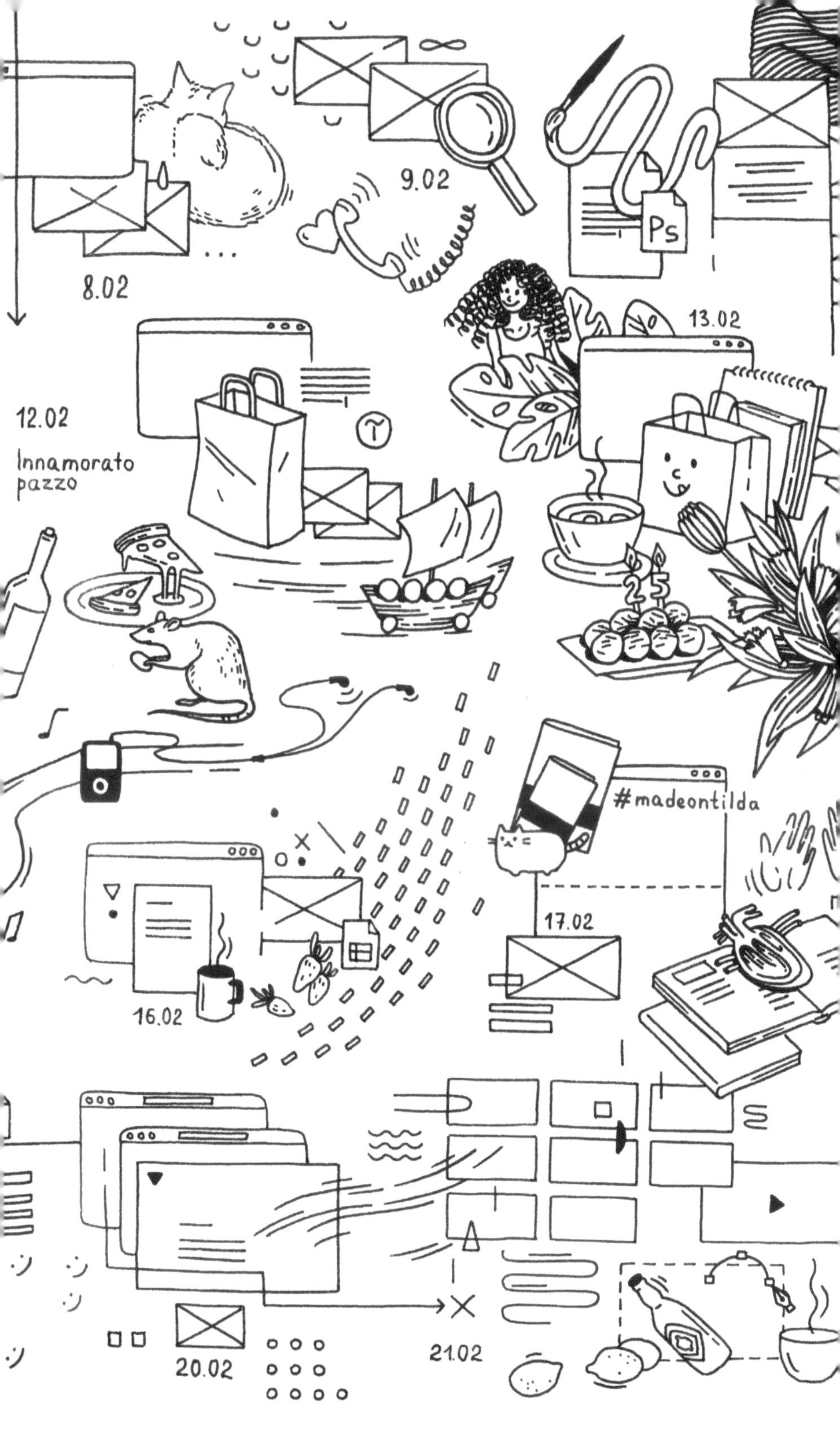
8.02
9.02
Ps
13.02
12.02
Innamorato
pazzo
25
#madeontilda
16.02
17.02
20.02
21.02

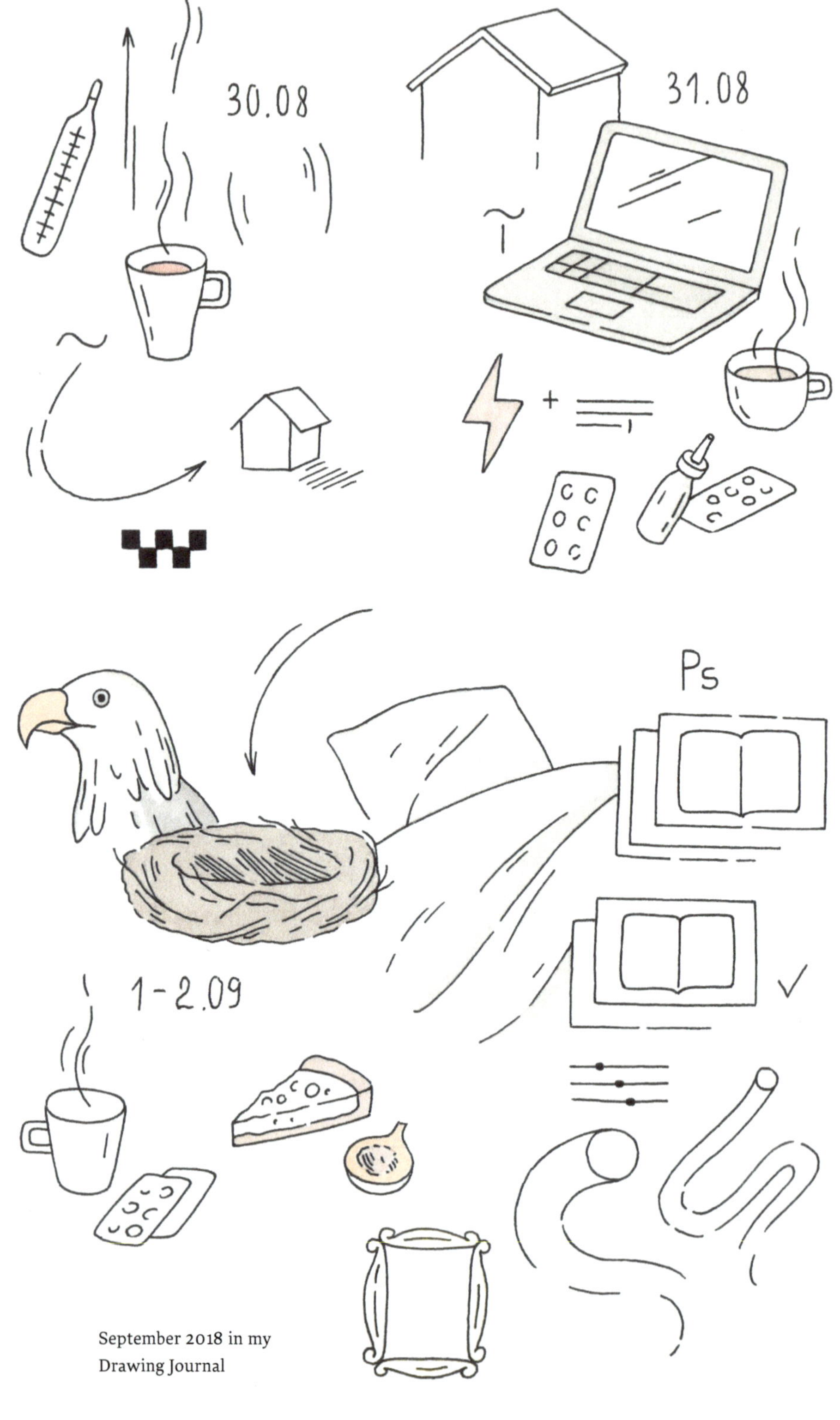

September 2018 in my Drawing Journal

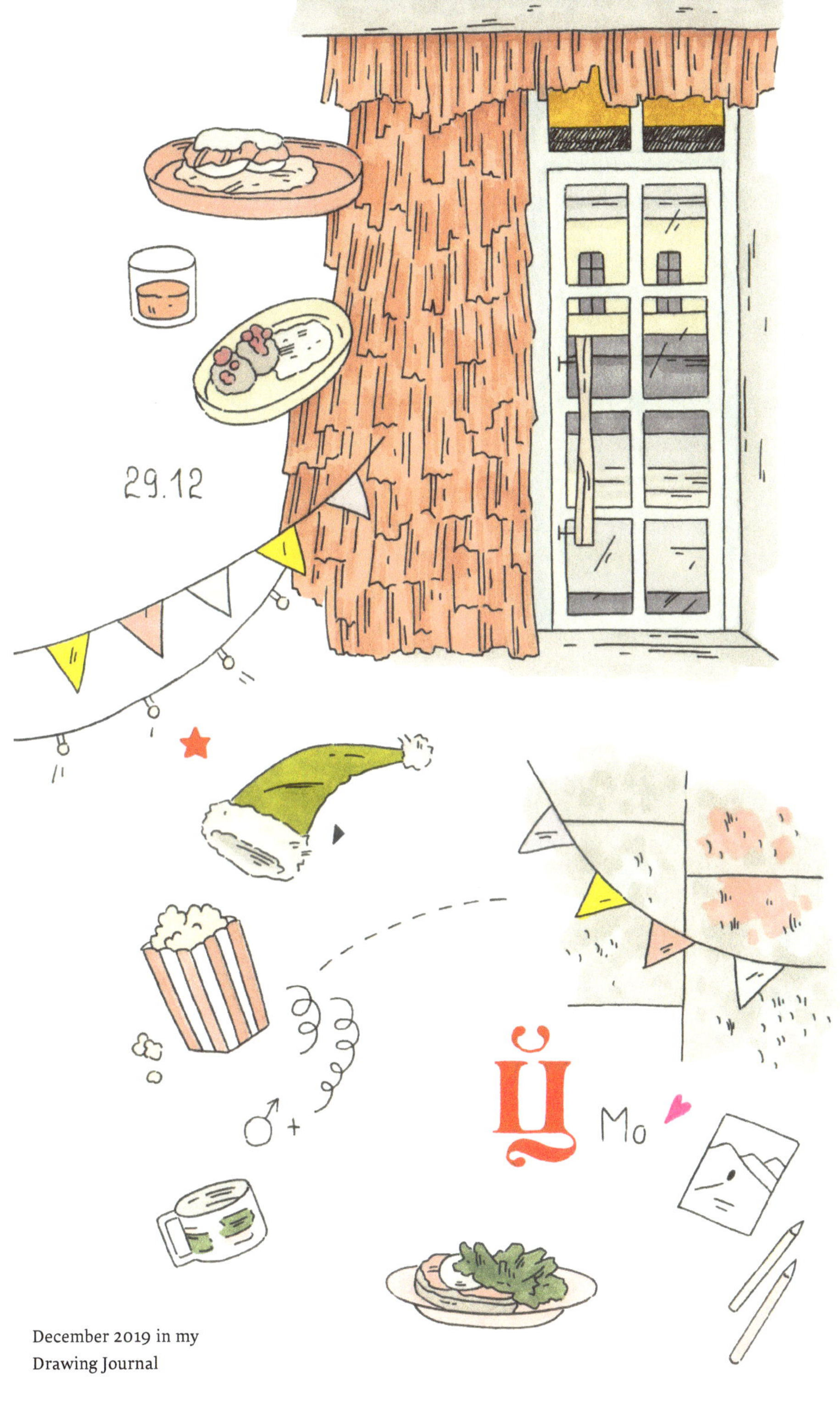

December 2019 in my
Drawing Journal

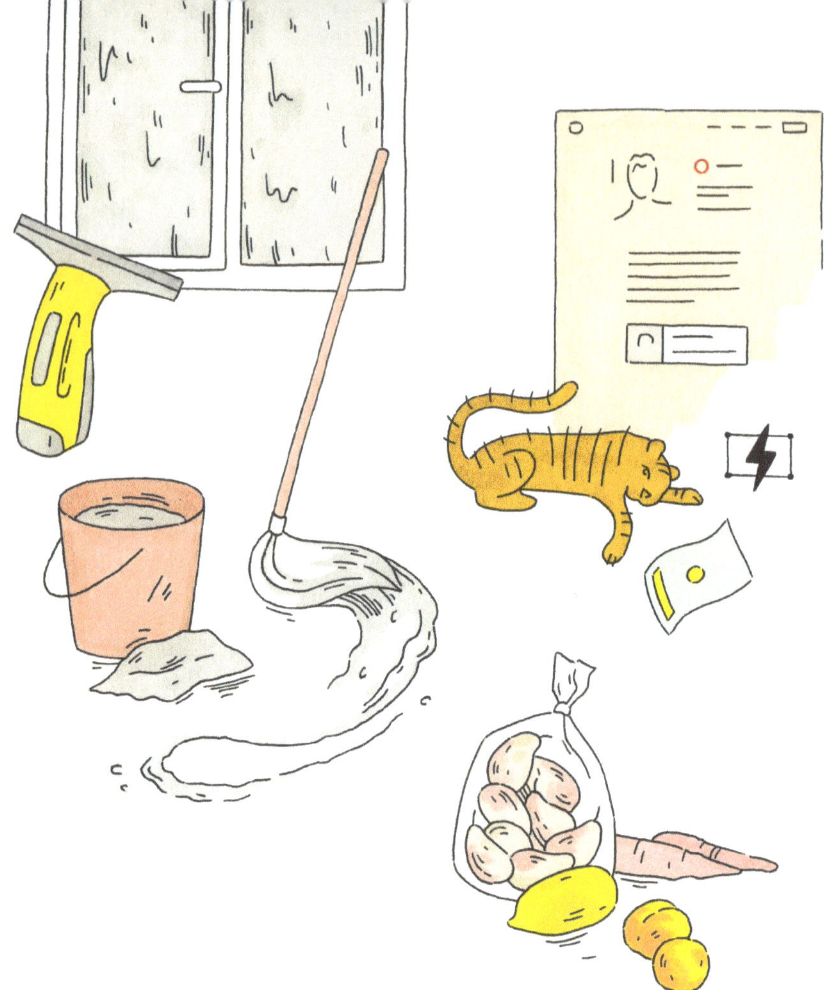

You start to find interesting things in your daily routine

The necessity to fill the space on a page develops your intuition to notice beautiful and interesting things in your routine. At first, it will be hard and unusual to seek out originality in your well-worn environment, but once you learn to do it, there is an endless world of inspiration and beauty.

You remember every day of your life

This one I love the most. Usually, we tend to remember only significant events of our lives. Meanwhile, small moments that happened between our regular routine tend to disappear from our memory. Each of these moments is unique and won't happen again, they are important too.

Drawn events work as vivid reminders for me. Once in a while I look back at old illustrations and they immediately trigger memories from that day. These memories spark beautiful details, which were hiding in my head.

Occasionally these memories can be practical too. For example, sometimes I check in my Drawing Journal when it's time to get a haircut or visit a dentist.

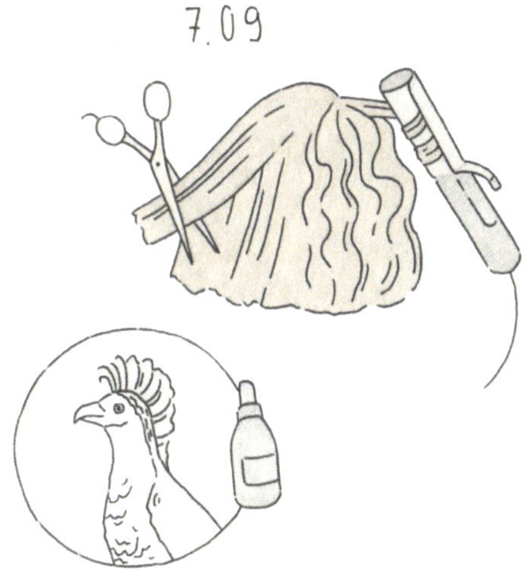

You will always have inspiration for drawing

It can be hard coming up with a plot for an illustration when you want to draw something badly but don't know what to choose. For me it was always a struggle, I was spending a significant part of my drawing time thinking about what to draw rather than drawing.

With Drawing Journal you don't need to spend a lot of time when you desire to draw. You can start creating at any moment because you already have memories and events from your day. It gives you the opportunity to create right away.

You will have a bit of art in your daily routine

Living an active life, especially in a big city can be pretty busy and non-creative. There is never enough time for personal development and drawing because you always have more important things to do. It is valuable to do important things that you like. And if you have a solid plan and challenge to draw every day, it will be easier for you to find time for it. Otherwise, you will always postpone your artistic plans.

There is one benefit that I discovered for myself but have kept to the end because I'm not sure it will work for everyone but I sincerely hope it will...

Your life will change significantly

Drawing Journal taught me to be curious, investigative, more active, and confident in my abilities. It motivated me to choose art and adventure instead of laziness. I started doing interesting things more often, so I could draw them in the evening.

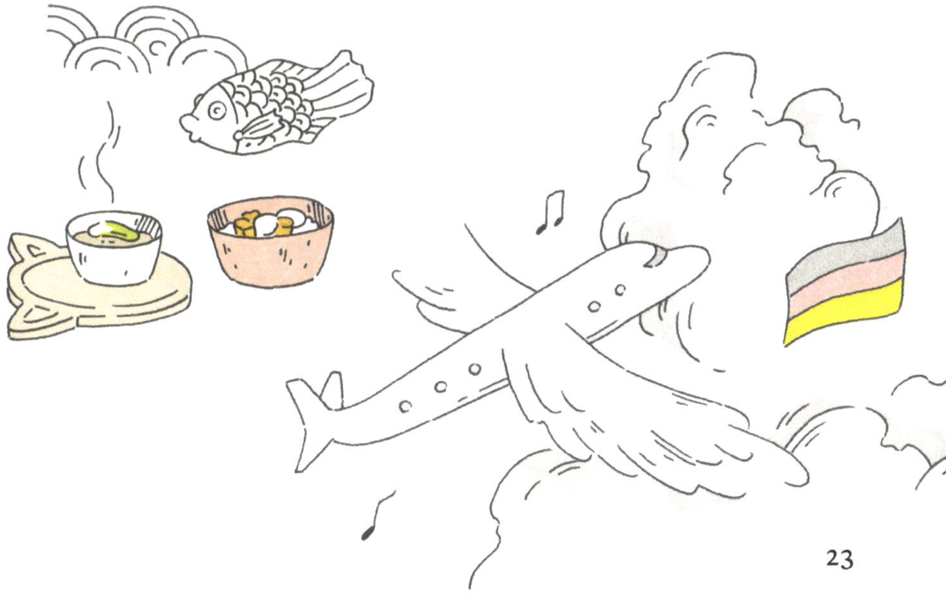

Before starting, I wouldn't travel alone, go out much, or think about self-development. Since then, I've noticed what opportunities I've ignored, bad habits I should work on, and things I need to appreciate more. I've had so many incredible memories and visited more events, new cities and countries than I ever had before.

Now I perceive the world differently and feel a constant desire to see something new or discover the hidden beauty in familiar moments and routines.

I hope that you are now inspired, motivated and ready to learn how to create your own Drawing Journal!

CHAPTER III

Choose the right materials

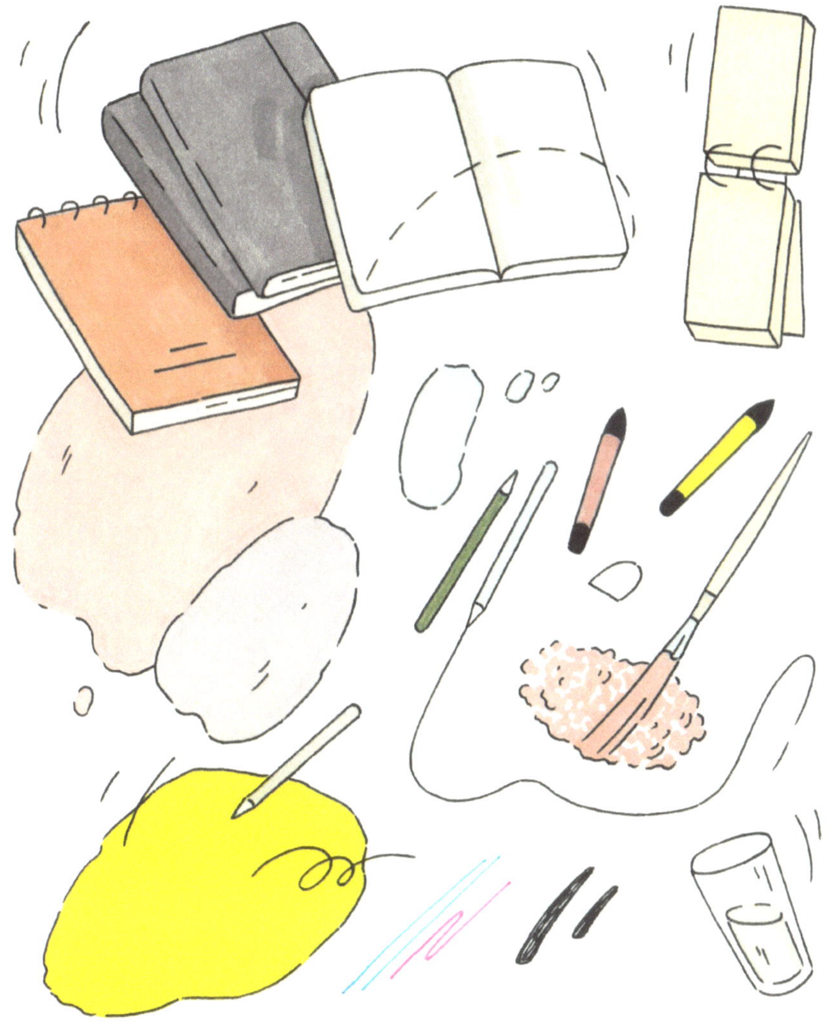

The right instruments are an important part of the daily drawing practice. They should be handy, compact and enjoyable. Don't put too much pressure on yourself if this is your first time starting a project like this. Start with simple and budget options until you feel comfortable. Once you feel that things are progressing nicely, you can always purchase more advanced materials if you want.

If you already have your favorite drawing instruments and can't wait to start your Drawing Journal, skip this Chapter and go to the Chapter IV.

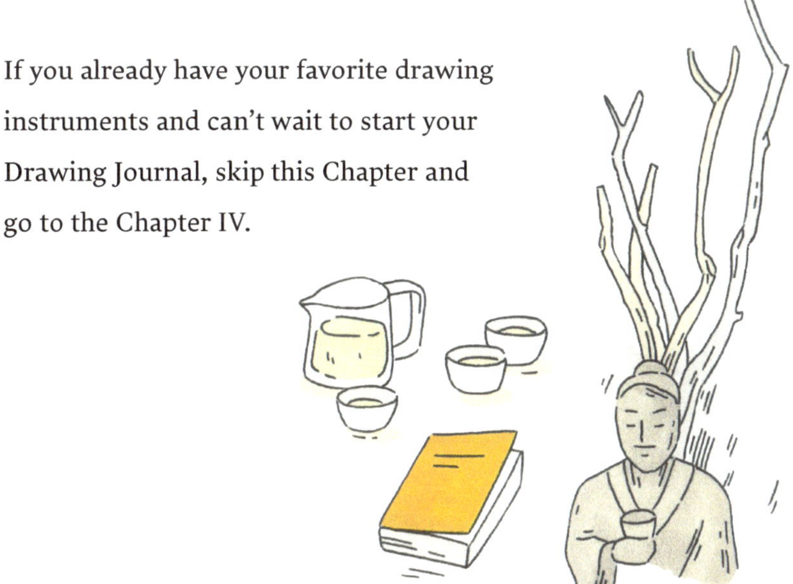

Sketchbook

A good sketchbook is an essential and most actively used instrument in this project, so it's important to choose the right one.

I use a Talens Art Creation Sketchbook with A5 size, hard black leatherette cover with an elastic band. The density of its paper is 140 g/m².

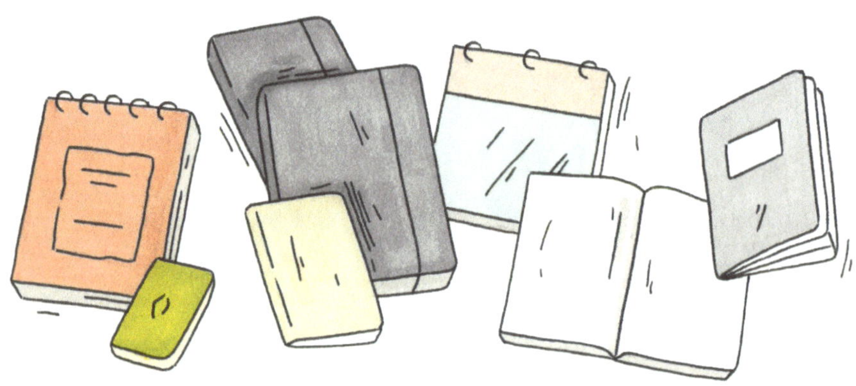

When choosing a sketchbook, keep a few things in mind:

Compact size. A sketchbook should be compact and easy to put in your regular bag or backpack. The easiest way to find your perfect sketchbook size is to go to an art shop, compare sketchbooks in stock and choose one in person.

I think that A5 format (the same as this book) is the most comfortable sketchbook size. It is big enough to draw a few days on each two-page spread and at the same time small enough to take it everywhere with you.

Hardcover. There won't always be a table to draw on. Sometimes you see something interesting on the street or subway and want to draw it right away. With hardcover, you can do it anywhere while standing. Hardcovers also stay stable much longer and protect your drawings better than soft covers.

Leatherette cover. Consider choosing a sketchbook in a cover made from a leatherette material which isn't afraid of dirt and is easy to clean. I suggest a dark color, or at least, not too light. Otherwise, it might get dirty pretty quickly since you will be using it every day.

Opens 180 degrees. The ability of an opened sketchbook to lay flat gives the opportunity to draw on two pages as a single area. It's also handy as there is no need to hold pages down while you're drawing.

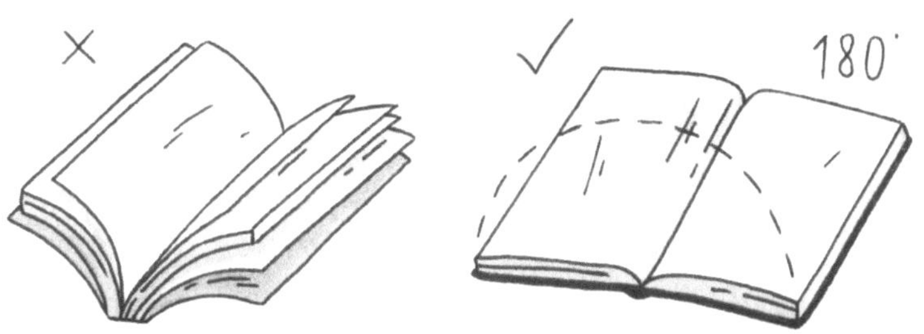

Dense paper. Select paper density according to the materials you will use. For drawing with graphite pencils or pens choose paper with a density of 80–100 g/m^2.

If you decide to draw with markers, select a paper with a density of no less than 130 g/m^2 otherwise it will bleed. If you want to use watercolor or watercolor pencils select a sketchbook with paper made for these mediums.

An elastic band or other type of sketchbook closer. Keeping a sketchbook tightly closed and safe during transportation prevents pages from creasing and getting dirty. It also helps to not lose scattered notes and objects collected for a collage.

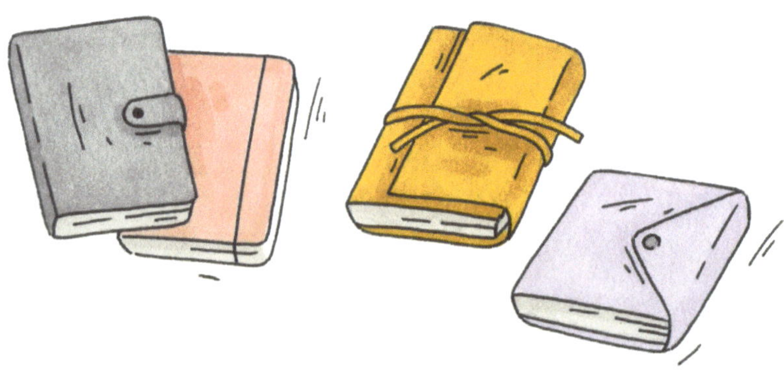

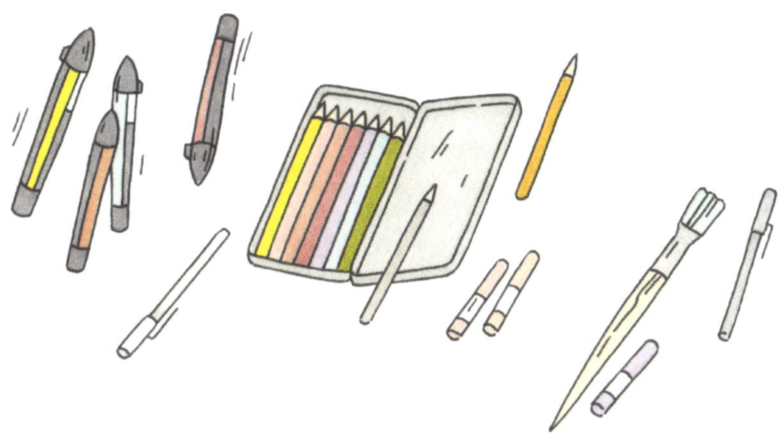

Drawing materials

The choice of drawing materials depends on your experience and preferences. While choosing instruments for drawing keep in mind these things:

- It shouldn't take a lot of time to use
- It should be easy to carry around on a daily basis
- It shouldn't require additional prep before or clean up afterward
- It shouldn't require time for drying

For the first year-and-a-half I drew with a Faber-Castell 3H graphite pencil and a Faber-Castell capillary pen for the lining. After a while, I wanted to make my drawings more clear and interesting, so I added color markers and replaced my capillary pen with a Muji Gel Ink Ballpoint pen. It made the composition more balanced and helped distinguish one object from another.

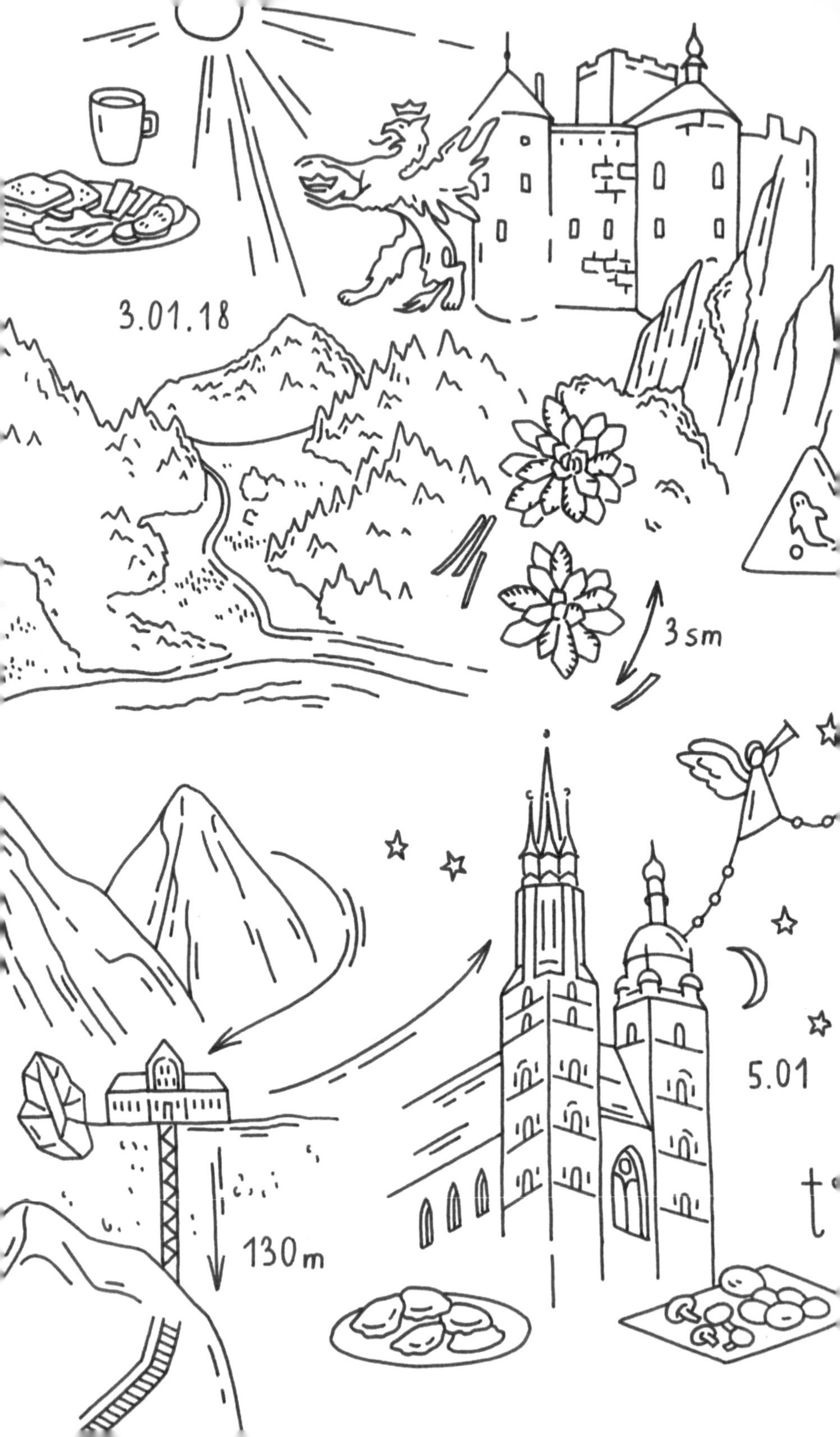
3.01.18
3 sm
130m
5.01

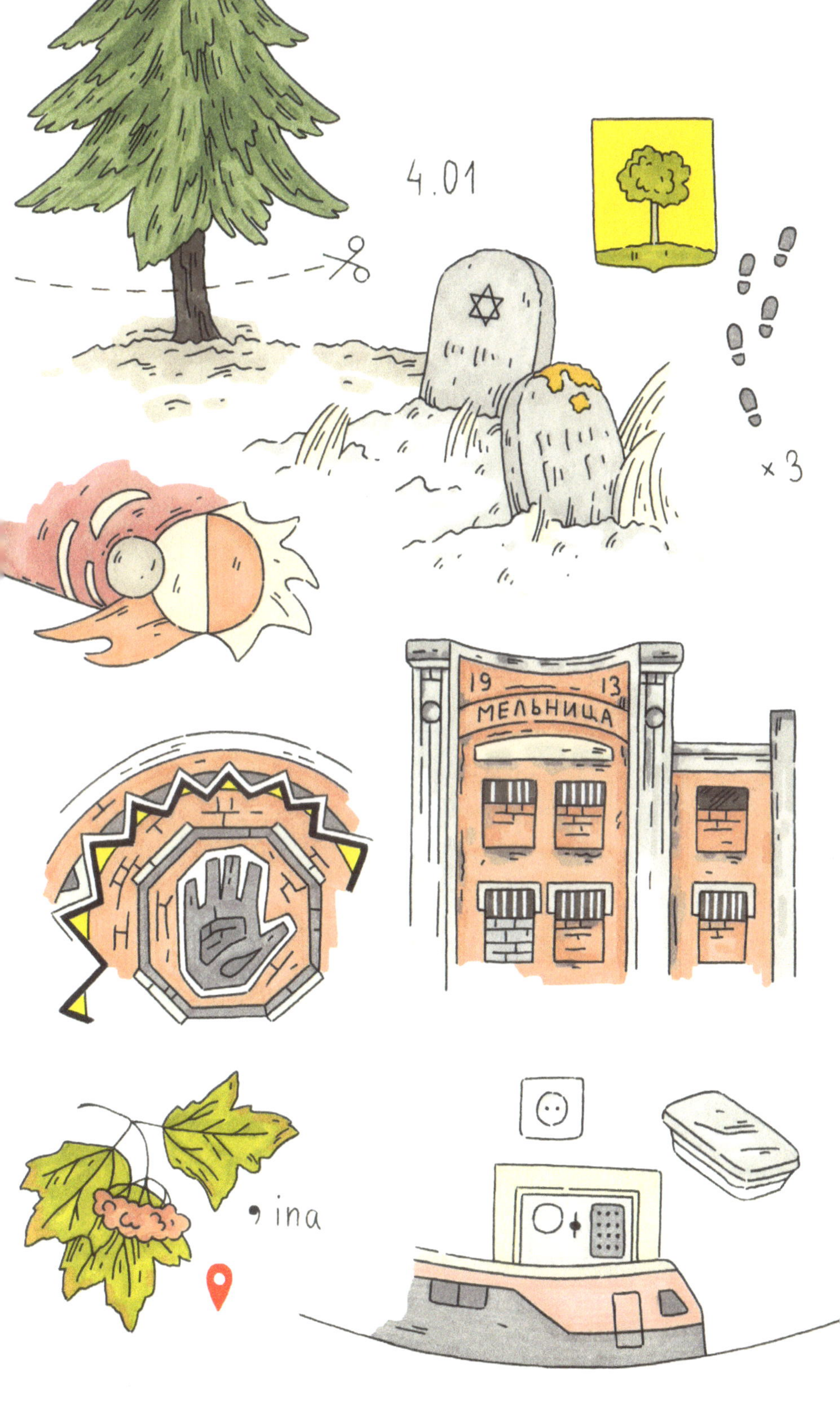
4.01
×3
19 13
МЕЛЬНИЦА
ina

Here are a few convenient instruments for Drawing Journal, which are quite easy to start with and use on a regular basis. They don't take a lot of time and don't require prep or clean up.

Graphite pencils

A pencil is indispensable in creating a drawing's skeleton if you aren't comfortable with drawing with indelible materials right away. For this purpose, it's better to use a pencil with a hardness in the range from HB to 3H. The exact choice of a pencil's hardness will depend on your preference and experience since 3H can seem too scratchy for some and HB too soft for others.

Every pencil is a part of the HB graphite grading scale which measures the hardness of the graphite core. The scale goes from hard to soft; 9H is the hardest and 9B is the softest. Grade B pencils have more graphite in their composition and leave a dark, saturated mark. These soft pencils can also be smudgy while grade H pencils have more clay in their composition. Hard pencils leave a light non-smudging mark and the hardest types can scratch paper.

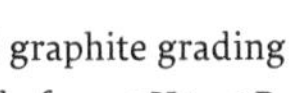

HB graphite grading
scale from 9H to 9B

I draw in a clean minimalistic style, so for me, 3H is perfect because it leaves a light (but visible enough) mark which isn't smudgy. If you want to create a free and "sketchy" style, choose softer pencils.

If you want to use pencils as your primary drawing instrument, use a few types with varying hardnesses. It will create contrast and add a dynamic look to your illustrations. For finding your perfect set of pencils, try a few combinations and look at how they work together. For example, you can use 3H for making a skeleton, HB for basic tone, and 3B for shading or visual emphasis.

Graphite pencils are an inexpensive medium. Consider buying a set with all the hardnesses and try them to find those which will be the most suitable for you.

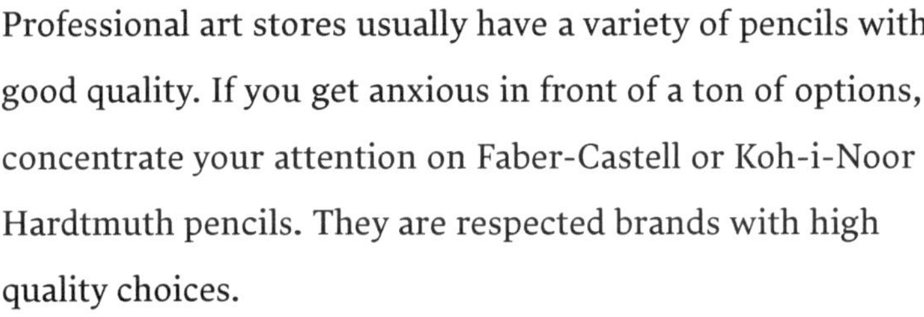

Professional art stores usually have a variety of pencils with good quality. If you get anxious in front of a ton of options, concentrate your attention on Faber-Castell or Koh-i-Noor Hardtmuth pencils. They are respected brands with high quality choices.

Pens

Using a pen in your Drawing journal helps to add definition and clarity to drawings. While there are plenty of pens on the market, I suggest using a felt-tip or gel pen.

If you would like to work with a pen but aren't confident with your drawing skills yet, try erasable pens. They are bright enough and comfortable to use. Muji has a good collection of erasable pens in different colors.

A felt-tip pen (also called a marker pen or a fineliner) makes uniform stable lines that dry fast and won't smudge when touched or erased over. There is a decent variety of line types from 0.1 mm to 2 mm.

They can come with different tips that replicate types of nibs such as a brush, which creates a line of different sizes depending on the pressure on the paper. It can be a calligraphy nib, which will make a different size of a line depending on the angle of a pen. There are also waterproof versions available if you want to combine it with watercolor or watercolor pencils.

I have tried Faber-Castell and Sakura Pigma Micron felt-tip pens. They have various line sizes, good uniform colors and can be used for quite a long time.

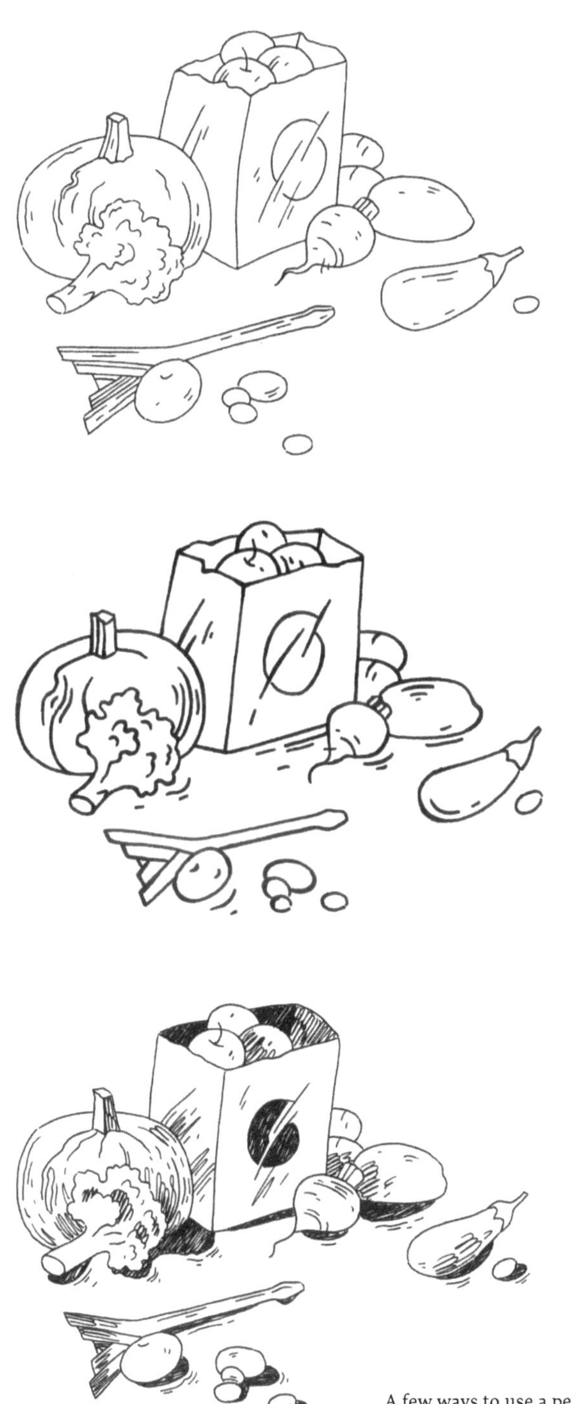

A few ways to use a pen
in a Drawing Journal

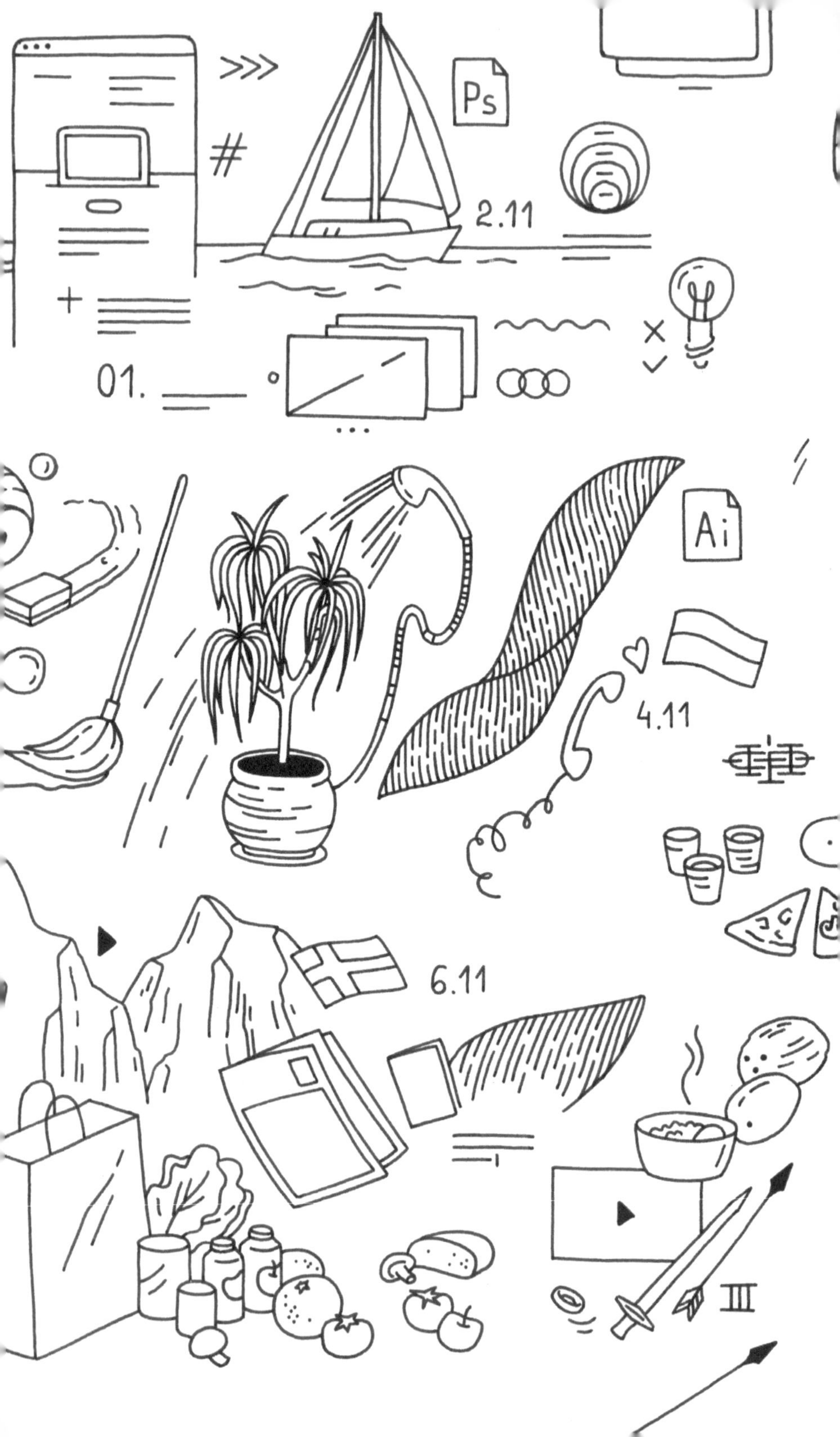
Ps
2.11
01.
Ai
4.11
6.11

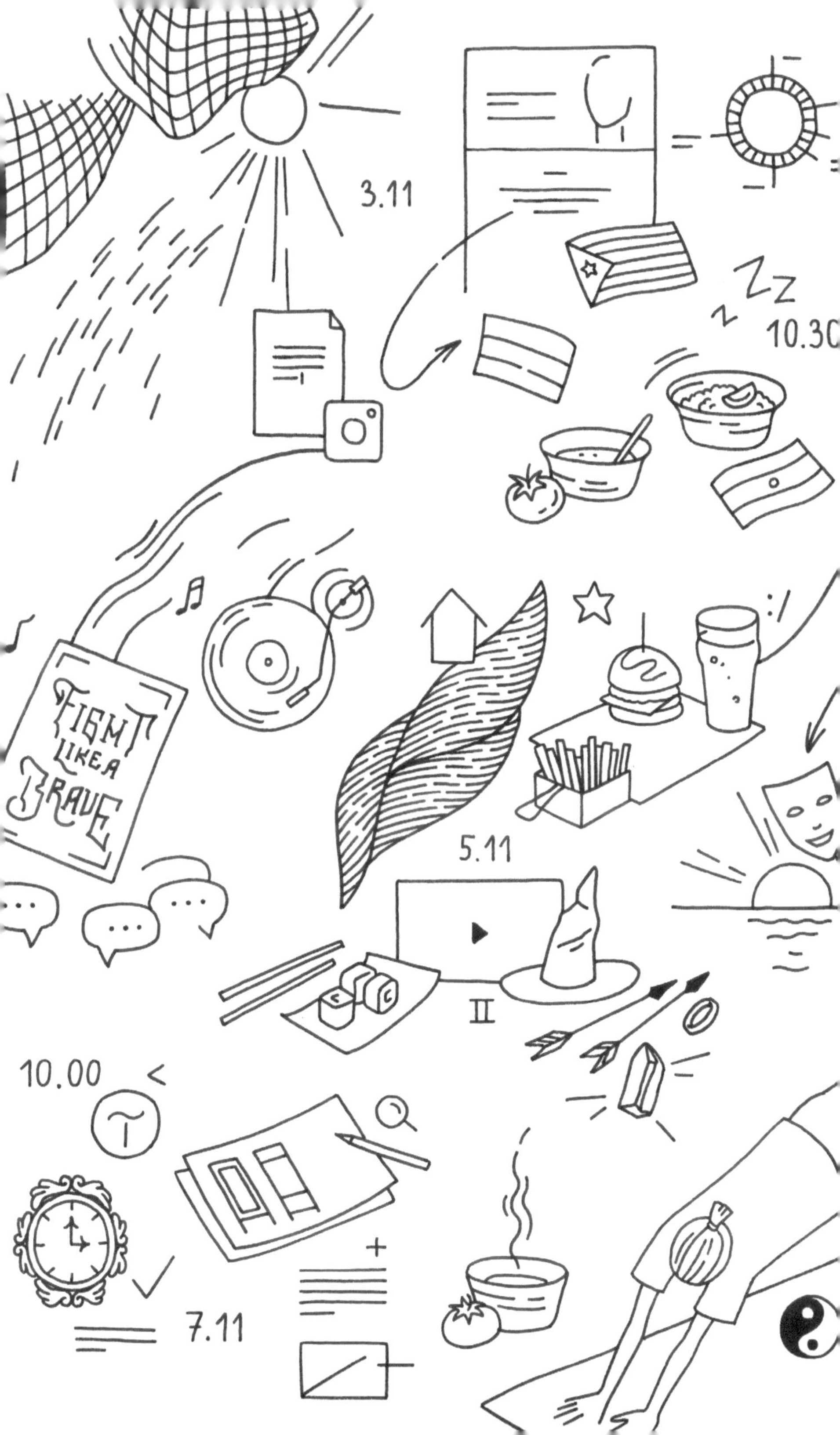
3.11
10.30
FIGHT LIKE A BRAVE
5.11
10.00
7.11

A gel pen is suitable if you want deep, saturated colors and neat thin lines. Some gel pens say they are waterproof but be careful and let the gel dry for a few minutes, otherwise it will smudge. It also can smudge if you try to erase other lines over it.

I haven't used a lot of different gel pens because when I tried the Muji Gel Ink Ballpoint Pen 0.38 mm I fell in love with it. Muji carries a good diversity of sizes, colors, and refills. These pens are perfectly balanced in terms of ink quality and design. They make smooth clear lines, and the refills make this pen budget and eco-friendly compared to others.

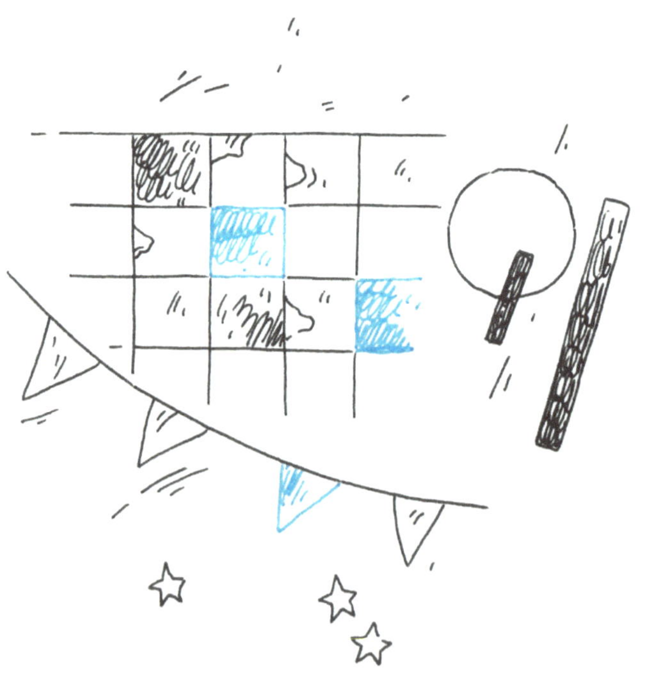

Color markers

With markers you can add color to drawings with minimal effort. They are easy to carry and don't require additional supplies or preparations before use.

Markers leave a translucent band of color which adds a lightness to the drawing and can be used for shadows and accents. You can add a sense of depth by applying a few layers of one color. When coloring with markers, start from the light colors and go to the darkest ones to make colors cleaner.

Markers can be blended to create a gradient or new color. In order to blend colors smoothly add a second color while the first one is still wet, otherwise, there will be a seam between the two. You may also use a dual-ended colorless blender marker. Although, in my opinion, the first option works better and looks smoother.

Examples of blending color markers with dry and wet layers

Because of its transparency, it's generally better to work with a marker on a small area — it's hard to make a big colored area seamless because the marker's ink dries out quickly, and the next layer will create seams. Also, be aware that markers may show up on the back of the page even if you are using a dense paper.

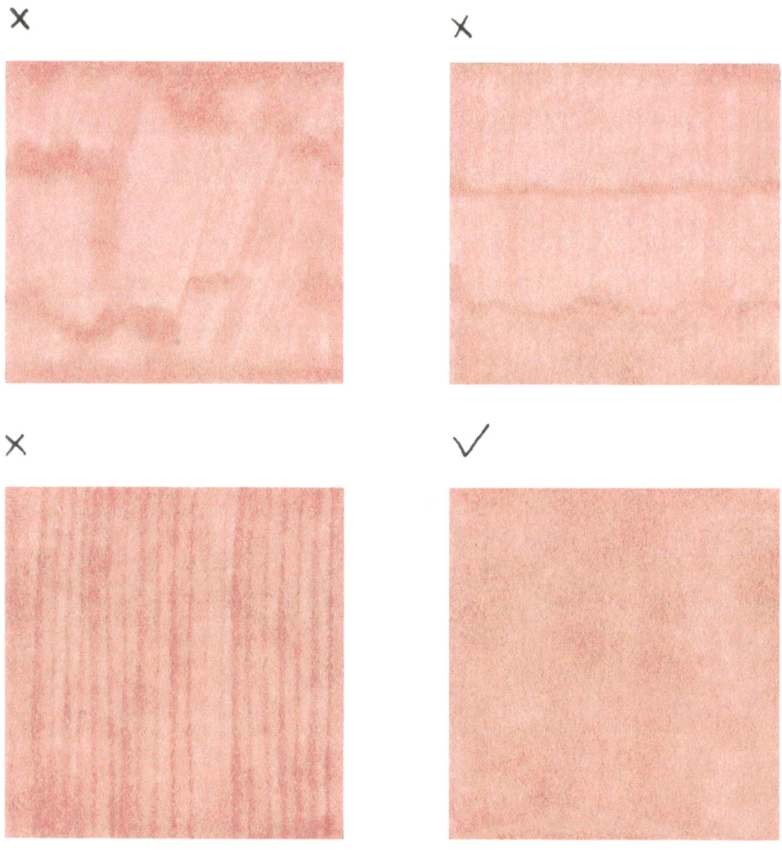

Draw parallel lines without layering each other along the entire area to make it seamless

There are many marker brands with different prices on the market. Take note of brands like Winsor & Newton, Touch Twin, Copic, Prismacolor and Faber-Castell. I prefer Winsor & Newton, they are reasonably priced and have nice brushes. Be aware that color markers are quite an expensive medium.

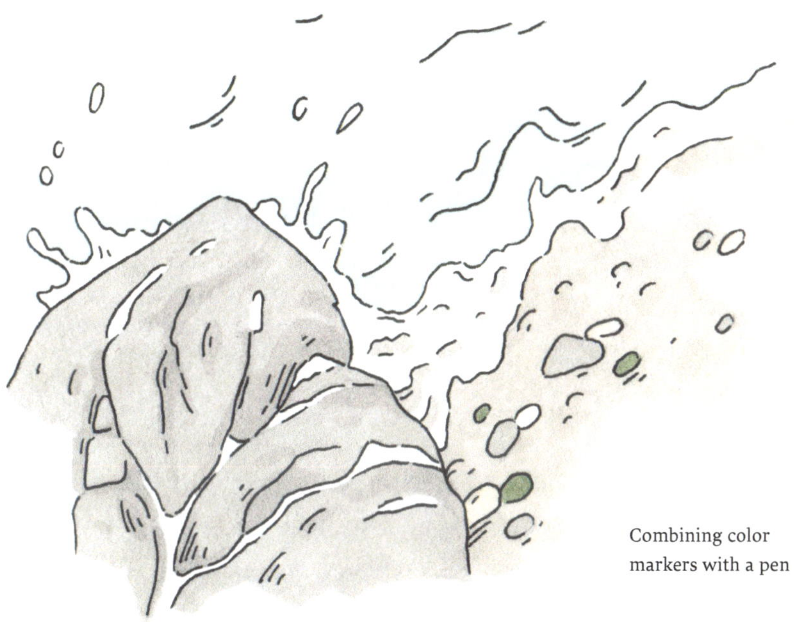

Combining color markers with a pen

Color markers are great for combining with different mediums, they can add depth and vivacity to the drawings. They create a soft color base which can be covered with other drawing instruments. They work well with pens, graphite, and colored pencils. The simplest option is to pair color markers with a pen. I'm applying this technique now, it doesn't take much time and livens up my drawings.

If you use color markers with graphite pencils, try adding shadows with different grades of pencil, it will make your drawing more realistic. Colored pencils can add accents and make a drawing more bright and textured. Although, it's better to use these complex techniques after you have started your Drawing Journal and become more confident and faster in your drawing.

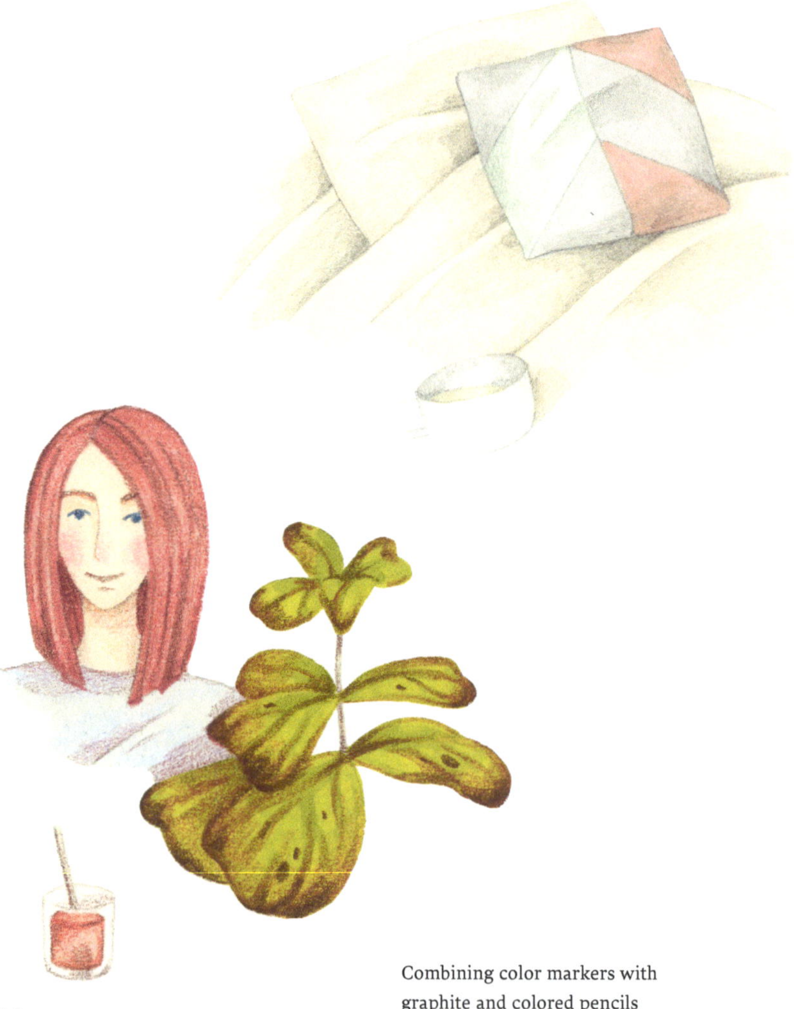

Combining color markers with graphite and colored pencils

Colored pencils

Colored pencils have many benefits for a Drawing Journal. They are durable, don't require much space, and don't need drying time. Colored pencils are also an inexpensive option, especially compared to color markers. For the same price you will get a lot more colors with pencils than markers.

Depending on the number of layers and pressure applied to a pencil, it can create a soft "fleecy" texture or saturated deep color. These features can be used together or separately to create interesting effects. Colored pencils can also be blended together to create new hues.

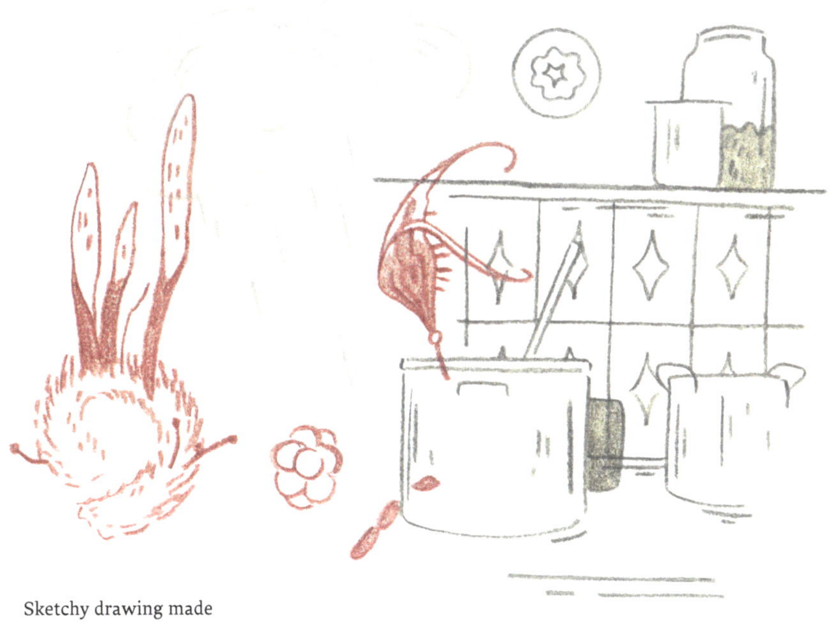

Sketchy drawing made with colored pencils

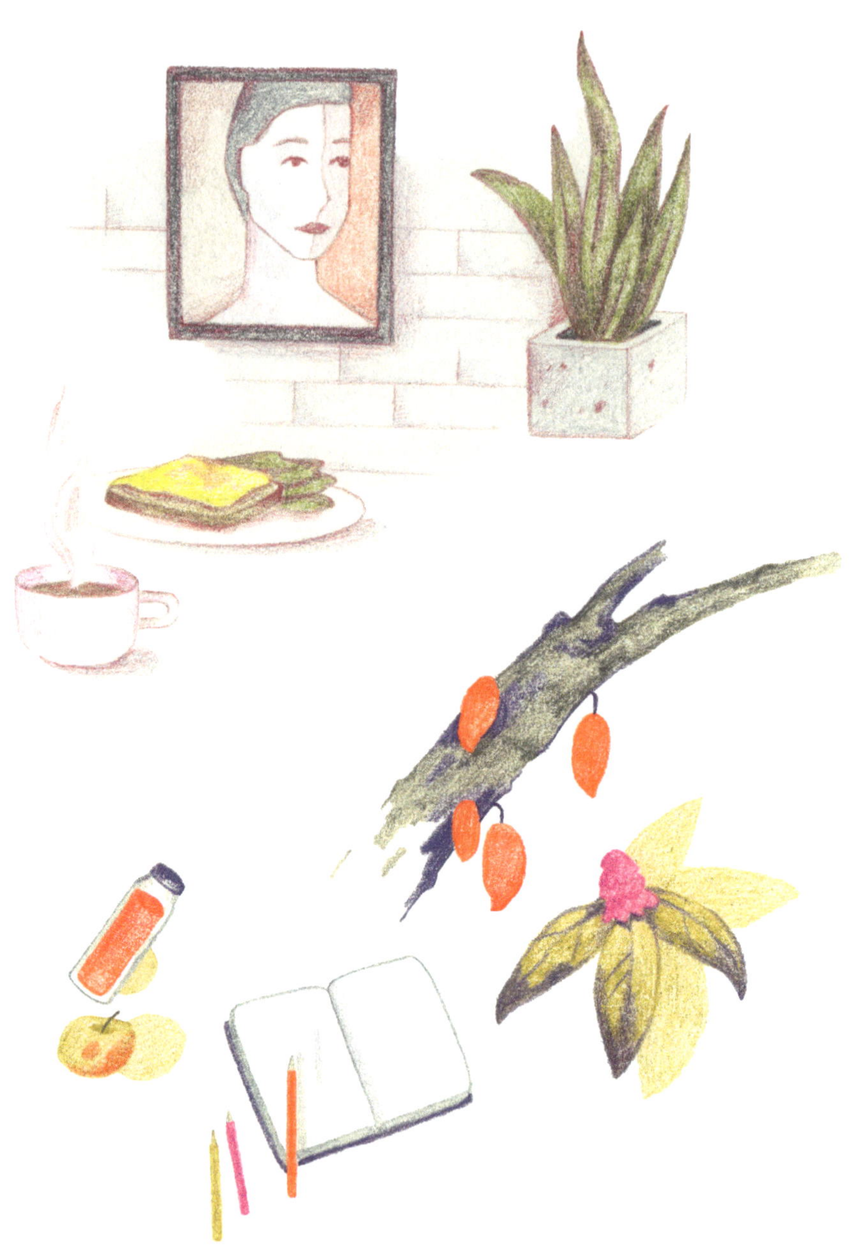

Faber-Castell, Prismacolor and Caran D'ache are just a few of the premier color pencil brands. I use Prismacolor Premier and enjoy its plentiful palette and soft, smooth layering.

Watercolor pencils (or water-soluble pencils)

Watercolor pencils are a great choice for creating a watercolor drawing with minimal effort. It's a perfect combination of painting and drawing in one medium. Watercolor pencils have the same qualities as colored pencils but behave differently when mixed with water. With this medium, you are free to choose when you want to finish your drawings. You can find something interesting during a day, draw it using watercolor pencils and then add water in the evening.

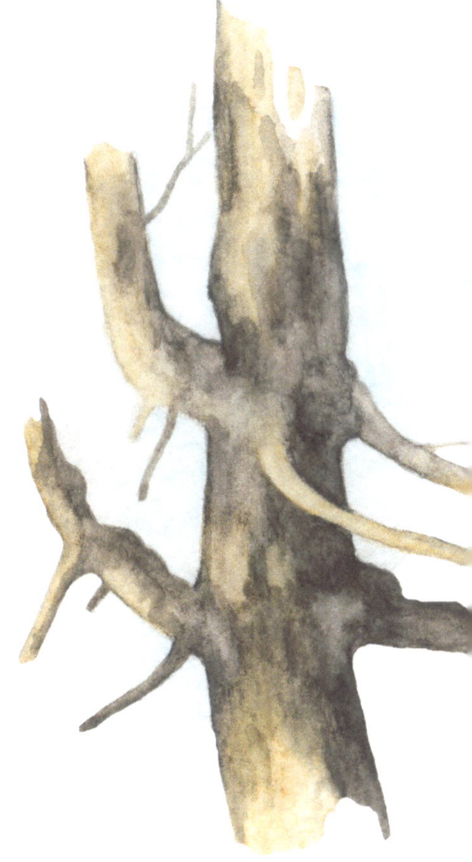

If you want to complete your drawings right away, try a water brush pen. Fill it with water and work with it anywhere, anytime, throughout the day. Before using, squeeze the water brush pen to make the brush wet and then apply it on the paper. To change colors, simply squeeze the brush and wipe on some scratch paper or fabric towel.

When using watercolor pencils, start off by coloring one area at a time. You can add shades and mix colors right away.

When you apply water with a brush, the pencil on the paper will "activate" and basically turn into watercolor. If you don't want neighboring areas to blend, carefully activate color within one area, let it dry, and then activate the second area.

To add more shades and depth to the area, let the first layer dry completely and then repeat the action of coloring with pencil and activating it with water. You can also vary this technique by using watercolor pencils with and without water. This way you can add more shades, brightness, texture, and highlight important details.

You can find good sets of watercolor pencils at Faber-Castell and Prismacolor. If you choose to apply watercolor pencils don't forget to use a sketchbook with an appropriate watercolor paper otherwise your drawings will be ruined.

Don't forget to explore and find what works for you. Don't limit yourself to only my suggestions of mediums and ways to apply them. They are only starting points to your experiments and discoveries.

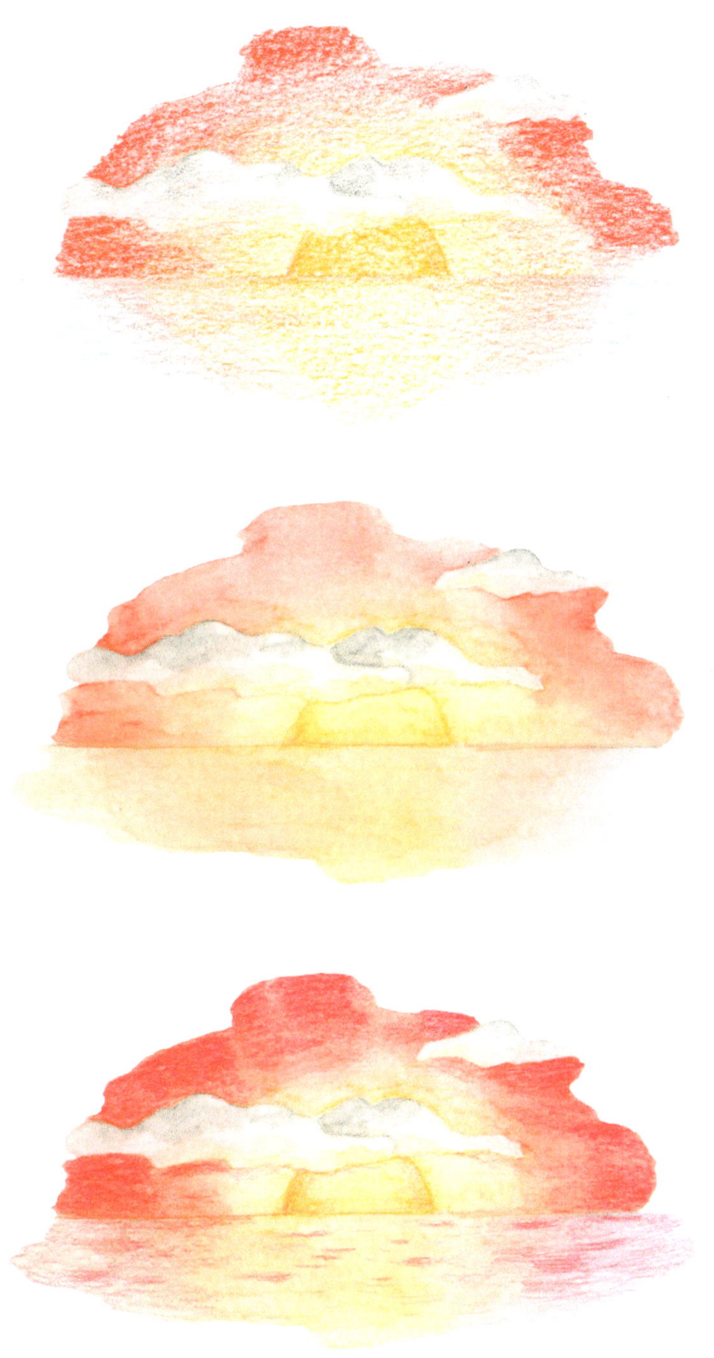

The process of applying
watercolor pencils

Tips for choosing a color palette

It can be scary to use colors at first. There are many choices and it can be difficult to combine them harmoniously. To save time while drawing, make your drawings balanced and feel less stressful, it's better to choose a limited palette and stick to it at the beginning of the project. When you feel more comfortable, you can decide if you want to expand.

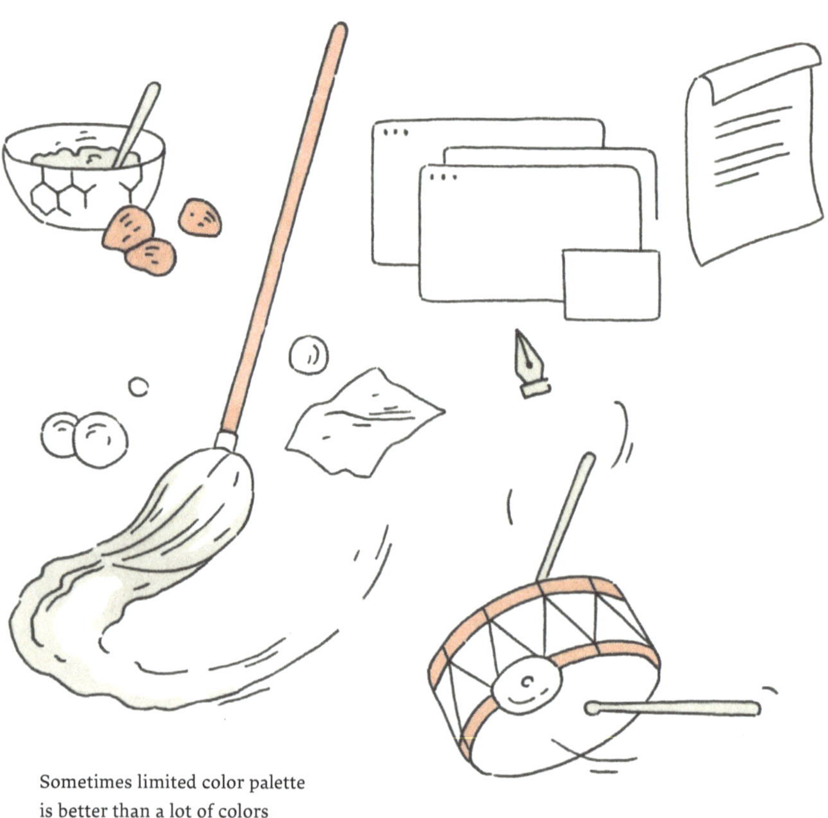

Sometimes limited color palette is better than a lot of colors

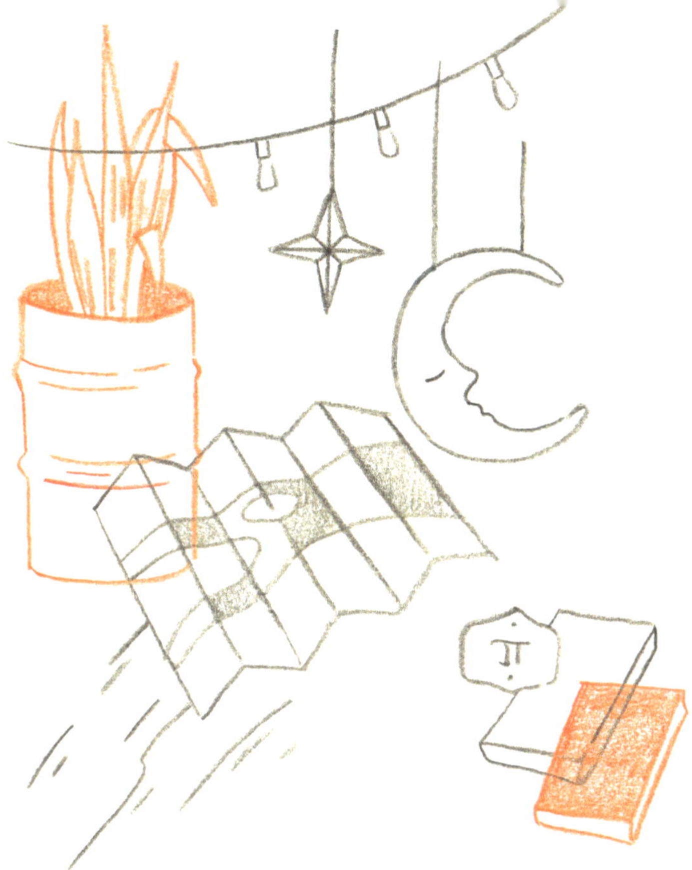

It's not necessary to use dozens of color pencils or markers to make a drawing interesting. It is more important for a color palette to be harmonious, than expansive. Even one or two colors can be enough. This focus can help illuminate important moments, add clarity, and create an attractive simplicity. It's also a more economical option. Go for quality over quantity of materials.

When I started to color my sketchbook, I added a few shades of neutral gray and calm pastels like blue, beige and peach. These are comfortable colors with neutral and light tones that can be applied to a lot of drawing elements.

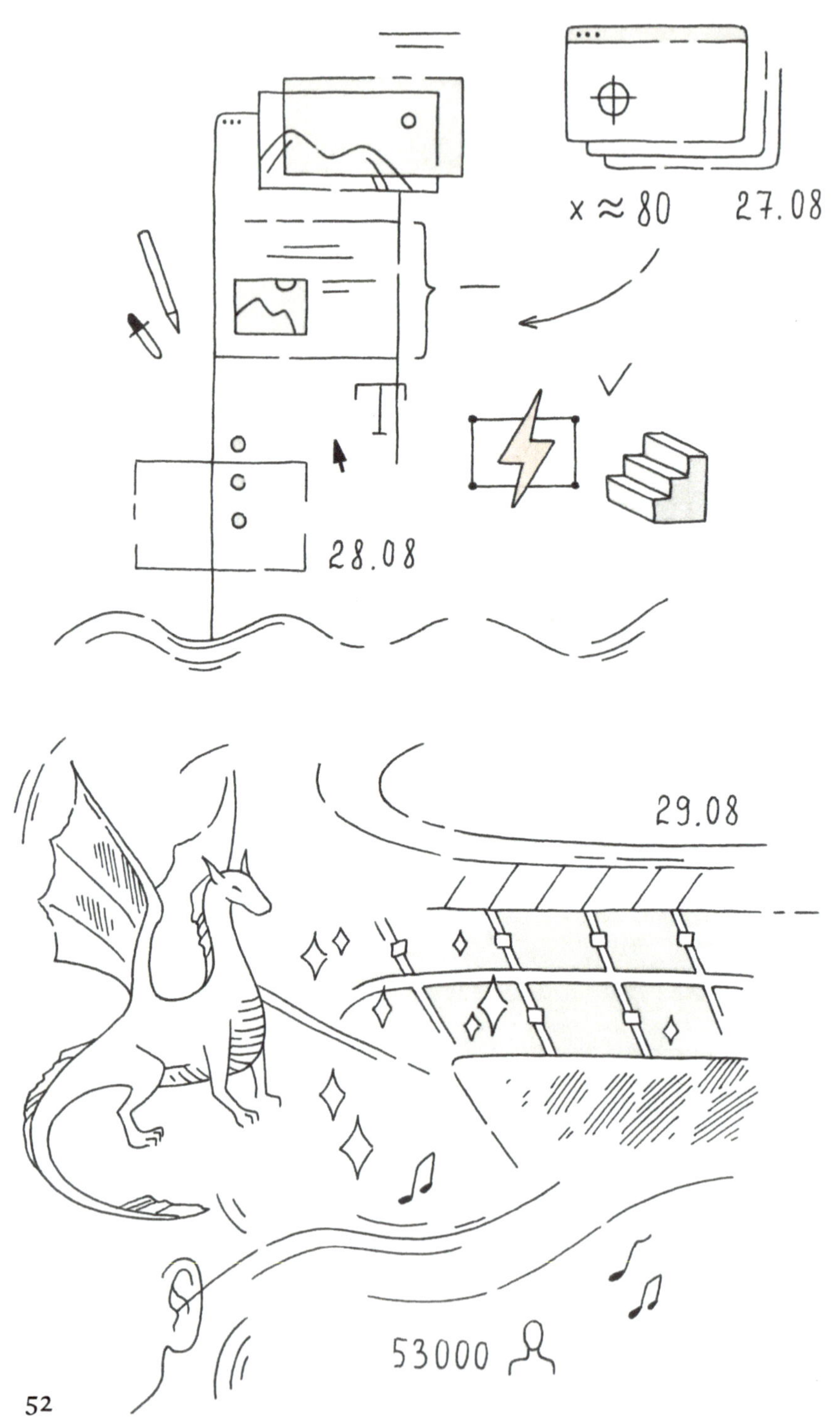
x ≈ 80
27.08
28.08
29.08
53000

If you want to go beyond this basic color range try a few bold or dark colors which can add contrast and accents into your drawings.

Basic color palettes you can start with

The color palette I used when started coloring my Drawing Journal. I've noticed that gray color is universal and can be used for coloring many objects, so I've added it to all color palettes.

The same calm palette but with one bright accent color. The accent can be replaced with any other bold color you prefer.

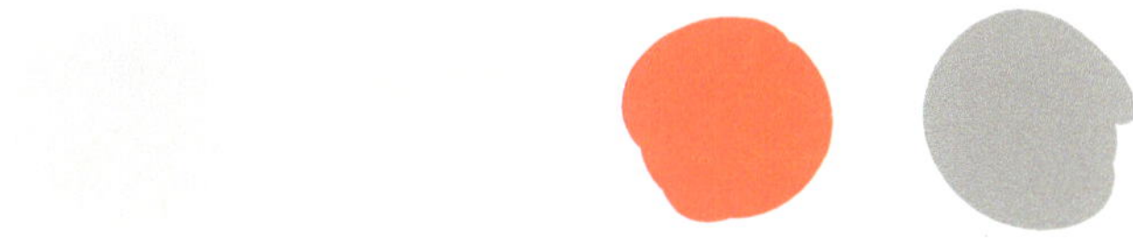

The more various but still calm palette.

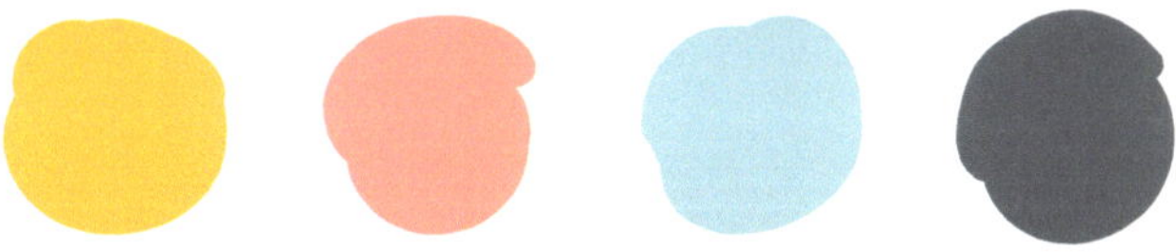

The more universal and bright palette if you prefer simple clean colors.

The color palette I use right now (2020) after two years of coloring Drawing Journal.

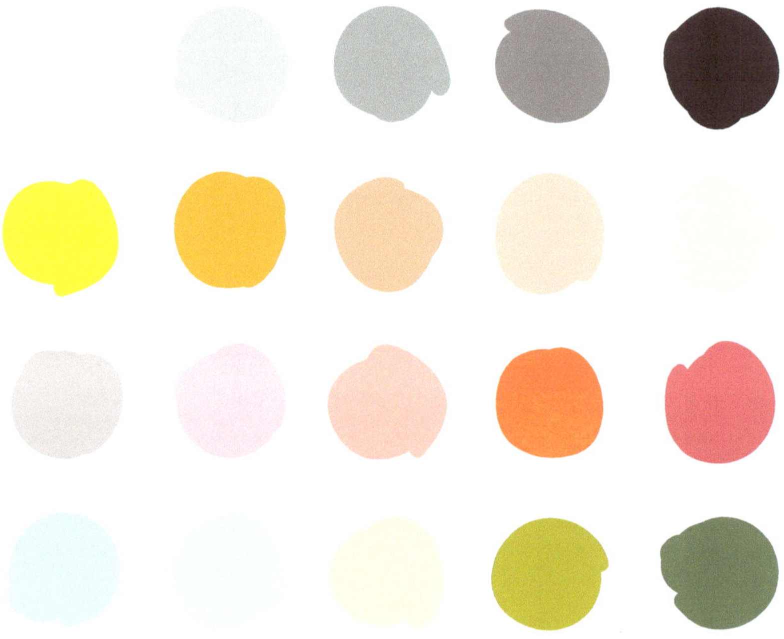

In an art store try colors on one piece of paper and see how they look together. Here is a space you can use for creating your own palette and comparing it with the options above.

After a while, you'll begin to notice whether your color palette suits your needs. I added new colors little by little when I felt I needed a certain color in my drawings.

Don't pressure yourself while choosing the first palette. Try different colors and enjoy the process. You can always adapt over time.

CHAPTER IV

Explore and find things to draw

A Drawing Journal can help you to be inspired by ordinary life, and it also motivates you to strive for something bigger. The first step is to recognize beauty in the things around you.

Remember that absolutely anything can be drawn in a Drawing Journal. From seemingly boring routines to your daily commute. One of the main ideas of this project is learning how to notice and absorb the interesting from the ordinary. It may seem hard but once you start paying attention, you will see the beauty around you.

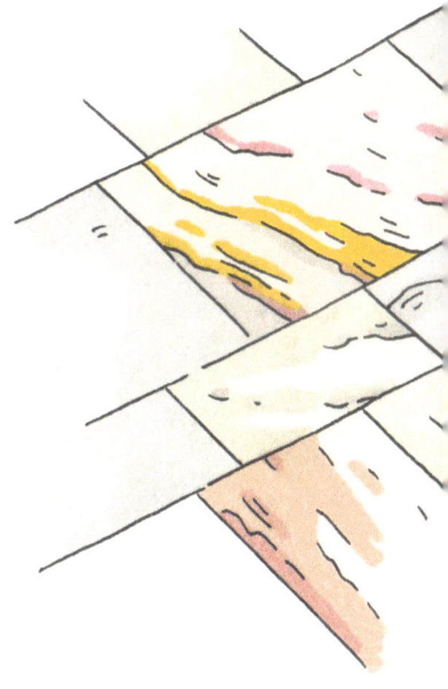

In general, look for oddity, and originality. Pay attention to patterns, textures, shapes, lines, and color combinations. Be investigative and curious.

Explore at school or college

Although being a student can have its dull moments, the constant flow of knowledge and new experiences is a prime time to explore.

Look at your lectures not just as information but as an amazing source of visual inspiration. Pay attention to unexpected facts, history, interesting characters, and biographies. Your research and projects can be full of exciting information that can be transformed into drawing ideas.

Explore your school's buildings, lecture halls, library. There are likely beautiful interiors, furniture, artworks, mosaics, fretworks, and other fascinating things inside. Even your textbooks can have interesting cover designs or illustrations.

I wish I would have started this project when I was a student, so I could have captured all the special moments of student life. On the other hand, now I enjoy learning even more and drawing from my personal studies and visits to museums, lectures and exhibitions with the excitement of a nosy investigator.

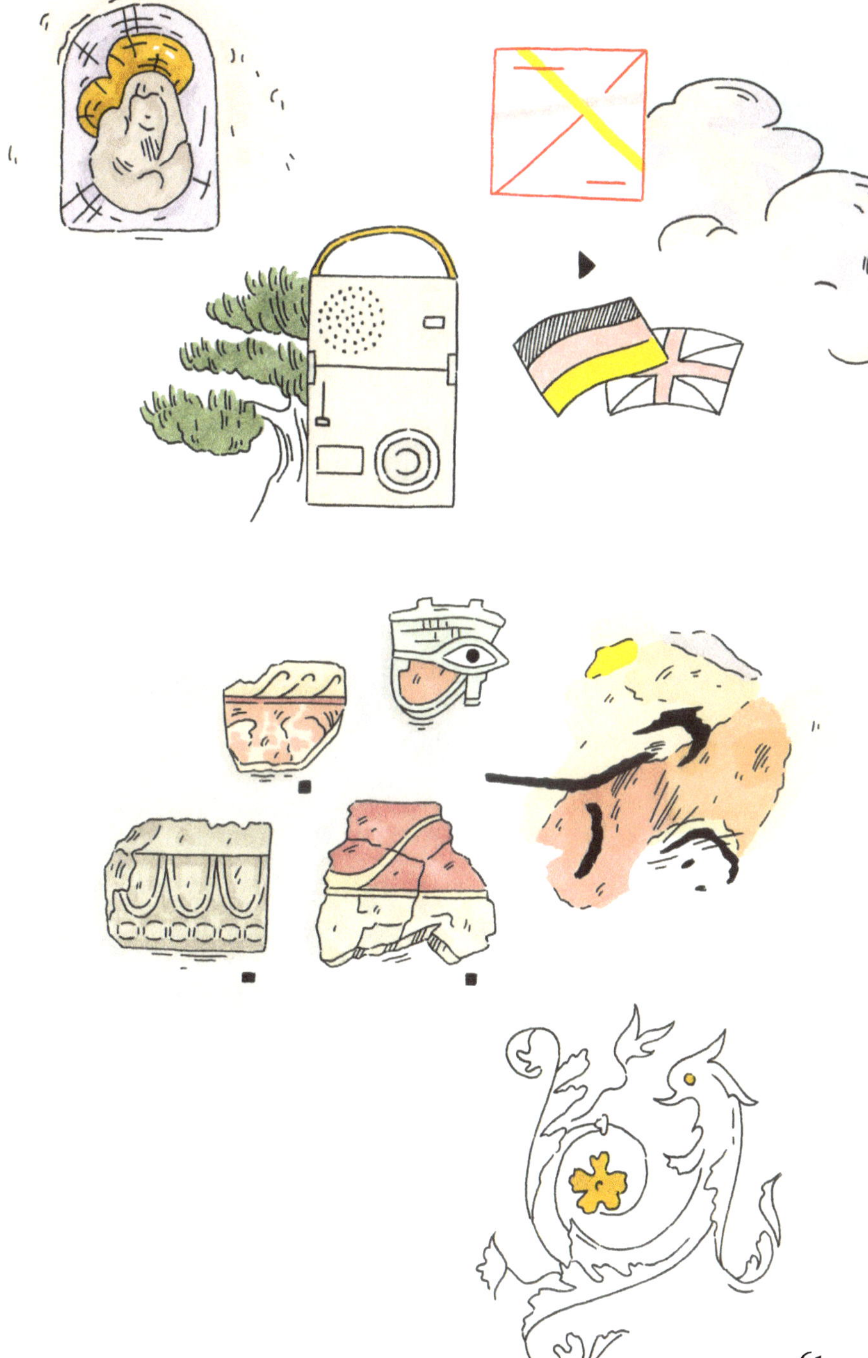

Explore at work

Most of my day seems to be spent at work and while it can often feel monotonous, there are moments that stand out. Pay attention to your environment, tasks, projects and activities. Communicate with your colleagues and take an interest in their work and lives. Look at your working space and an office interior. If you have an ability to listen to music, podcasts or lectures at work, these are big inspirational resources too.

You could draw your colleague's funny new sweater, lunchbox or story. Become inspired by your new client's business. Discover that a broken printer made cool patterns on a printed document. It could even be a new interface or feature of a program you regularly use at work.

As a web designer, I work a lot on visual content and so I often capture my working process with new designs and illustrations that I make. This way I integrate the digital part of my routine into my offline life. I like how these two parts intertwine in drawing with each other.

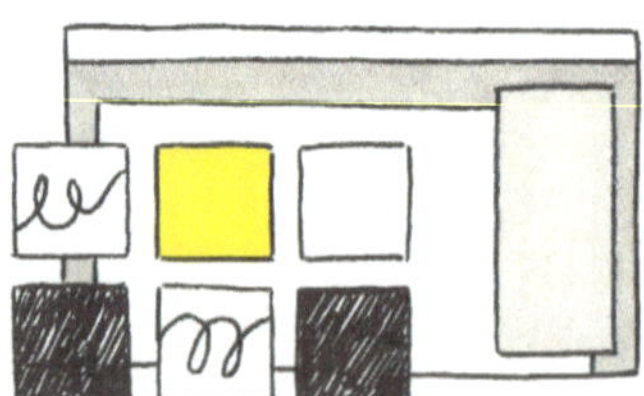

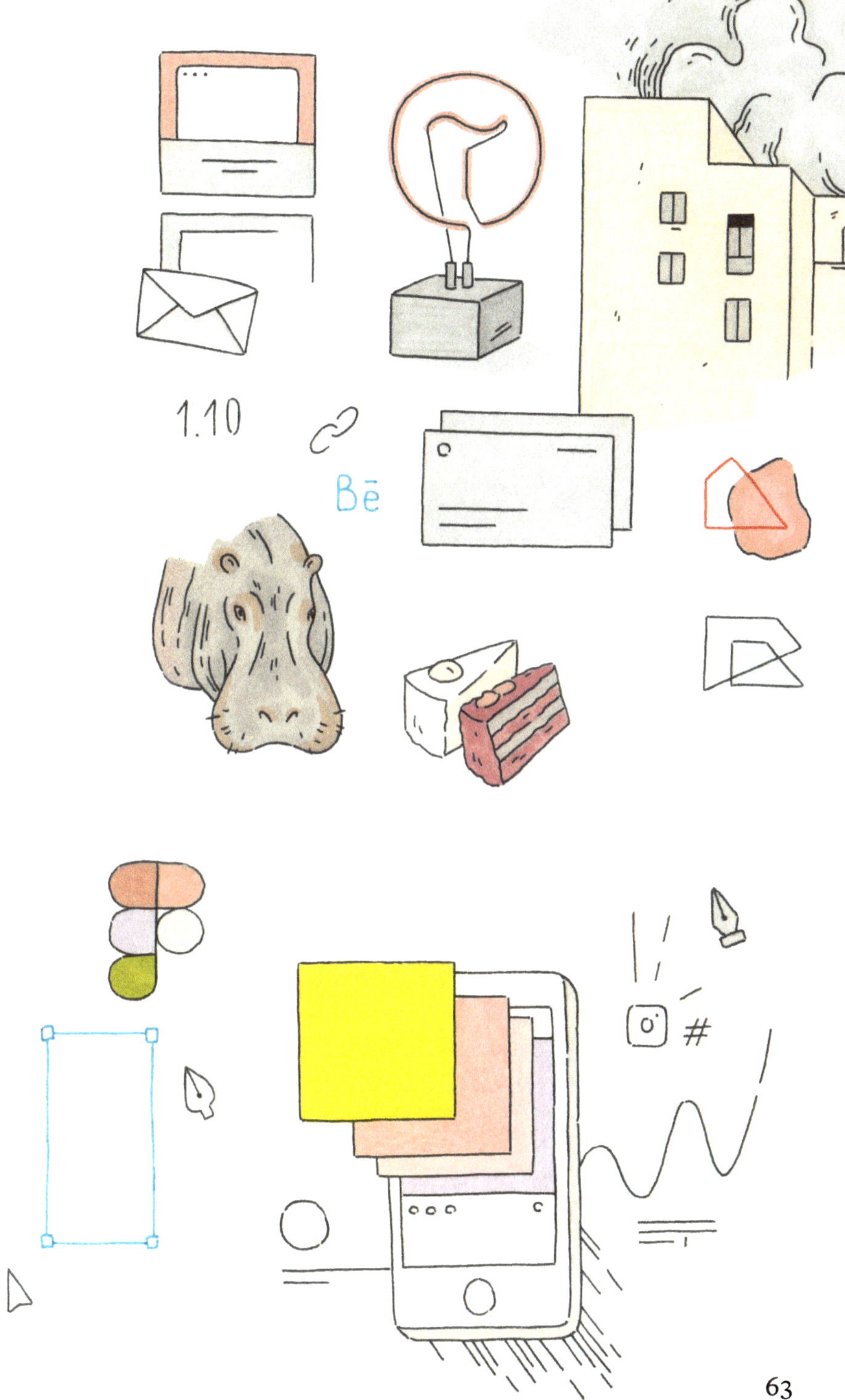
1.10
Bē
#

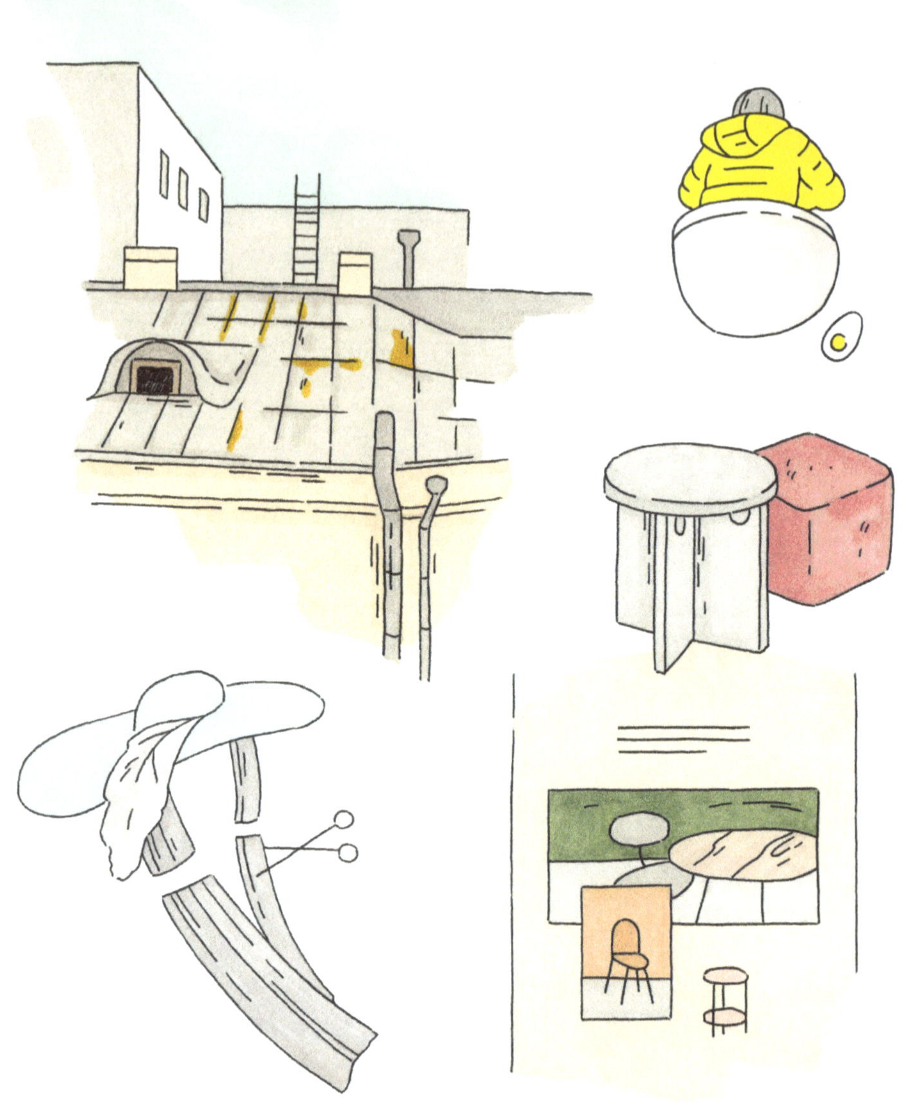

To make these drawings look more alive I enjoy adding something fun like a playful cat that I've seen on some website or my colleague sitting in the white chair in the yellow jacket and reminding me of an egg. One of my favorite themes is to capture my colleague Yana in the d'Artagnan's hat because her name resembles the musketeer's.

If you still don't feel inspired, try to bring some changes. Make your working space cozy and pleasant, surround yourself with things that you love. Suggest your colleagues to add some innovations into your working process to make it more pleasurable. Develop your professional skills so you could take on new challenging projects, which will bring you new impressions. Initiate change to make every moment a potential source of creativity.

If you truly and absolutely feel there is nothing worthy and interesting in your work, maybe it's a sign to make some changes in your life.

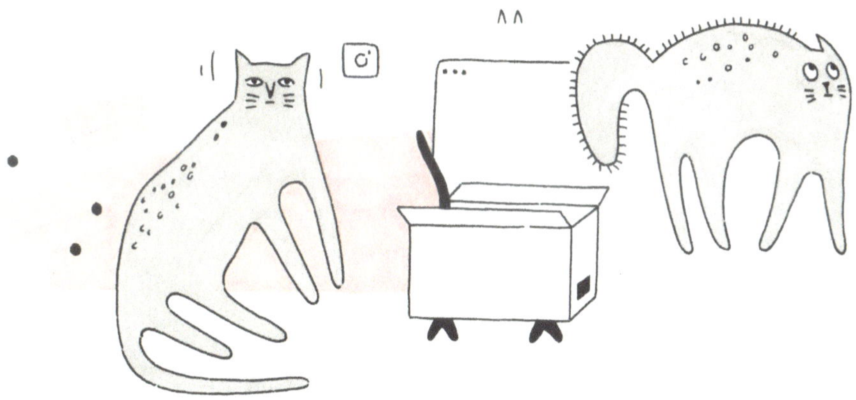

Connect with people

Each person is unique and everyday is a symphony of interesting characters. Each with their own personality, clothes and ideas. Meet new people, listen to their stories and let them inspire your work.

While using public transport or hanging in public places pay attention to people around you. Someone can have a hilarious hat, a cute dog or unusual shoes. Although, be careful and don't stare at people too much.

When I draw people, I don't usually draw the exact person, I think it's more interesting to represent the person in objects I associate with them. Instead of a person I can draw his or her pet, a pattern on their clothes or some distinctive feature.

I'm lucky enough to have three friends with gorgeous curly hair — Tanya, Masha and Masha (Yes, two Mashas!). Luckily, they all have different haircuts and often I draw them with the help of just a few springy curls — short strands for Tanya, long ones for Masha, and pink ombre for my other friend Masha.

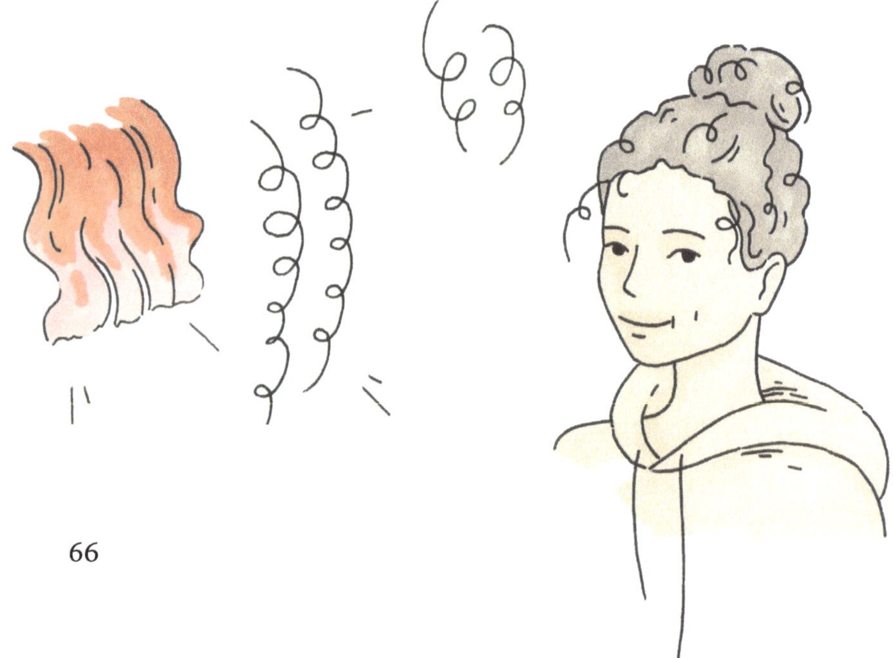

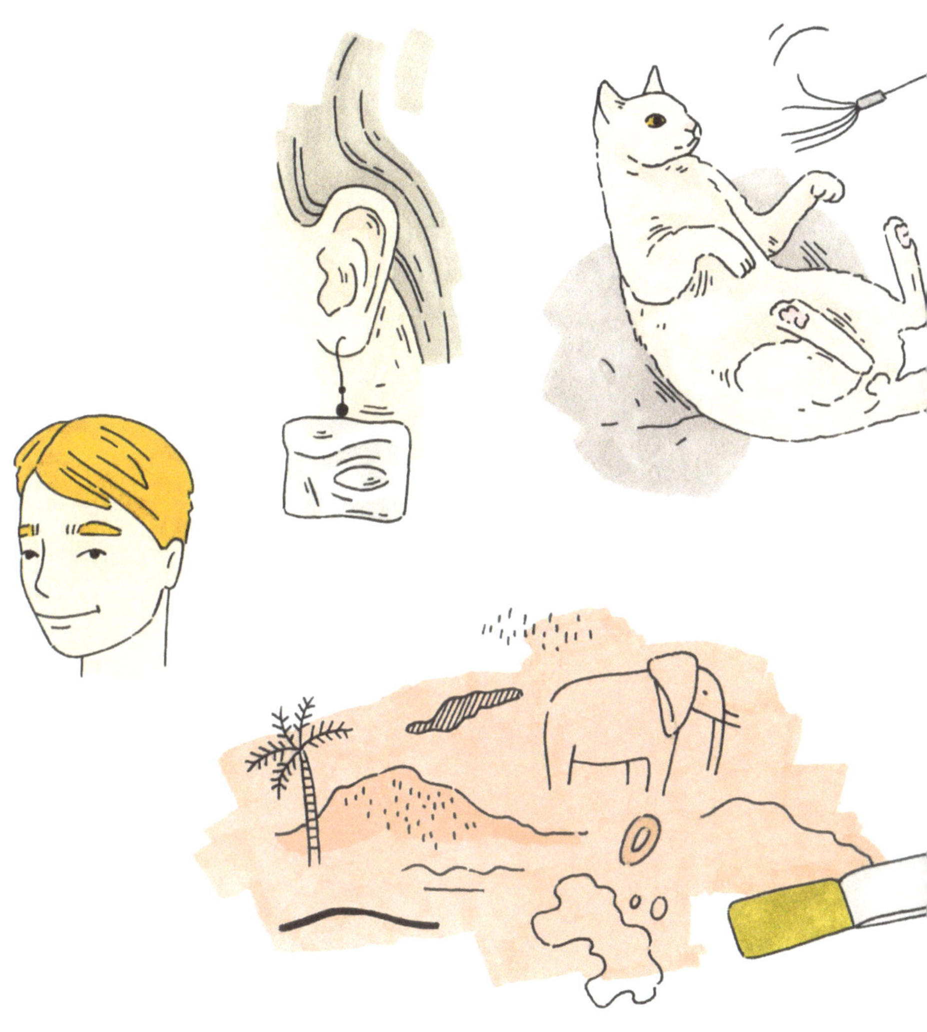

Capture feelings and emotions

Draw your happiness, your moments of peace and of sadness. When you draw your problems, they become physical, easier to understand and perhaps even solve.

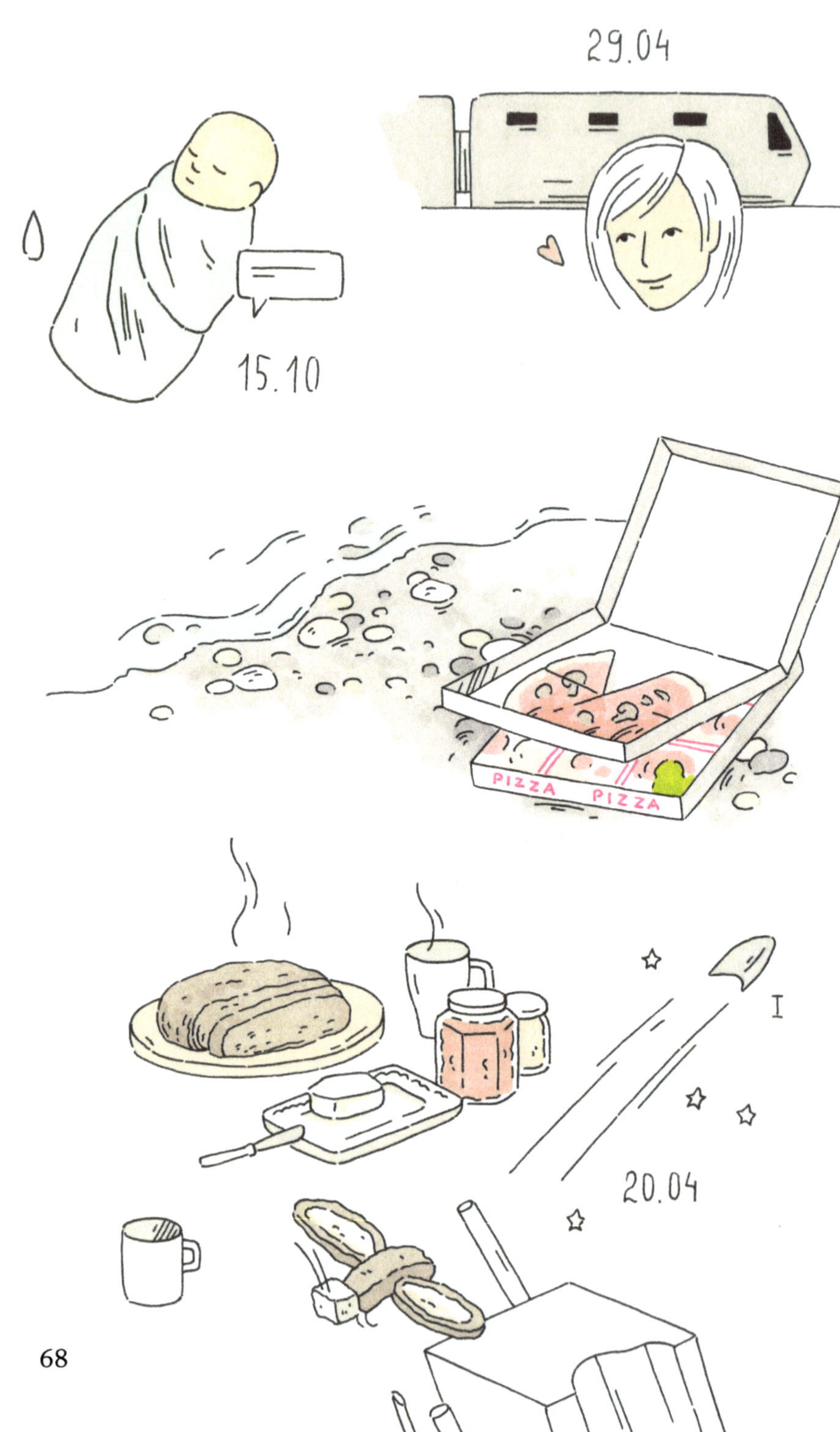
29.04
15.10
PIZZA PIZZA
20.04

Your drawings don't have to be literal expressions of emotions like a smiling face or red eyes with tears. Try expressing emotions by drawing the environment you are in at the moment and the atmosphere that made you feel that way. This way you can reflect more shades of feelings and later vividly remember why exactly you had them.

It can be anything with different levels of importance — a message from your friend with news that she just gave birth to her first child, meeting with mom after half a year of separation, eating delicious pizza on the shores of Lake Garda in Italy or just a cozy morning in bed with flecks of sunlight on a blanket.

Explore your city

Whether you live in a big city or a small town, there is a unique spirit and tradition to the place.

Architecture is a huge insight into this spirit. Try comparing different architecture styles in your drawings. Pay attention to a building's details, not necessarily the whole thing, this is where the most interesting elements are. Search for interesting windows, doors or facades. In many towns, there are tiny pieces of art that can be found on buildings' facades — sculptures, painted tiles or drawings.

Look at signboards, tiles, street art, and store windows. When you are walking down a street and see an intriguing store, a corner or a small lane, go there and soak in your hometown.

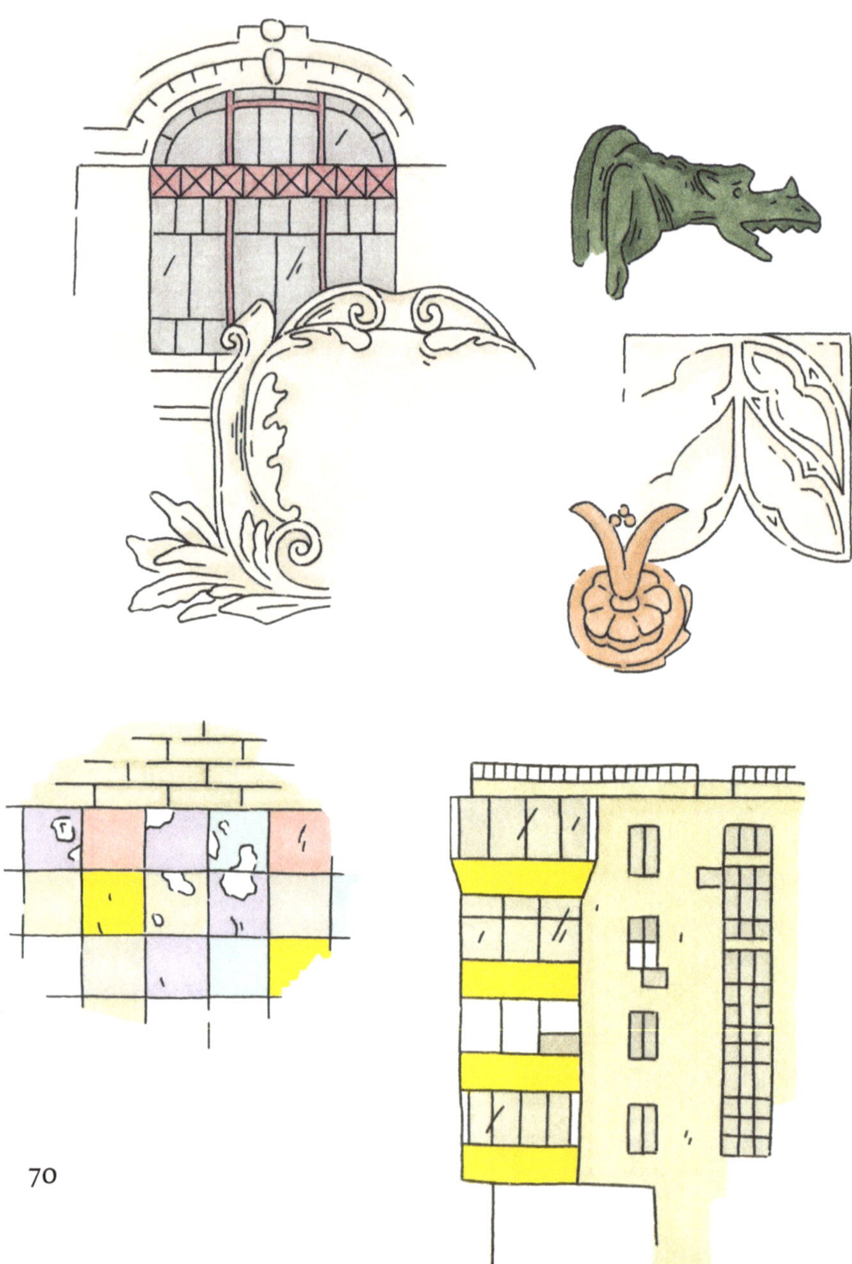

Look at nature

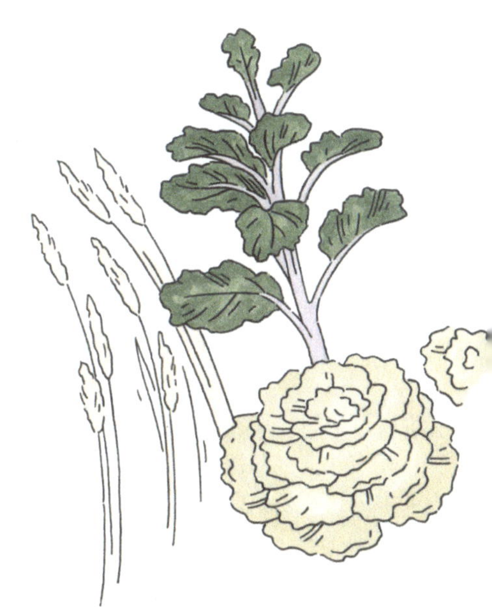

When you look closely at the complex structure of a leaf, a marble pattern or the winding texture of a tree you can see how perfect and elaborated nature is. Even if you live in a city, communicate with nature which is always beautiful and exciting to draw.

Drawing nature is one of my favorite aspects of the Drawing Journal. Its unique and vivid shapes make pages more dynamic and contrast well with geometric forms and stark shapes of the big city where I live.

When you encounter nature during your day, breath in the freshness of flowers and look at the details. Look around when you're passing by parks, alleys, and landscapes. Pay attention to leaves, rocks, water, branches and bark on trees. You can find perfect symmetries, compositions and interesting patterns there.

Strive to have a rest in green places more often. For example, instead of having lunch at a cafe during a workday, take food out and go to a park or a beautiful alleyway.

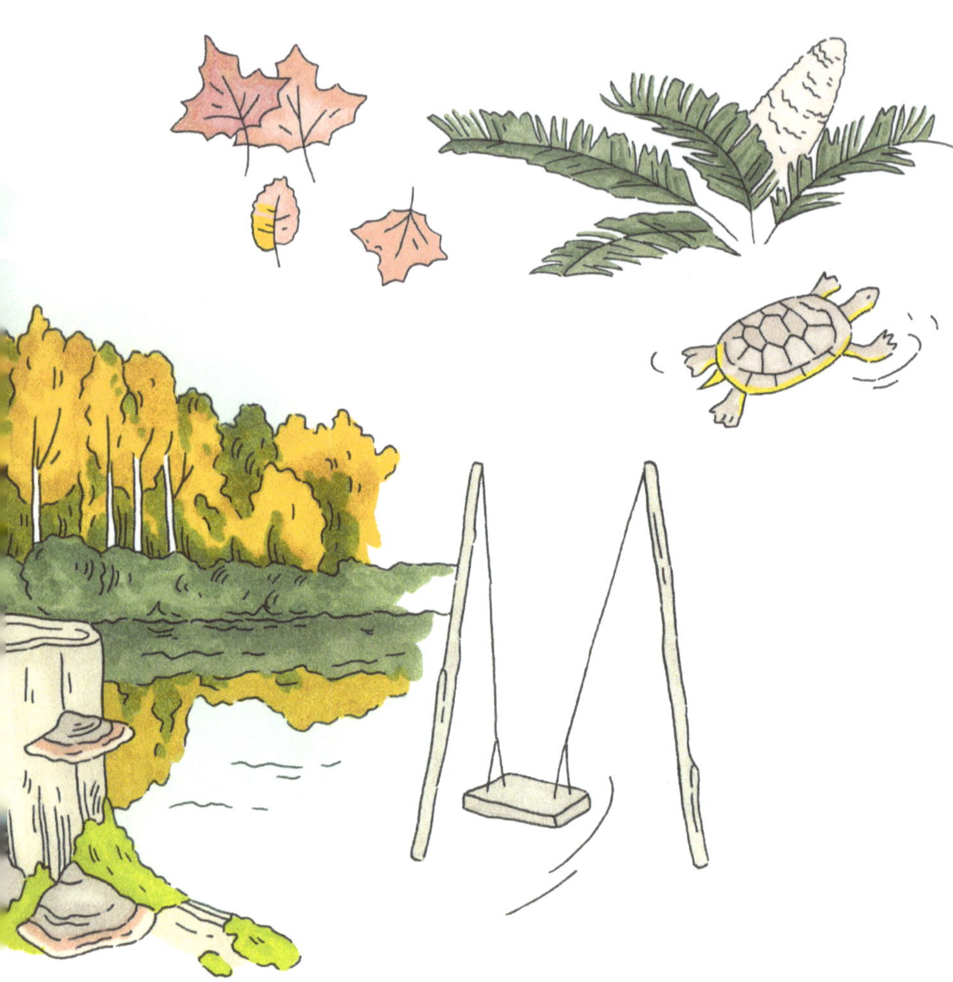

Enjoy food

When you visit a cafe or a restaurant, look at their interior, table setting and meal design. When you buy groceries think about a beauty of food. Just look at pasta in bizarre shapes, a cabbages's wavy curves, the bold color of a tomato, a rosy bread or shiny glass bottles of milk.

I love to draw food, and especially groceries in my Drawing Journal. Inadvertently, when I started my daily drawing journal, I became more careful with my nutrition choices because I strived to surround myself with aesthetic foods which I could draw later. This eventually turned out to be good, not only for my drawings, but also for my health. Fruits and vegetables bring me a special joy because of their interesting shapes, colors and structures — they're so beautiful.

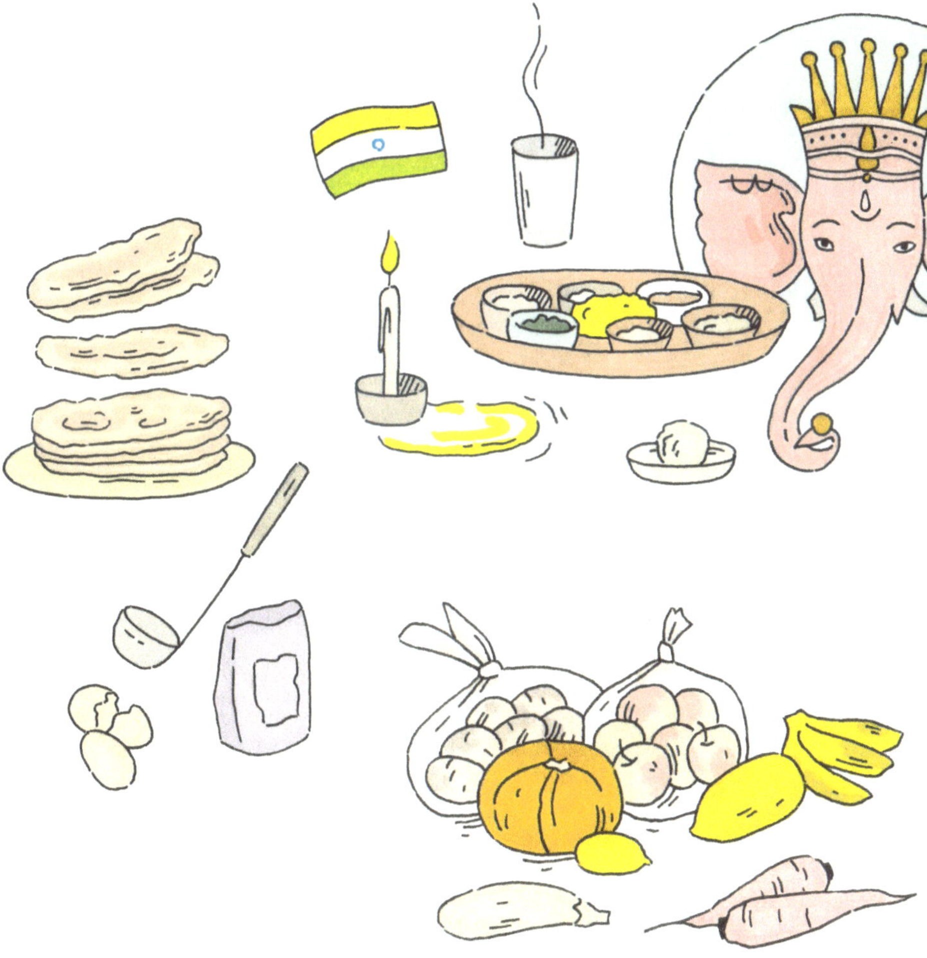

Draw the weather

The weather and the seasons are our inalienable companions. And in these natural phenomena, inspiration can also be found. Beautiful clouds, heavy rain, a colorful sunset, or the first snowfall capture the atmosphere of a day.

I especially enjoy drawing rain with dark clouds, abstract puddles and dynamic raindrops. Sometimes I play around with metaphorical representations of the weather like a flipped bucket to show that the rain is so heavy it feels like water being poured from a bucket.

Don't forget about the temperature either. Add clothing items and your emotions about how frigid or sweltering hot it is. All these details round out a memory and add that bit of uniqueness. For example, when it was 5 degrees celsius in Moscow in the middle of June, which is quite unusual for this time, I added my winter shoes with the warm socks I was wearing that day to demonstrate just how cold it was that day.

We see seasons changing and feel joy or sadness about it. When spring comes we observe how the snow melts, birds start to sing, and how buds turn into leaves. We notice how a day becomes longer in June and how the first leaves start to fall in September. All these things can be beautifully captured by your drawings.

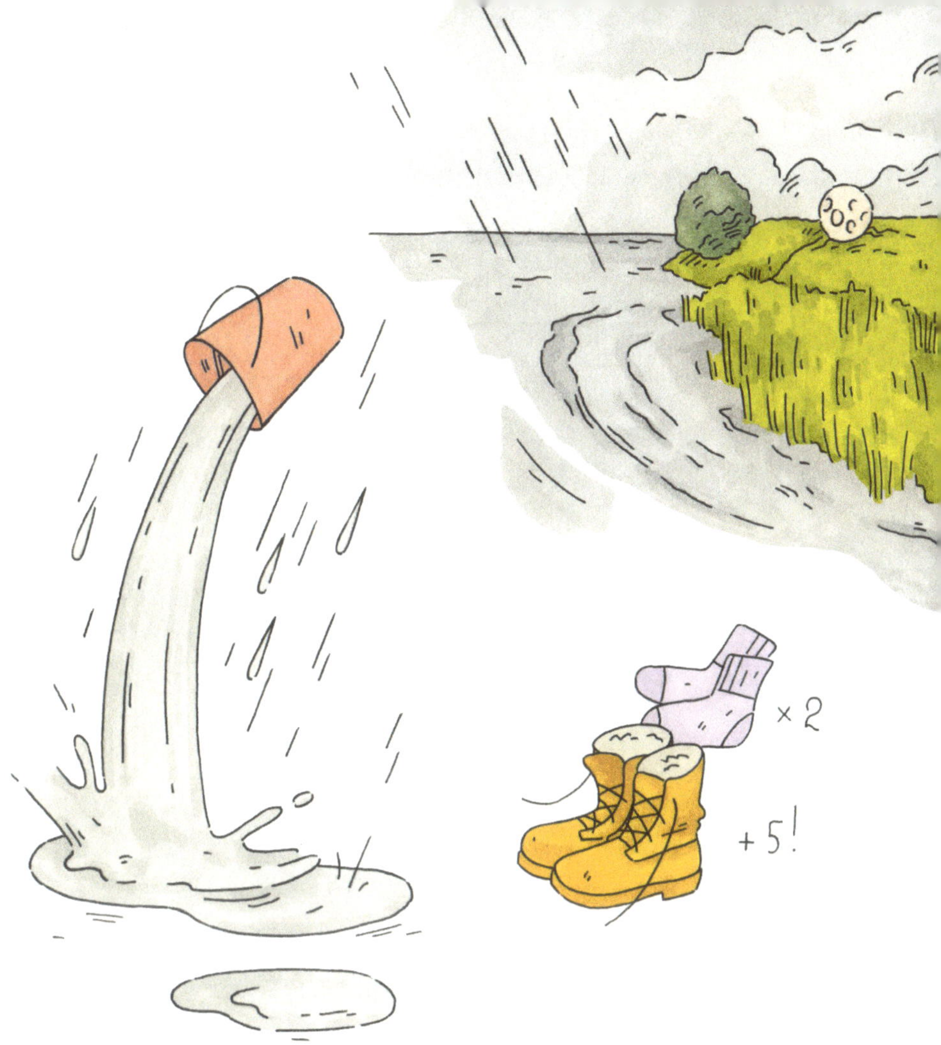

Capture your journeys

Traveling is the best time for drawing and being inspired. Being in a new place is always exciting and you notice details faster and more precisely. One of my biggest pleasures is to draw during my trips. It seems like the pages with my travel drawings are the most interesting and diverse because they have all these beautiful places with architecture, nature, local food, sights, plus a spirit of freedom and adventure.

Many cities, towns or regions have their own distinctive features expressed in local architecture and urban design. Paris has its pixel art tile mosaics and there are so many bronze dwarfs in Wroclaw. Search for these features and depict them in your Drawing Journal. They are a great source of local heritage and references for your future creations.

Don't hesitate to visit popular tourist places. It is always better to create your own memories and build your opinions rather than accept others'.

While traveling we can find not only unknown beautiful views but also face unexpected circumstances and challenges. Sometimes it's even more fun to experience and then draw these moments than to have a calm, well-planned trip.

Once during a vacation in the Czech Republic my family and I hadn't booked a hotel beforehand. After searching for a good place to stay for ages, we eventually booked a creepy, shabby hotel in the backwoods with no mobile connection, WiFi, adequate lighting in rooms, or English-speaking staff. We eventually distracted ourselves with walks in the forest and in the evenings I drew outside with a phone flashlight. This experience still was great and definitely outstanding for me. I will recall it with a special joy.

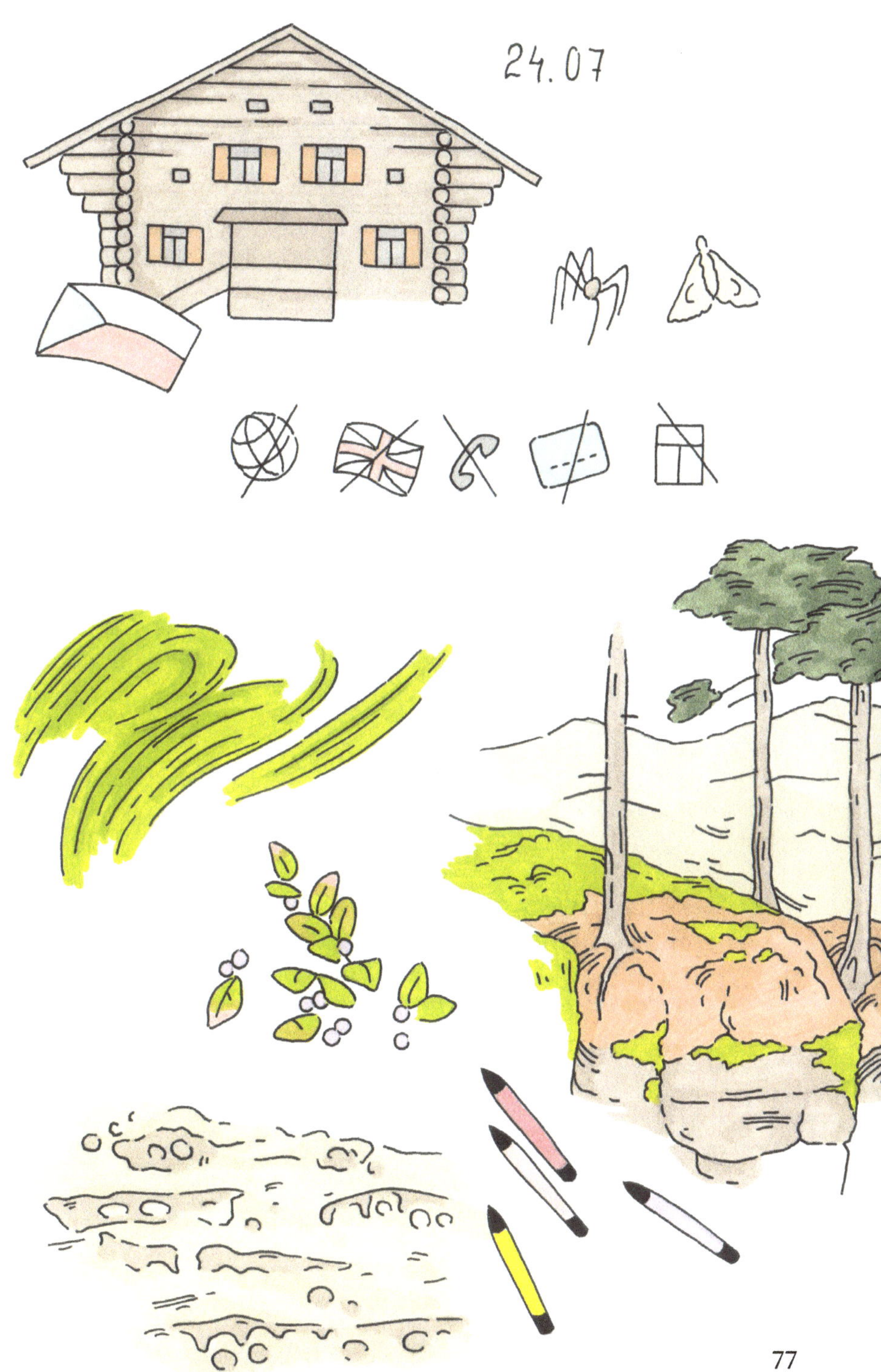
24.07

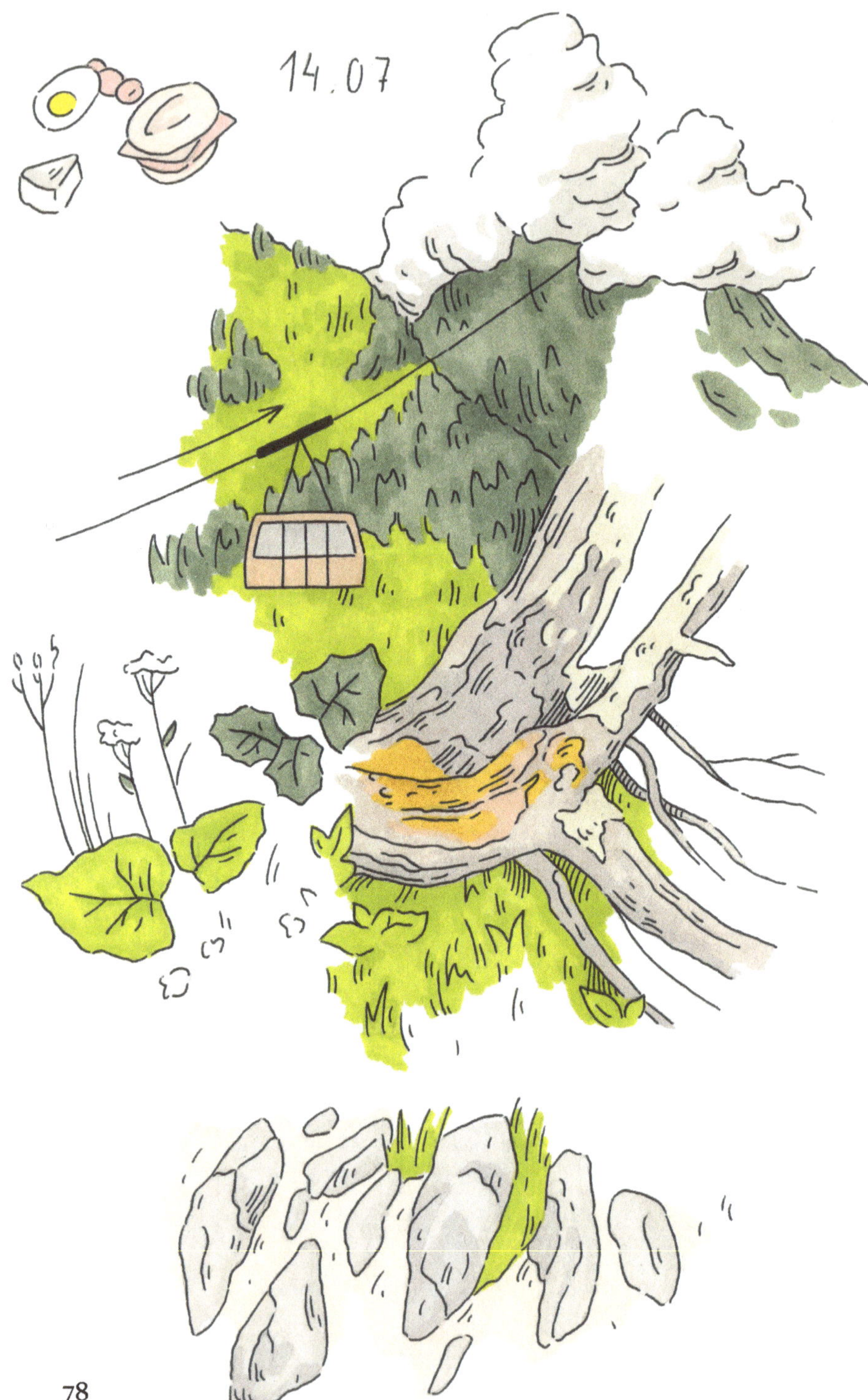
14.07

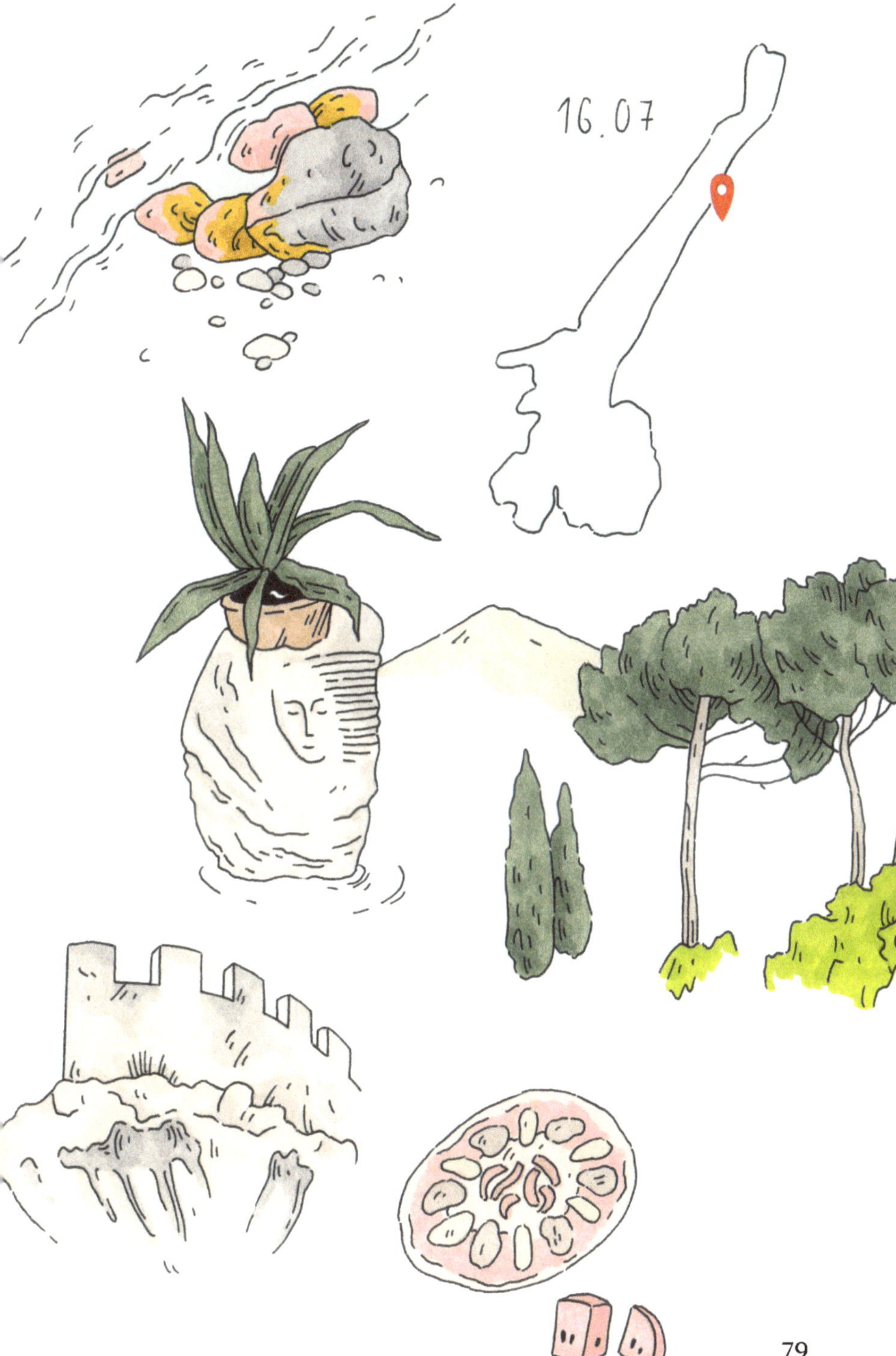
16.07

EXERCISE I

Developing attentiveness

As we go about our day, there are often beautiful things we ignore. They may seem boring or mundane but if you pay attention and look closely, you will be surprised by what you were missing the entire time.

During your usual day, find at least 5 visually or emotionally interesting things and draw them.

On the next two pages, you can see my version of this exercise I drew on December 26th, 2019. I intentionally found things that I hadn't captured before to show that if you just look closely it's always possible to see the beauty in things that you pass every day.

I have a 30 minutes commute to work. First I take the subway with one transfer to another subway line and then I have a 5 minute walk in the city center to the office. On my way, I have found 7 interesting things, which I have never drawn before.

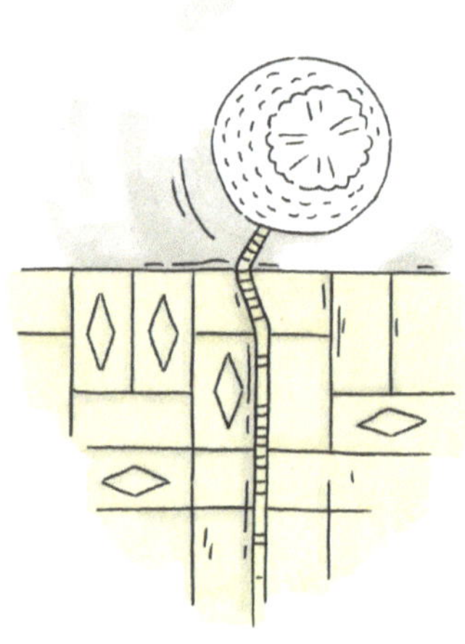

A lamp in the hallway of my house

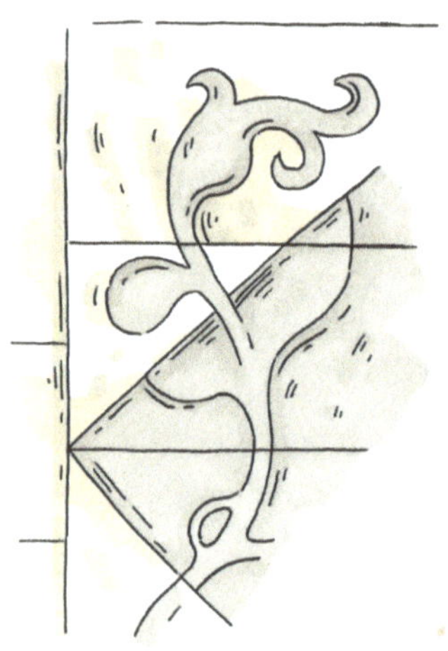

A bas-relief in the Perovo subway station, near which I currently live

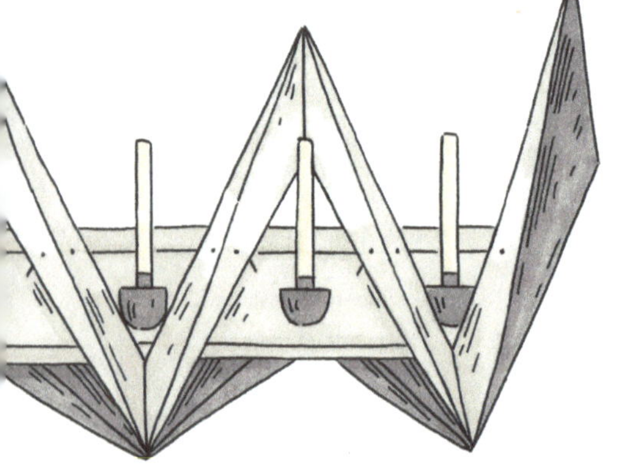

A lamp on the Marksistskaya subway station where I make the transfer to another subway line

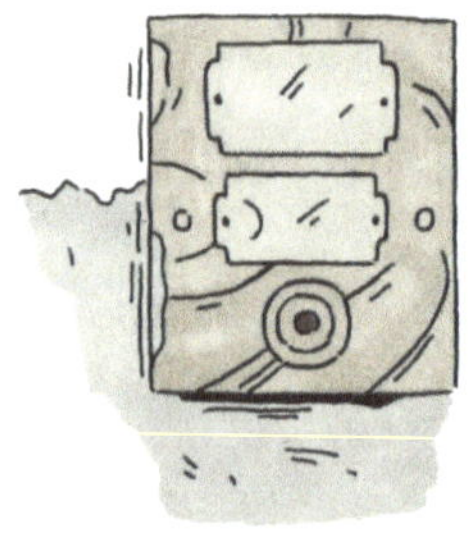

An old wooden doorbell next to my office door

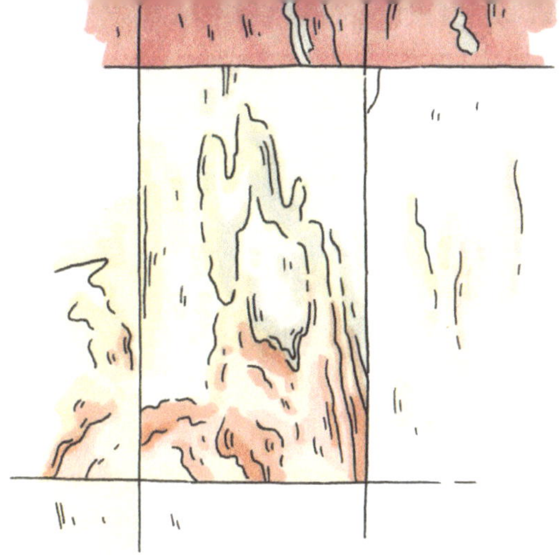

A marble tile on the Taganskaya station

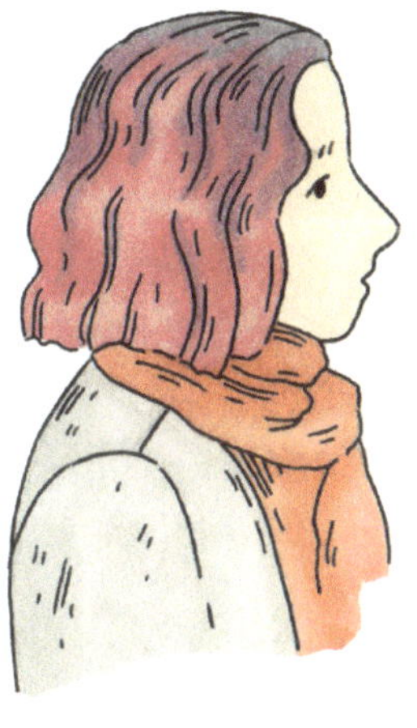

A girl with beautiful pink hair in the subway train

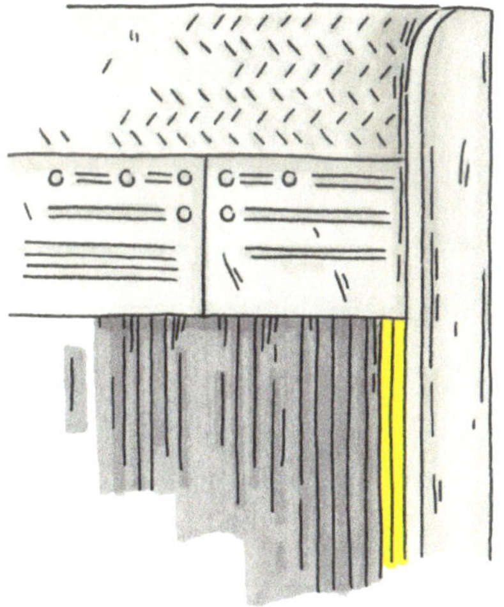

The top of the escalator on the Kuznetskiy Most station where I work. A view from above

CHAPTER V

Get started

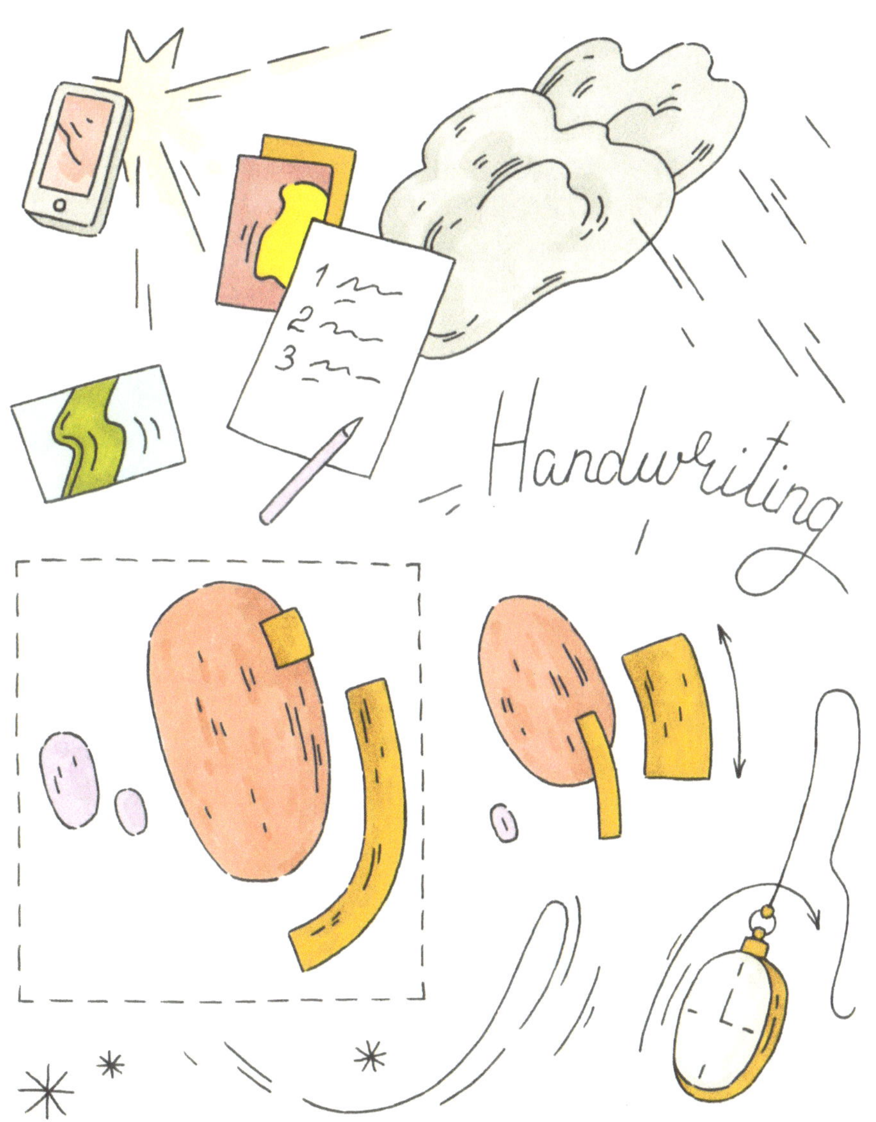

Now, when you got inspired, have chosen materials to draw, and learned how to find beauty in your routine, it's time to start drawing.

Take notes and photos

It can be difficult to remember everything you want to draw, especially detailed objects. Taking quick notes and photos can help with this problem. I usually use Apple Notes or Google Keep. If that doesn't work for you, you can use a dedicated section of your sketchbook or planner. What's important is to choose whatever is most convenient for you.

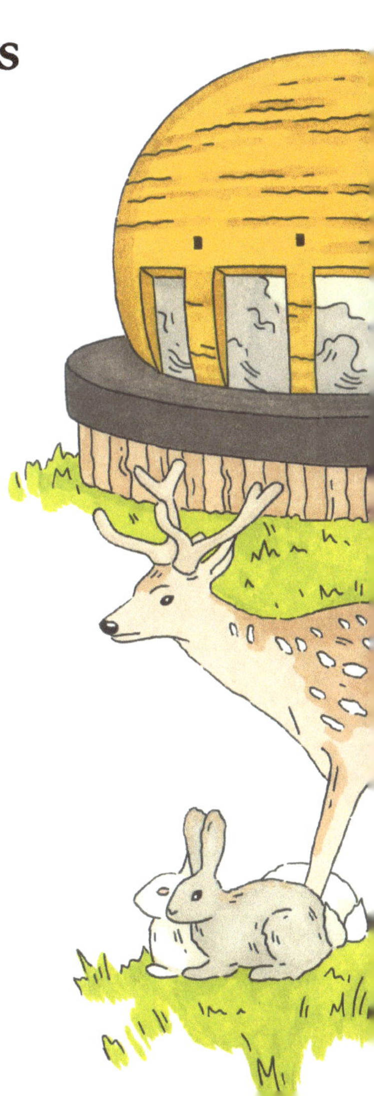

Sometimes I even send myself images in Messenger that will help me to draw a particular detail. If I find something during work, I take a screenshot. Also, sometimes I add googled images which will help me to draw some metaphor or detailed object which I haven't photographed and wouldn't be able to recover in my mind.

Taking photos is especially useful during trips. There are always a lot of impressive landscapes, detailed architecture pieces and intricate details in nature. Pictures will save every detail and provide a chronology of events, so you will be able to depict all your memories later, in a calm and more comfortable atmosphere.

Taking notes is a helpful practice, but remember to use this tool carefully. Don't get into a situation where you take 30 photos but don't draw in your sketchbook because there are too many choices.

My quick note from July 5th, 2019

Smoothie bowl with avocado
Podcast release (first screen)
Instagram post and text
Meeting with Masha
She gave me a tiny vase
Vietnamese place, rice
Malchik (cat's name) on a carpet
A cockroach

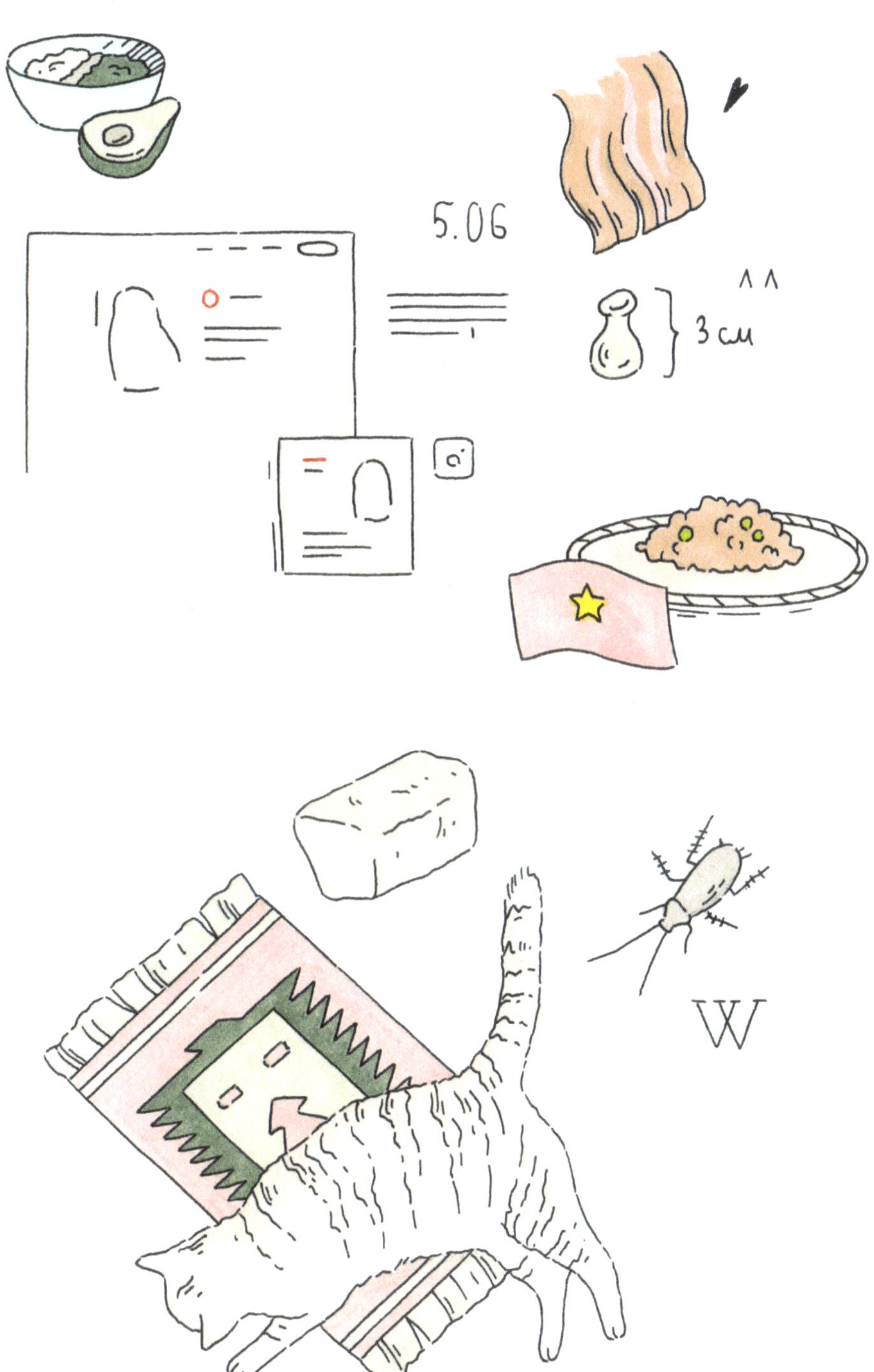
5.06
3 см
W

EXERCISE II

Making notes

Capture your memories of one day with quick notes and photos in any format suitable for you. Write a note for your drawing here, you will need it in the next exercise.

Start to draw

When I start to draw a day, I mentally return to the beginning of that day, look at my quick notes and photos, and piece together what has happened in my mind. Then I choose what moments I find the most memorable and draw them from the morning to the evening in a chronological order.

I don't aim to draw every detail, there is no need to remember everything. Besides, it would take too much time. If there is only one standing out element or thought per day — that's fine. The main thing is to capture things that are important to you.

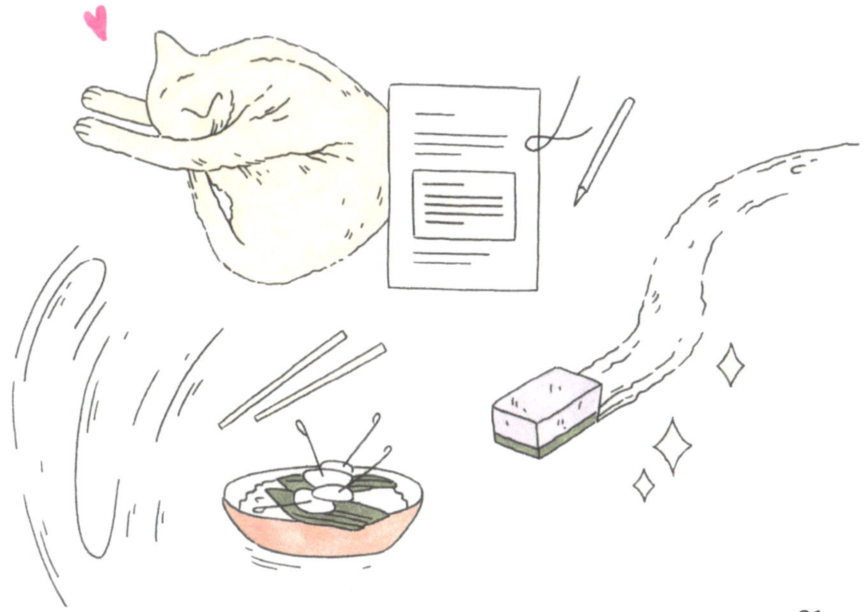

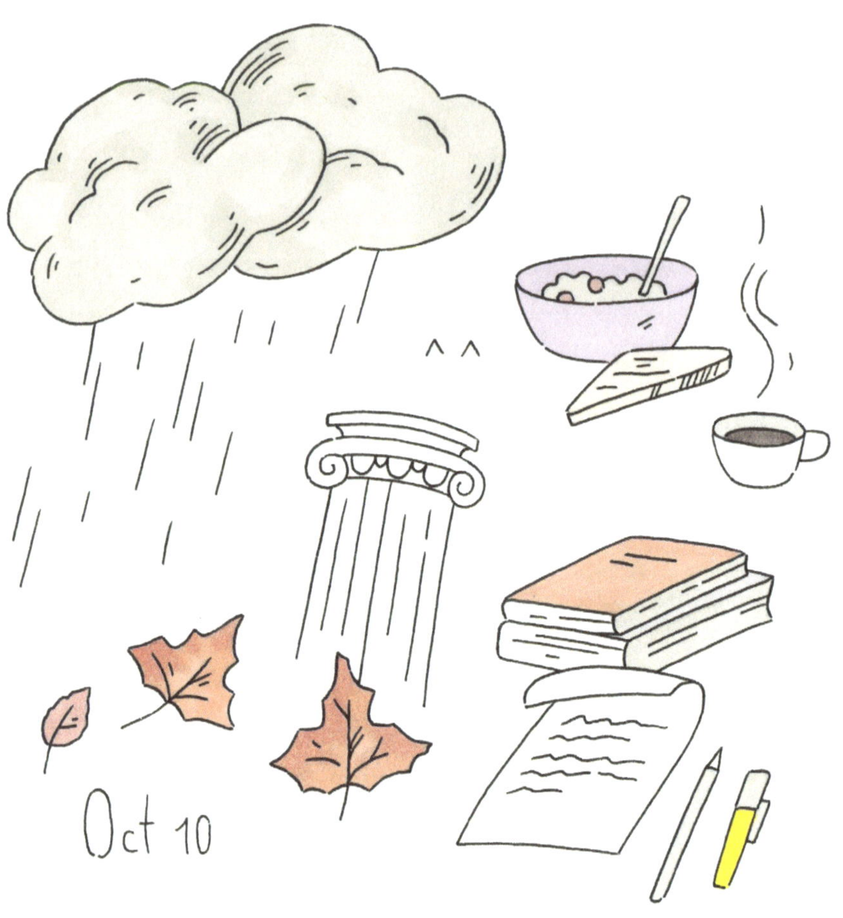

When I have chosen what I want to illustrate, I start to draw. First, I use a hard 3H pencil then I add color with markers and finish the drawings with a black pen. Sometimes the compositions in my sketchbook can be quite complex and using a pencil first is more comfortable for me because it prevents mistakes.

If a blank page makes you feel anxious, start with basic and everyday elements like the weather or your mood. Add a drawing of your breakfast, architectural details, or some piece of nature you saw during your day. Draw what you have been doing at work or school. Look at your notes and pictures, they will be especially helpful during the first few weeks of the Drawing Journal project. Also, don't forget to write down the date.

Don't worry about the quality of your drawings and don't be hard on yourself if something doesn't work. With daily practice, your drawings will evolve and become better. The most important thing is to keep going.

How to capture a memory

There are many approaches to capture your memories on paper.

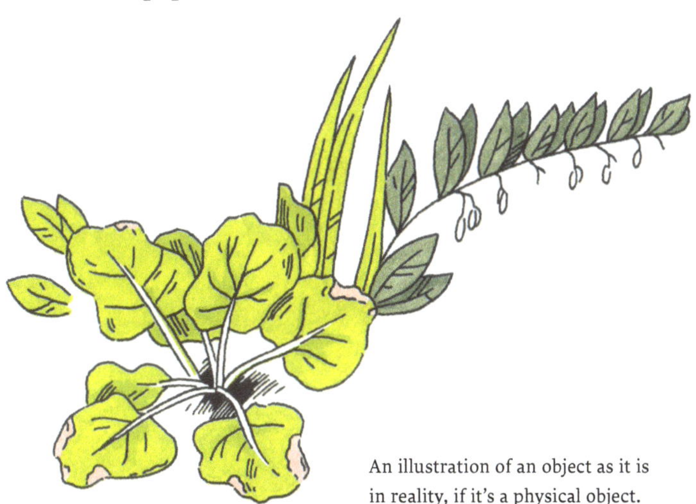

An illustration of an object as it is in reality, if it's a physical object.

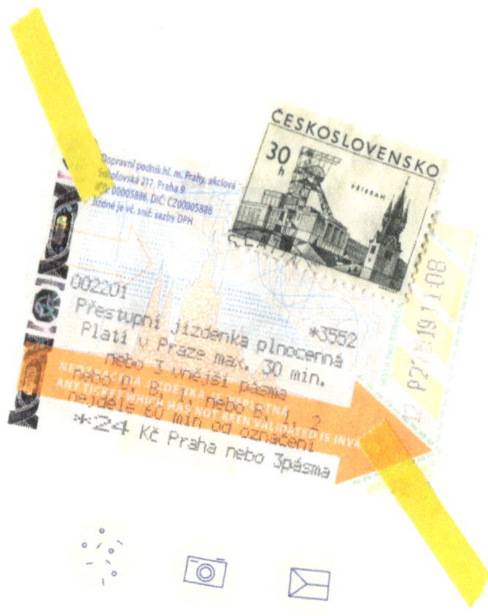

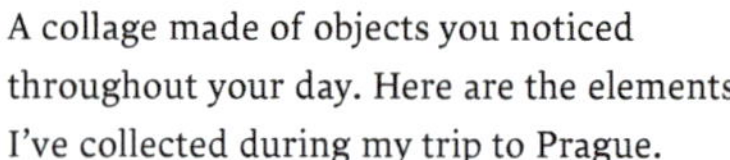

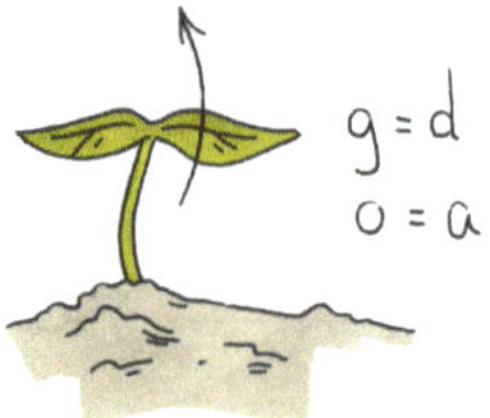

A collage made of objects you noticed throughout your day. Here are the elements I've collected during my trip to Prague.

A rebus encrypting the name of an object, event, or feeling you want to capture. The answer to this rebus is: growing = drawing.

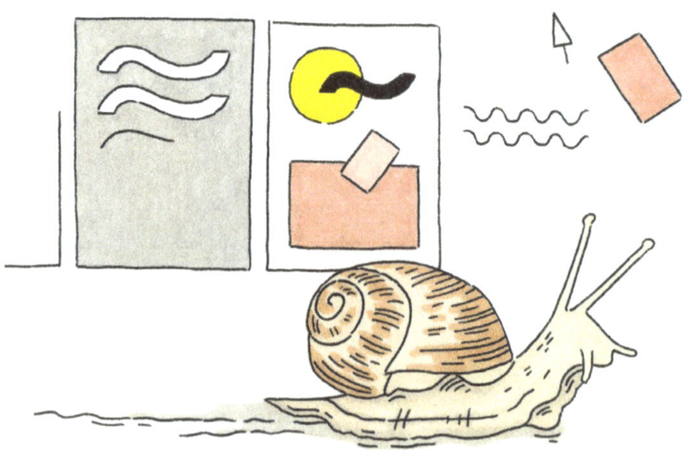

A metaphor of an impression. Here is the day when I was working very slowly and drew a snail to show it.

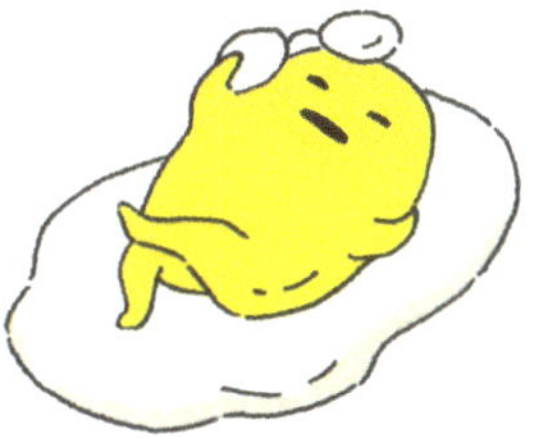

An association with a person, an object, event or feeling. Here is Gudetama, the Japanese cartoon character. I associate it with my colleague Nastya because she has a T-shirt with it, which she wears on Fridays.

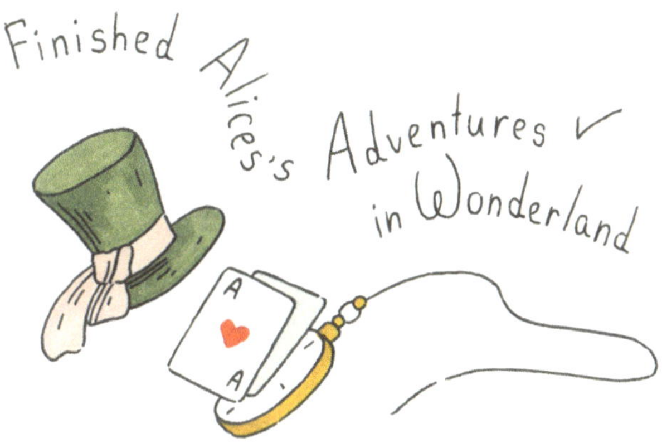

A word or a phrase made with simple handwriting or lettering.

It's not necessary to use the same drawing style on every page. Experiment and draw each day differently. On the next pages you can see a few examples. If you need more inspiration, look at other artists who are keeping similar projects. For example, it's easy to find them on Instagram by #drawingdiary or #drawingjournal tags.

Remember to make your first days easy and relaxed. The goal is to create a new habit and not to overdo it on day one.

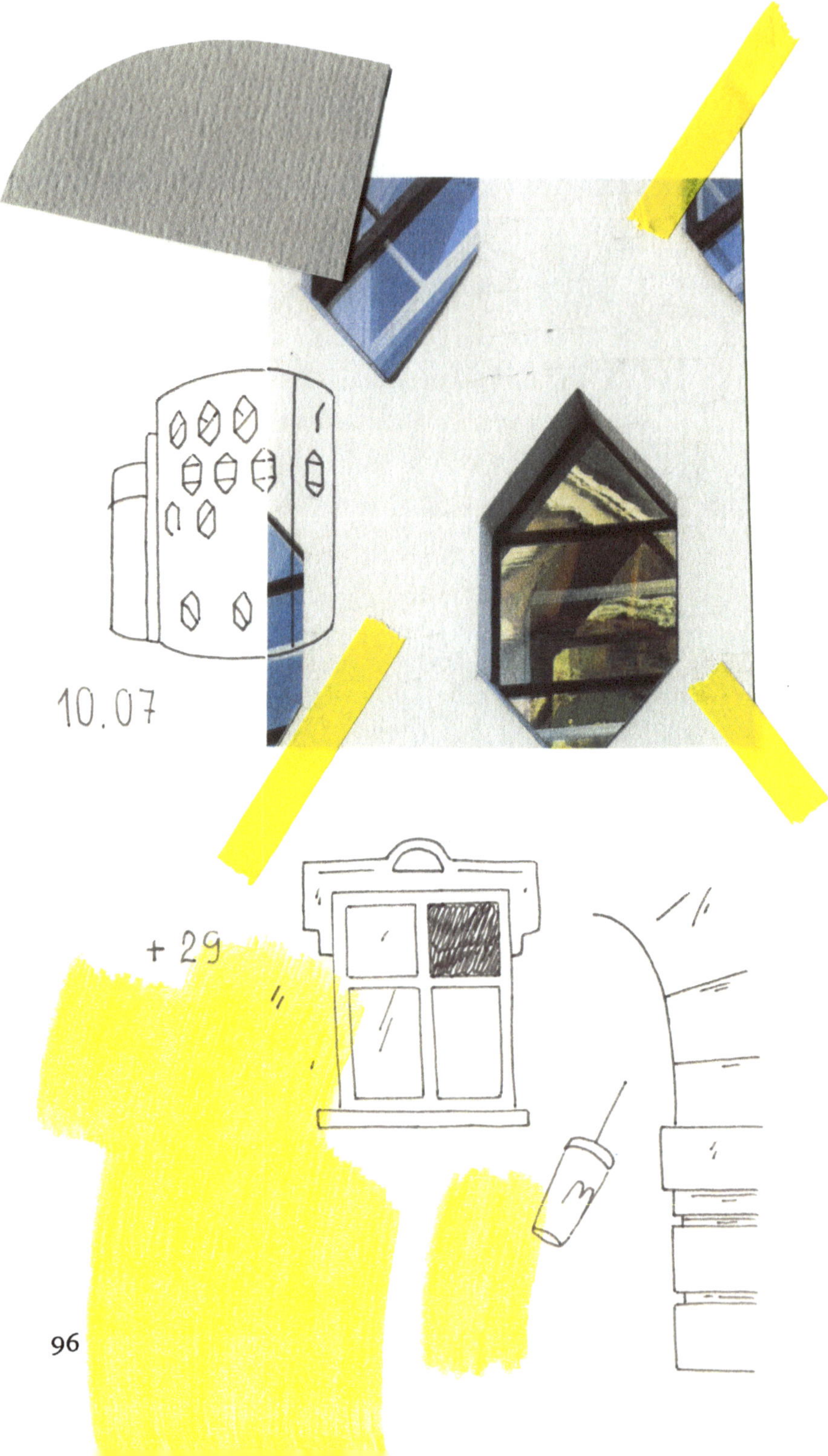

10.07

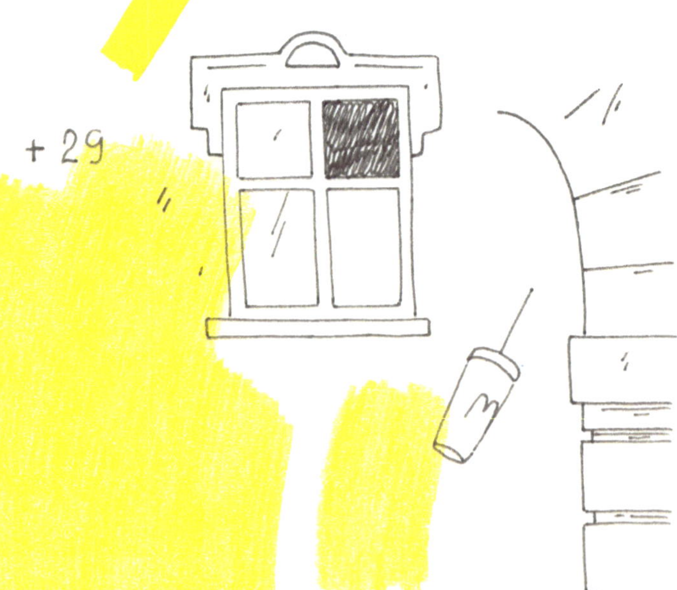

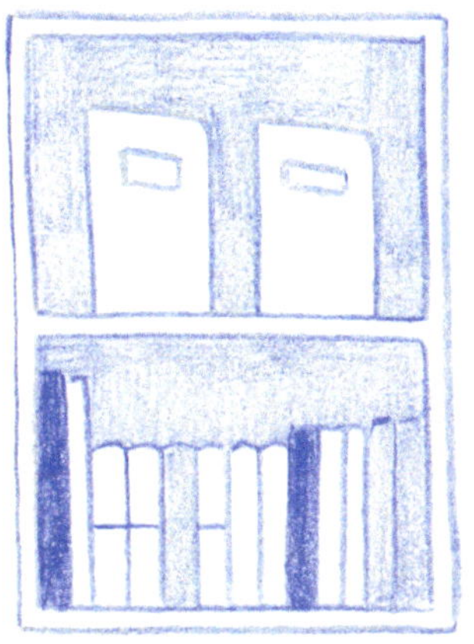

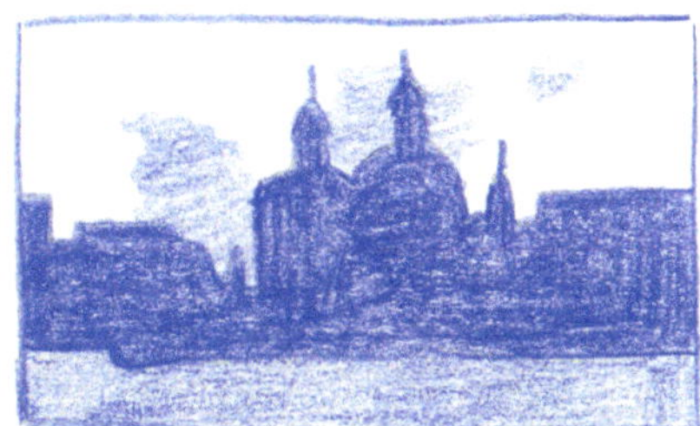

PAPELOTE

OLD TOWN SQUARE

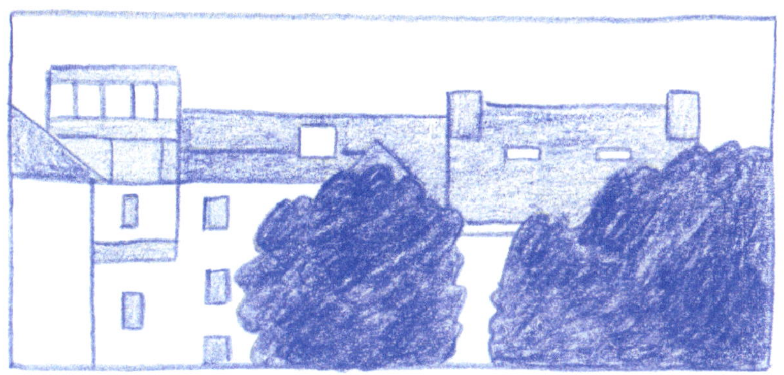

THE VIEW FROM OUR APPARTMENT

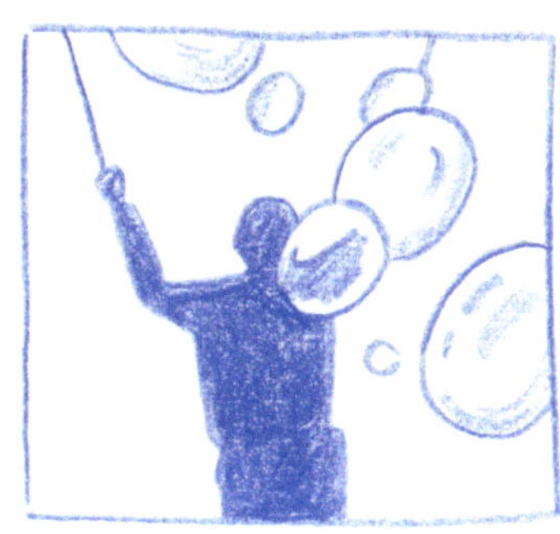

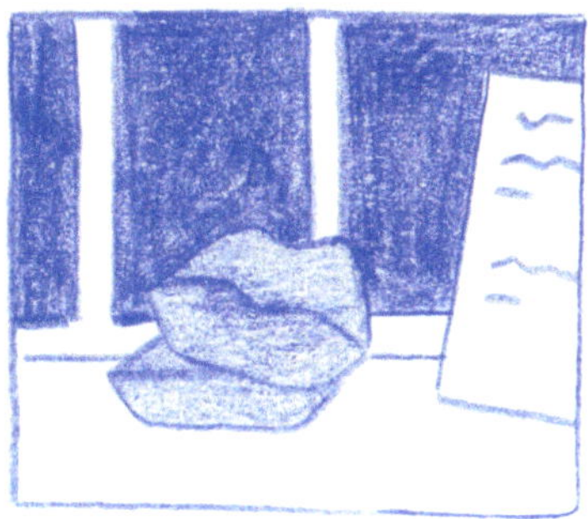

A MAN WITH SOAP BUBBLES

SOME CAFE EXTERIOR

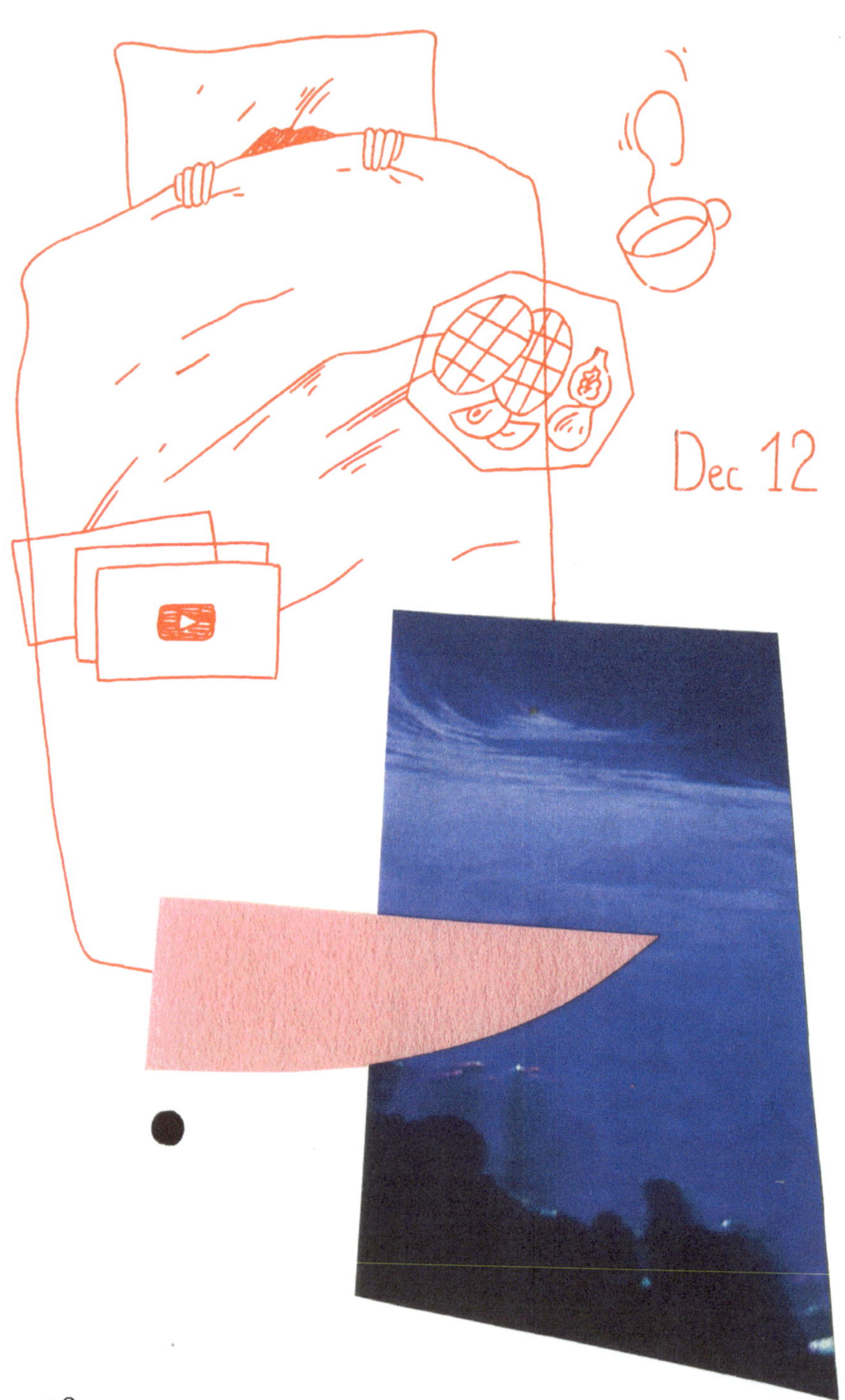
Dec 12

MONDAY

MAY 19th

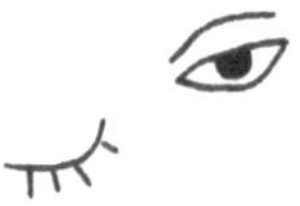

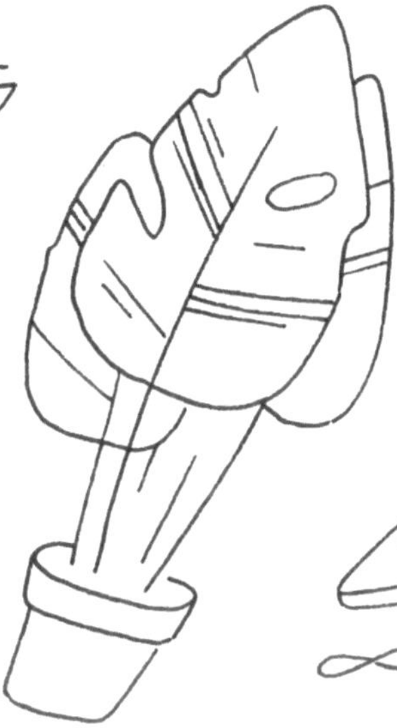

a new flower on my desk

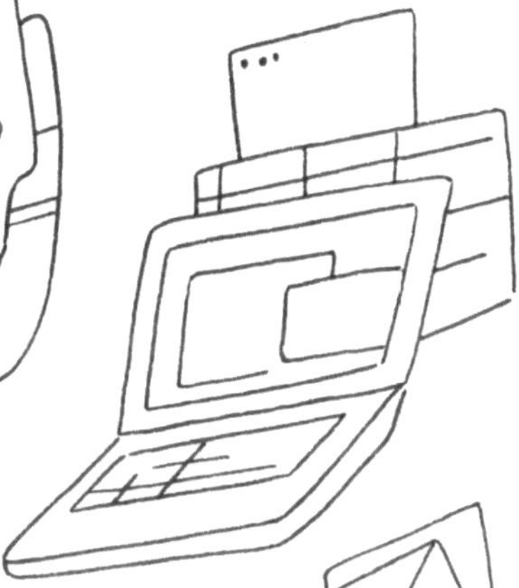

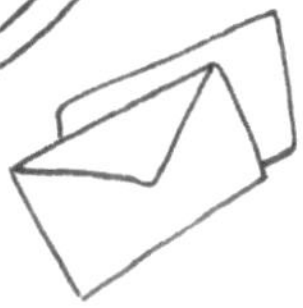

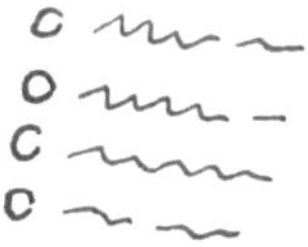

lots of tasks

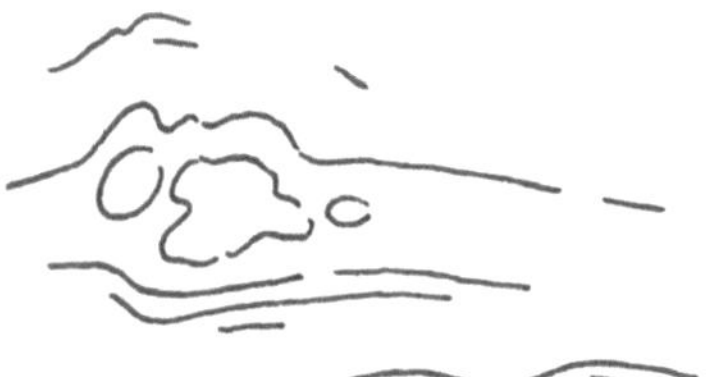

marbel pattern on a sabway station

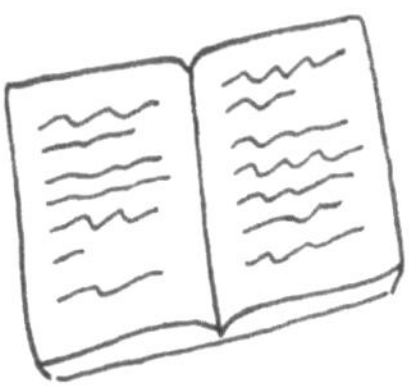

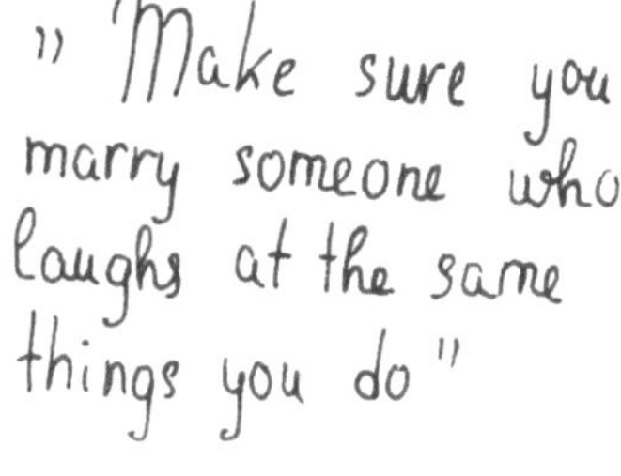

" Make sure you marry someone who laughs at the same things you do"

JD Salinger

If you're having a hard time visualizing what to draw on your first day, try combining handwriting with drawings. Try a 70% handwriting and 30% drawing blend to kick things off. With practice, you can change this ratio at a comfortable pace and train yourself to illustrate your memories in a variety of ways.

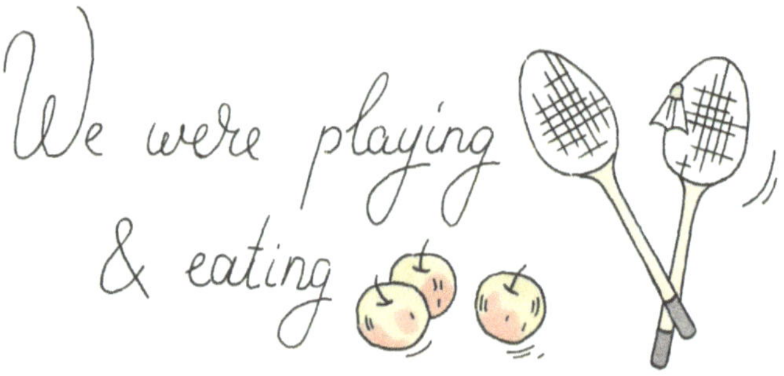

If you decide to do handwriting, try to write your words with curves that support your drawings and repeat their edges to make them look more interesting.

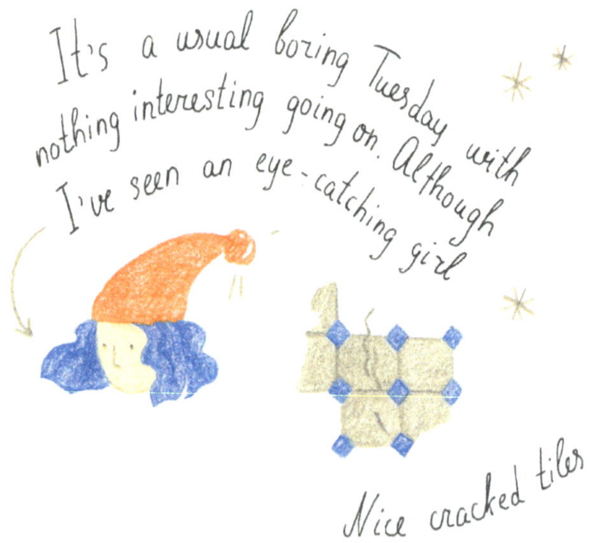

EXERCISE III

Capture your day

Try to illustrate one day with the help of simple drawings and handwriting. Don't think about style, neatness, or composition. For now, only the meaning is important. The next exercises will help you to develop your skills and make your drawings better.

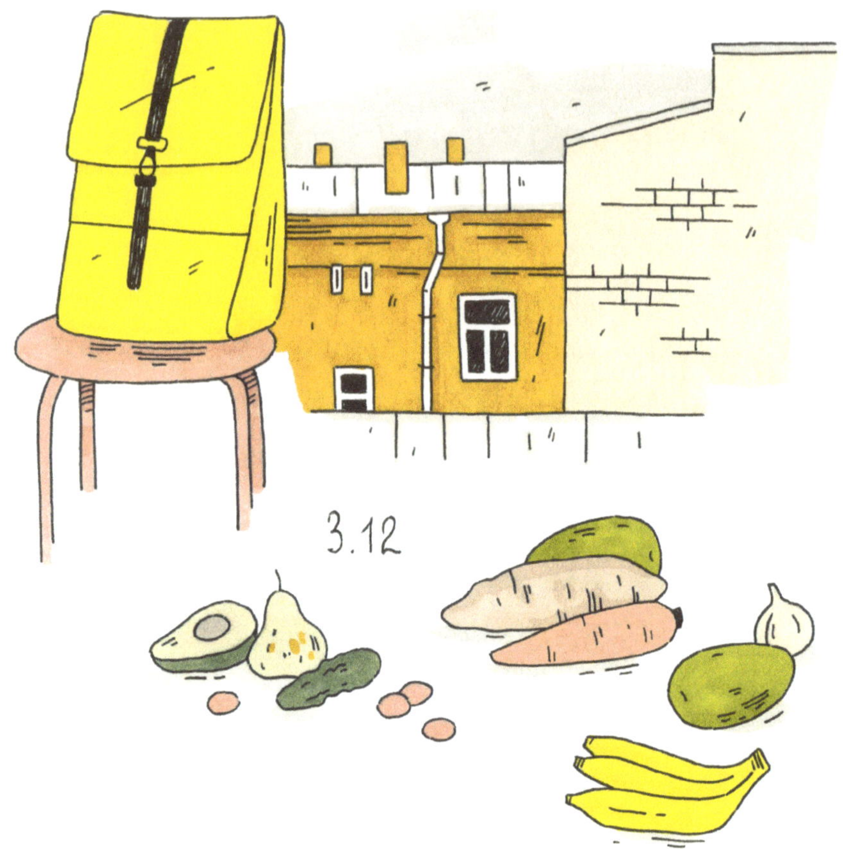

Build a composition

After you've drawn a few days, you may notice you have developed a style you're comfortable with. It then becomes time to think about how you can make your concepts better and more harmonious. A good composition makes drawings balanced and chronologically understandable.

Here are a few basic rules and my personal observations which will help you to make a composition clear and interesting.

Group objects by contextual relevance

There is an important basic rule in Design called "the Law of Proximity" and it's also very helpful in a Drawing Journal. It says that elements located close to each other are perceived as related when compared with elements that are separated from each other.

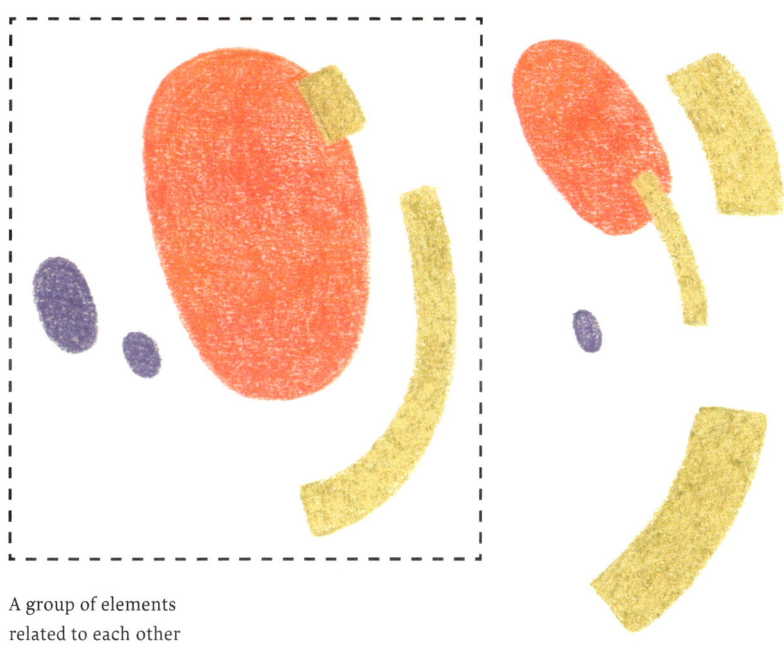

A group of elements related to each other

For example, your day's drawing could consist of: a group of tasks that you worked on at your job, a group of groceries, and a group of reactions you had from watching a movie. Separating these different parts of your day into small groups of drawings helps to reinforce the context and keeps the memories distinct from each other. Otherwise you may have a situation where the broccoli from your groceries is near a bar chart from your work. I mean, maybe they relate but probably not.

Besides space, drawings can also be united by additional elements like a unique background color, lines, patterns, or frames.

The fun part is that this rule can be used for both one day and a span of a few days on one page. I suggest spacing the events of one day closer than the distances between days. It will be easier to understand which event is related to which day.

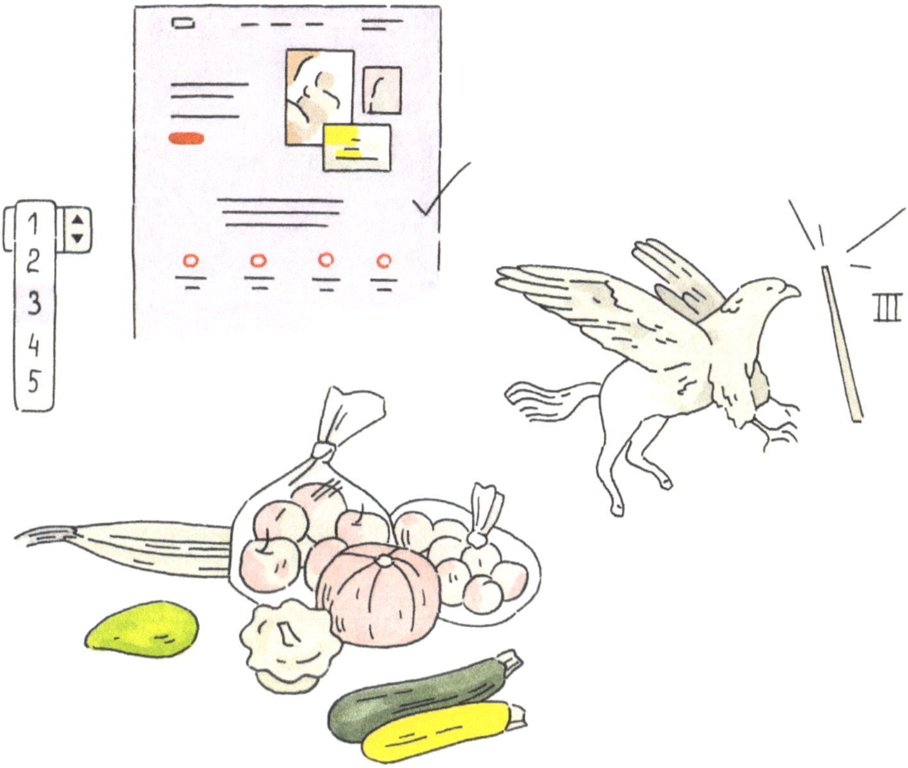

Groups of elements are separated from each other by their relevance to a day timeline

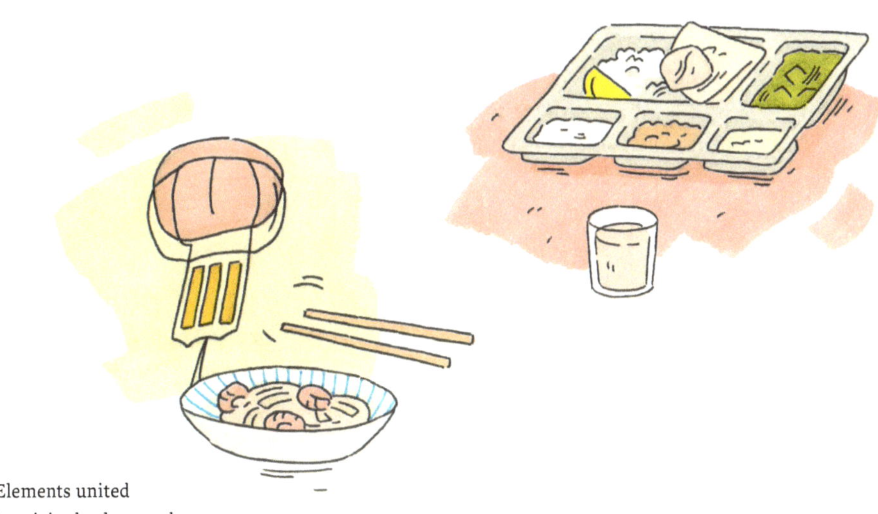

Elements united by a joint background

EXERCISE IV

Applying "the Law of Proximity"

Here is a group of graphic shapes of different colors. Regroup them by color so shapes of one color are visually united.

I left more space in the Composition Exercises for you to experiment and try a few versions of a composition. After finishing the exercise you can look at my version of this exercise on the next page.

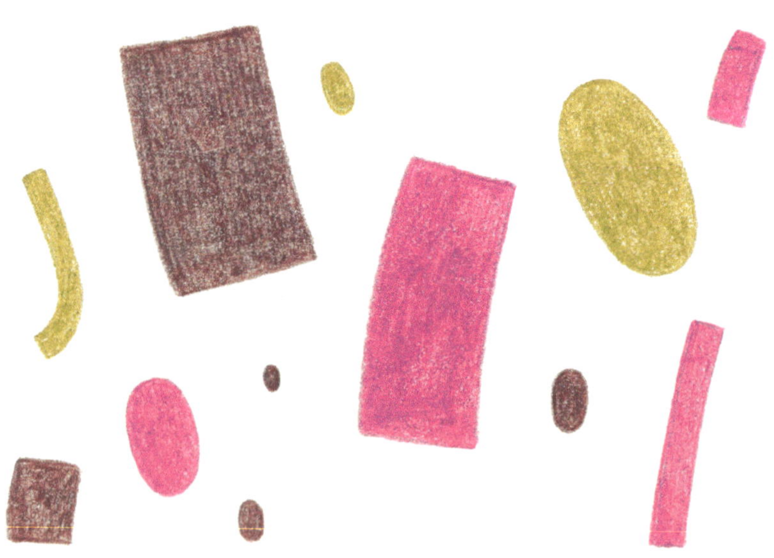

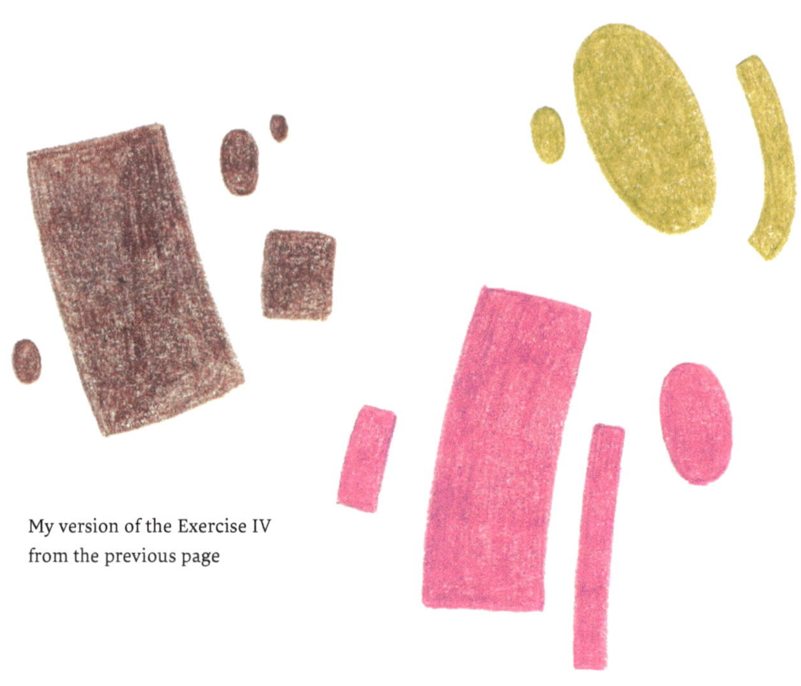

My version of the Exercise IV
from the previous page

Contrast neighboring objects with scale

To help objects look good together, put them close and contrast their sizes dramatically. Don't be afraid to use a big contrast, it will make your drawings more dynamic.

You may wonder, "What element should be larger and how big should it be compared to its small neighbor?" When you put a plate of macaroni next to The Eiffel Tower, obviously the original size of objects won't work here. Draw important and detailed objects larger. Less detailed and insignificant objects can be drawn smaller so the details of these neighboring objects look approximately the same scale. For example, a building facade with bas-reliefs should be a few times bigger than a book or another simple item. If the book has an intricately detailed cover, the contrast between it and a building should be less significant.

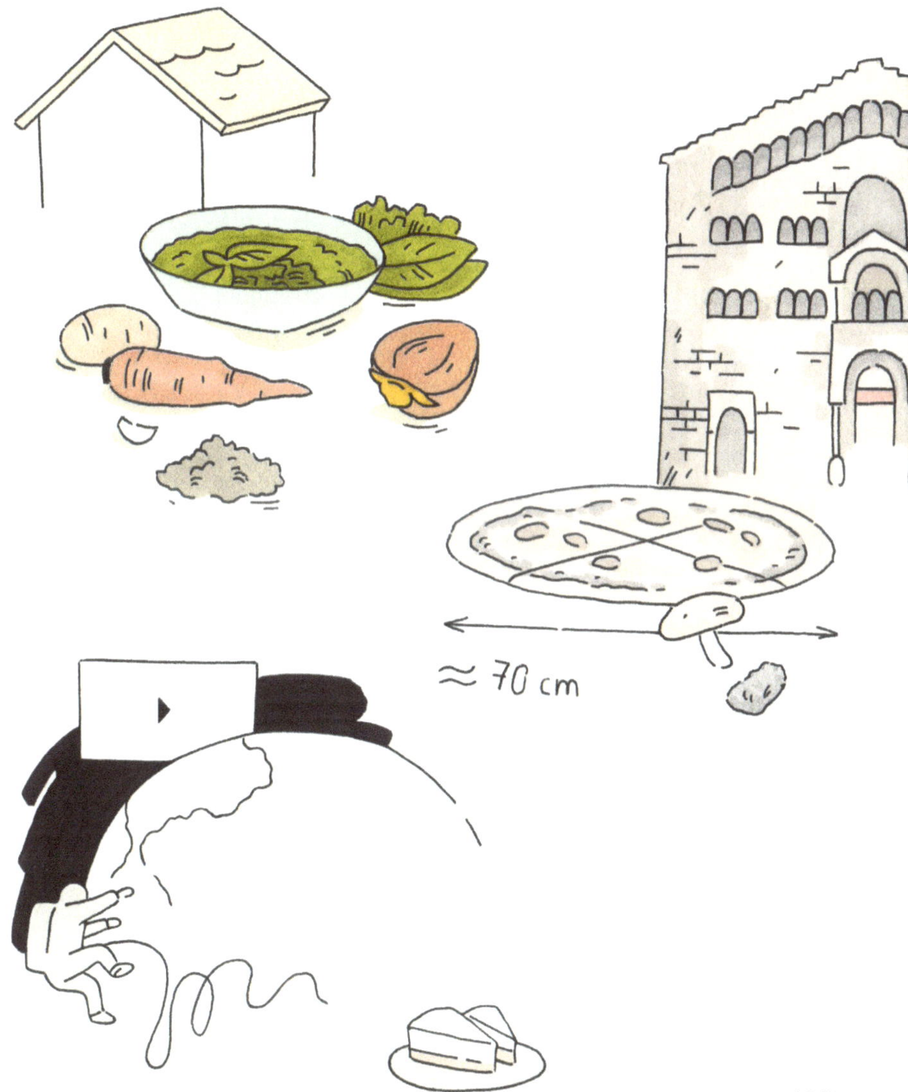

EXERCISE V

Making a contrasting composition

Here is a group of graphic shapes that have almost the same size. This composition lacks contrast between the shapes' scale. Draw a version where the elements have more contrast to each other. My example is on the next page.

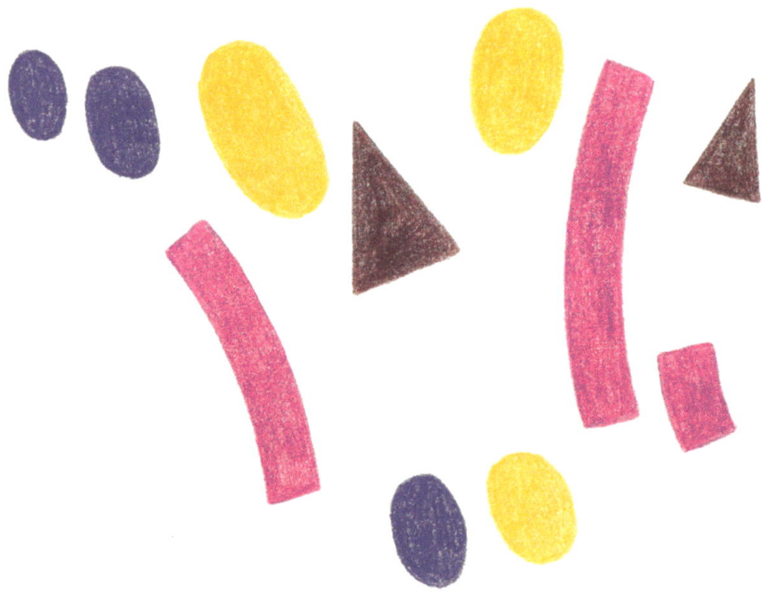

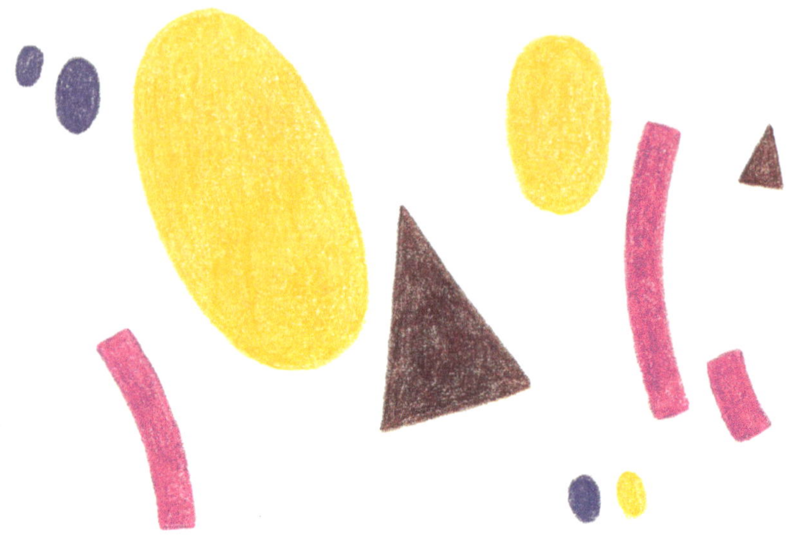

My version of Exercise V
from the previous page

Overlay one object on another

I love overlapping objects on each other, it helps to connect them accordingly to “the Law of Proximity” and give a composition more depth. You can multiply this method over and over to create groups of elements overlaid on each other.

It’s better to put a smaller object on top of a bigger one. Make sure not to obscure a big part of a background object and try to put the smaller object on the edge instead.

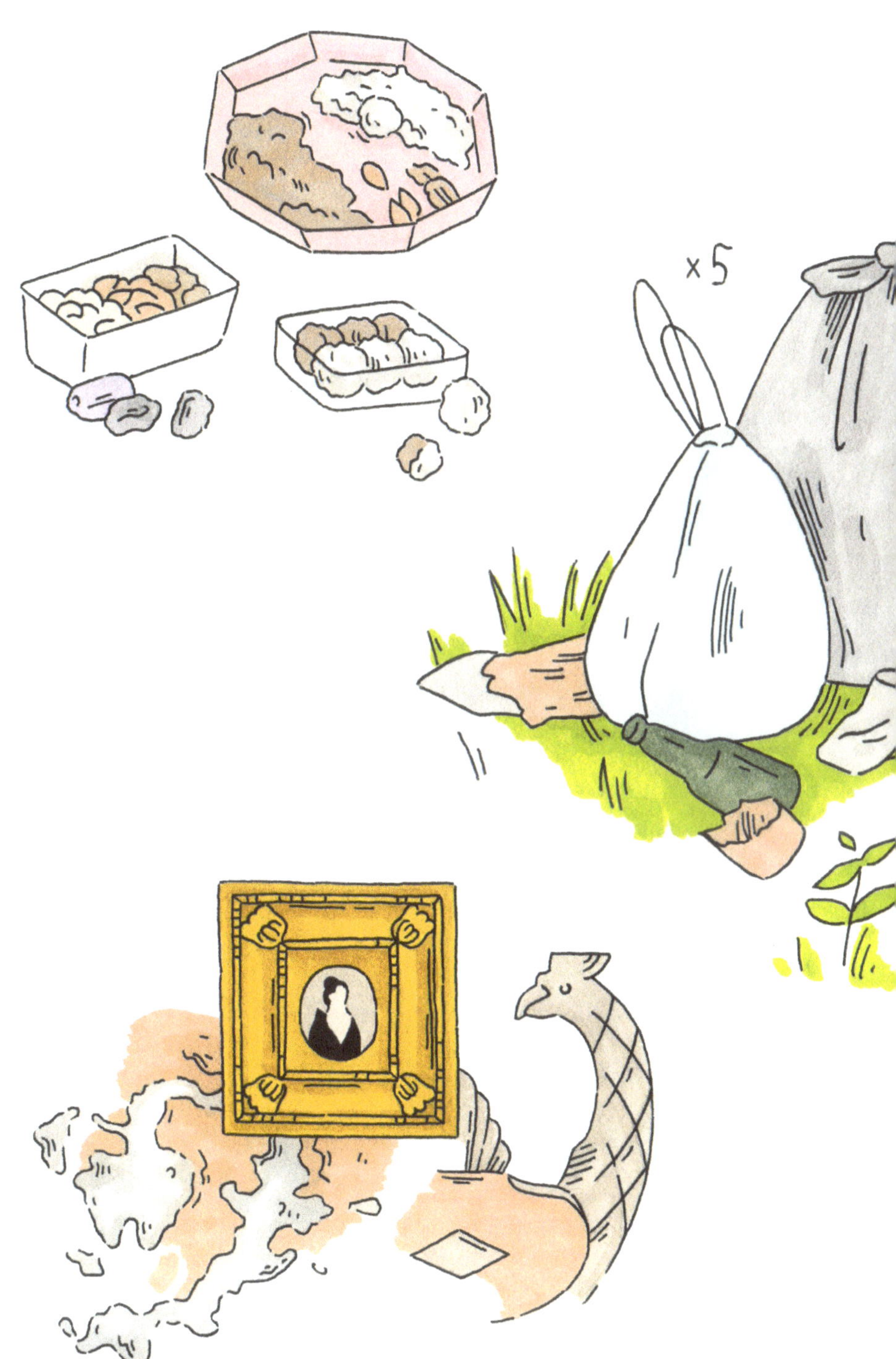
x 5

EXERCISE VI

Overlapping objects

Here is a group of graphic shapes that can be regrouped in a more interesting way. Redraw them so a few of them overlap each other. Try to connect two or more objects and don't forget to put smaller objects on bigger ones. You will find my version of this exercise on the next page.

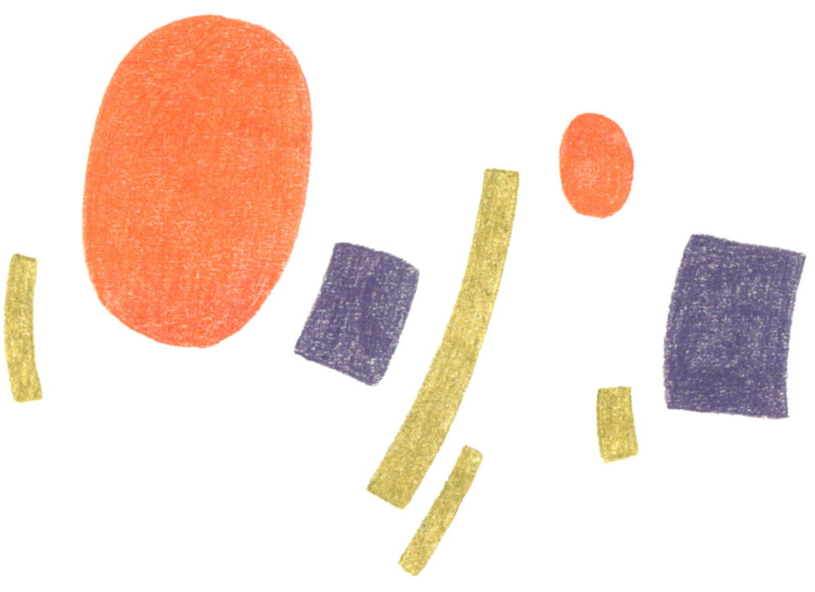

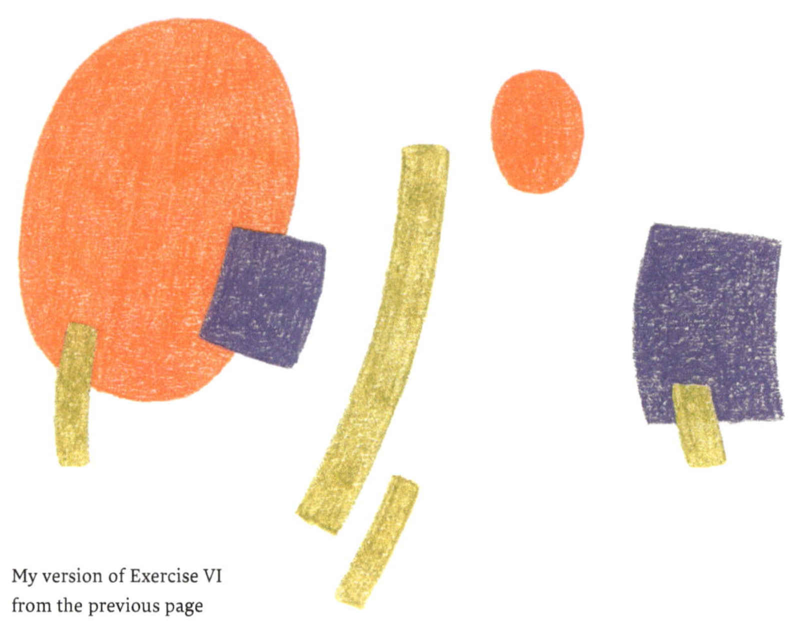

My version of Exercise VI
from the previous page

Add dynamics

Dynamics imply the presence of movement and energy in a drawing. They can be created by adding a “moving” flow of elements and playfulness of lines and shapes. It’s appropriate for elements that can be moved this way in real life, like clothing, book pages, long hair, rain or wind in the trees.

Instead of drawing static objects, imagine them flying in the air or being moved by wind. Try to create these “flows” in one direction, so the movements won’t be too chaotic.

Dynamics can also be used to craft a metaphor. If you had a crazy and hurried day or experienced a sudden and surprising moment, create a mess on purpose to show a dynamic atmosphere or your mood.

Use dynamics carefully. If you make all the objects in motion, the drawing can become an incomprehensible mess.

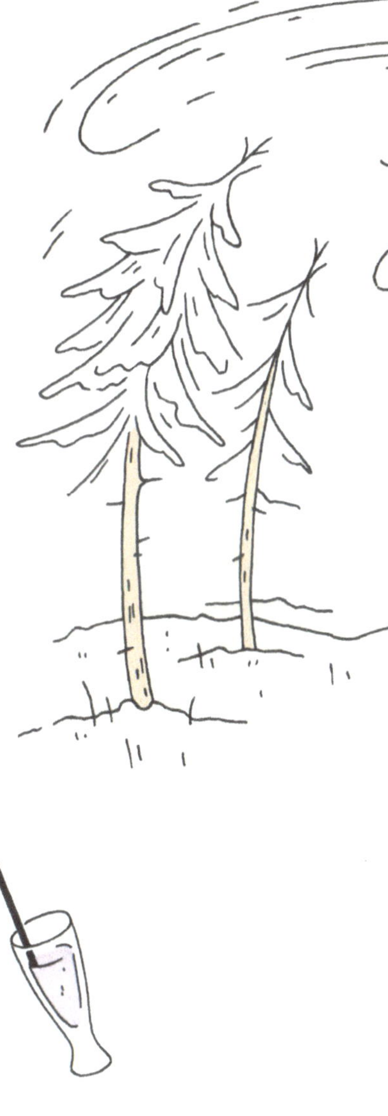

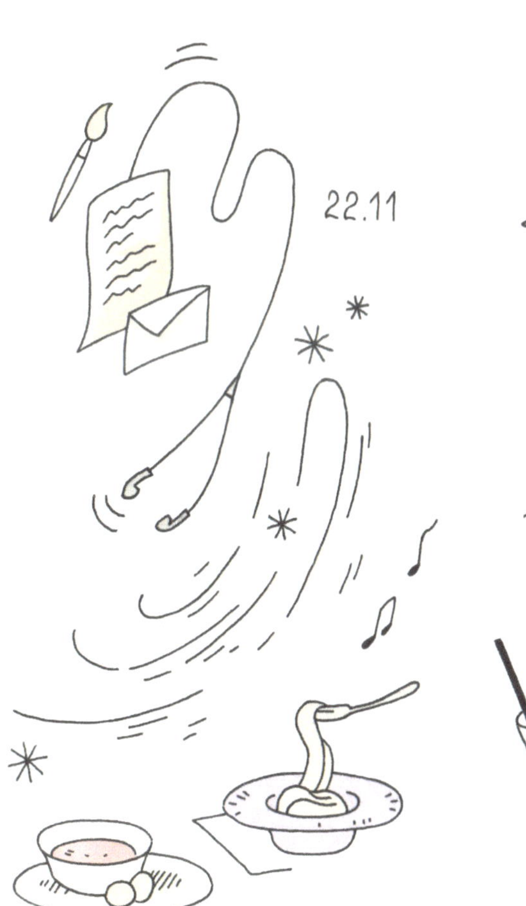

EXERCISE VII

Creating a dynamic composition

Here are graphic shapes combined in a static composition. Reorder them to be dynamic. Don't forget about creating "flows" of elements. Look at my version of this exercise on the next page.

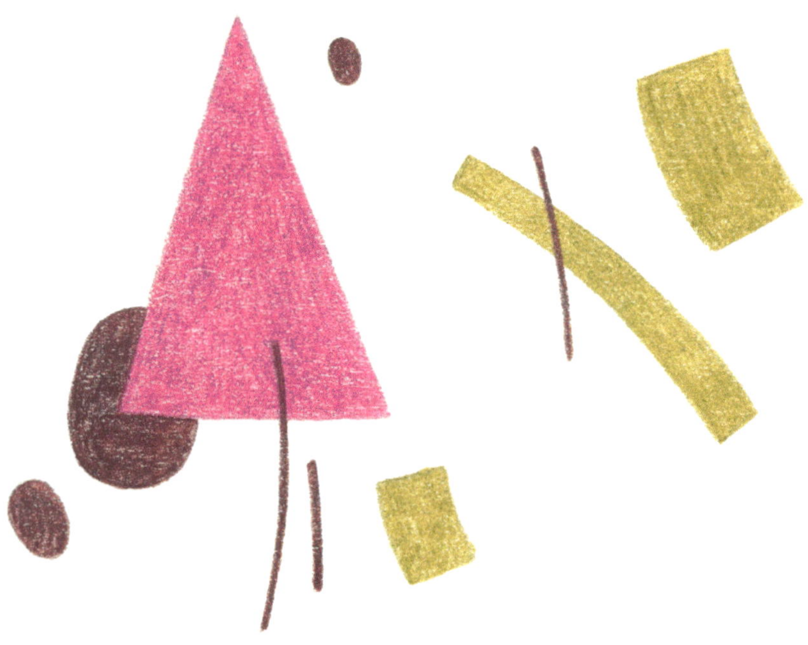

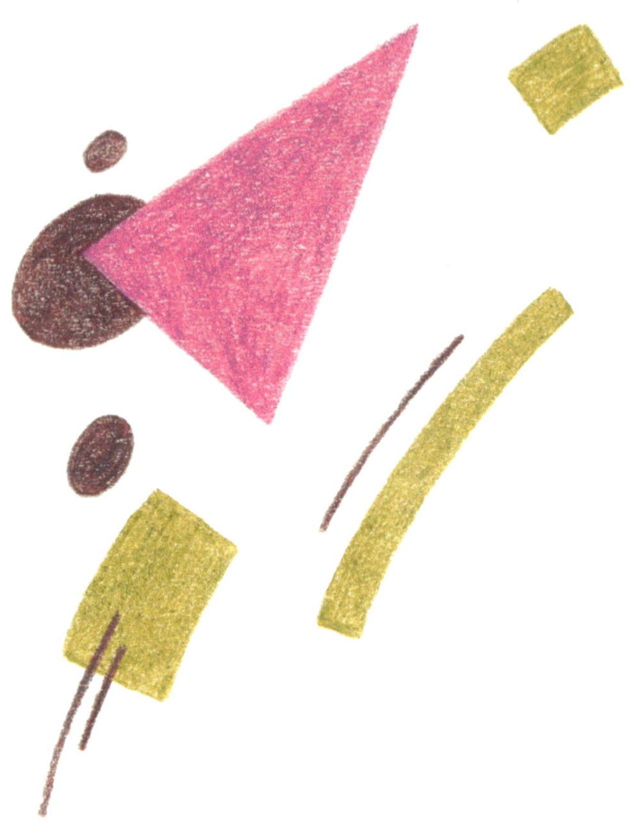

My version of Exercise VII
from the previous page

Use page edges

This method is easy but quite effective. Make some elements go off page to add diversity to your drawings. Edges can also be used to cut difficult elements that take a long time to draw or to cut large elements that are too big to draw full size but can't be drawn smaller because of their importance or detailing.

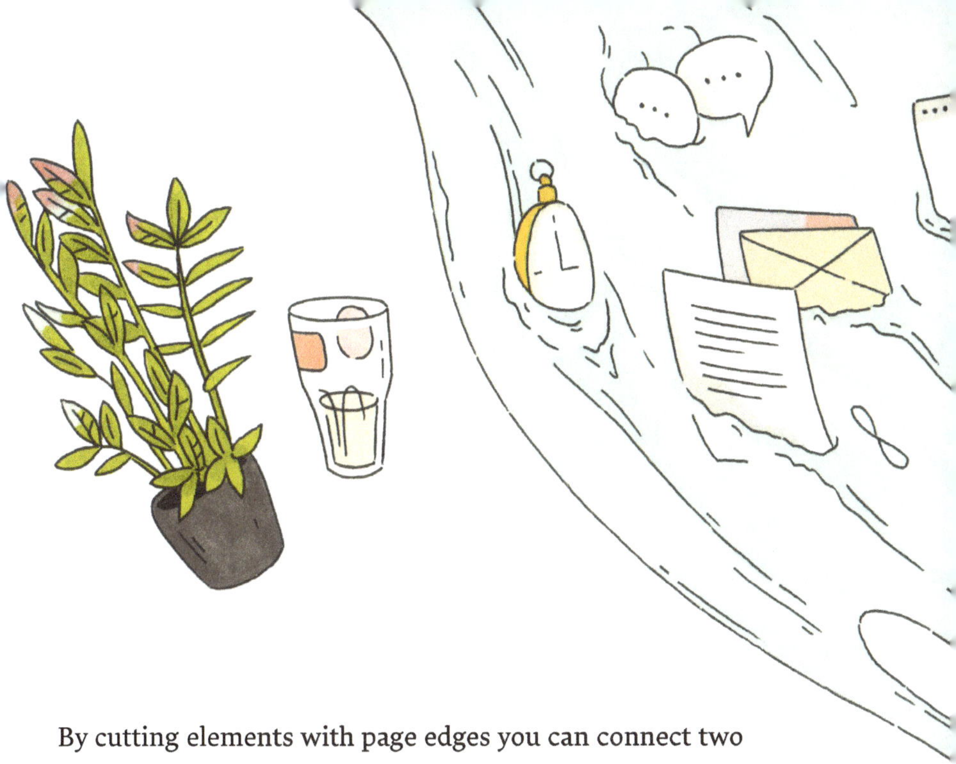

By cutting elements with page edges you can connect two days on different pages. For example, when I take a night train somewhere, I draw the rear half of the train on one page and the front part of it on the next one. If you have a half of a day on one page and another half on the next one, this approach will also connect these drawings.

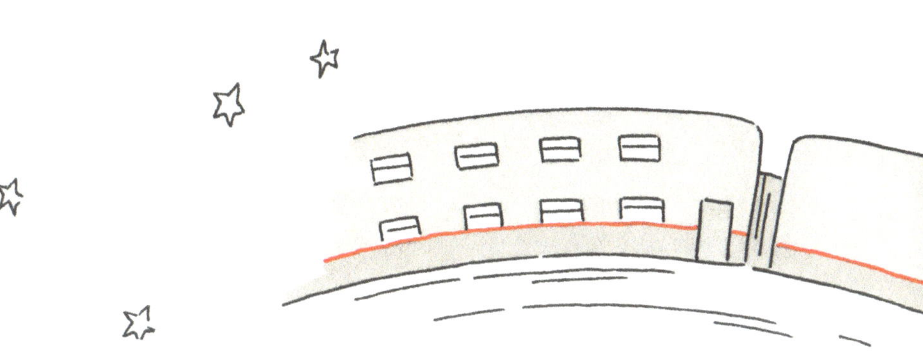

EXERCISE VIII

Using page edges

Use the edge of this page to create a cut composition. You can work with graphic shapes as in the previous exercise or any other objects. For example, the ones around you right now.

CHAPTER VI

Make drawings interesting & intriguing

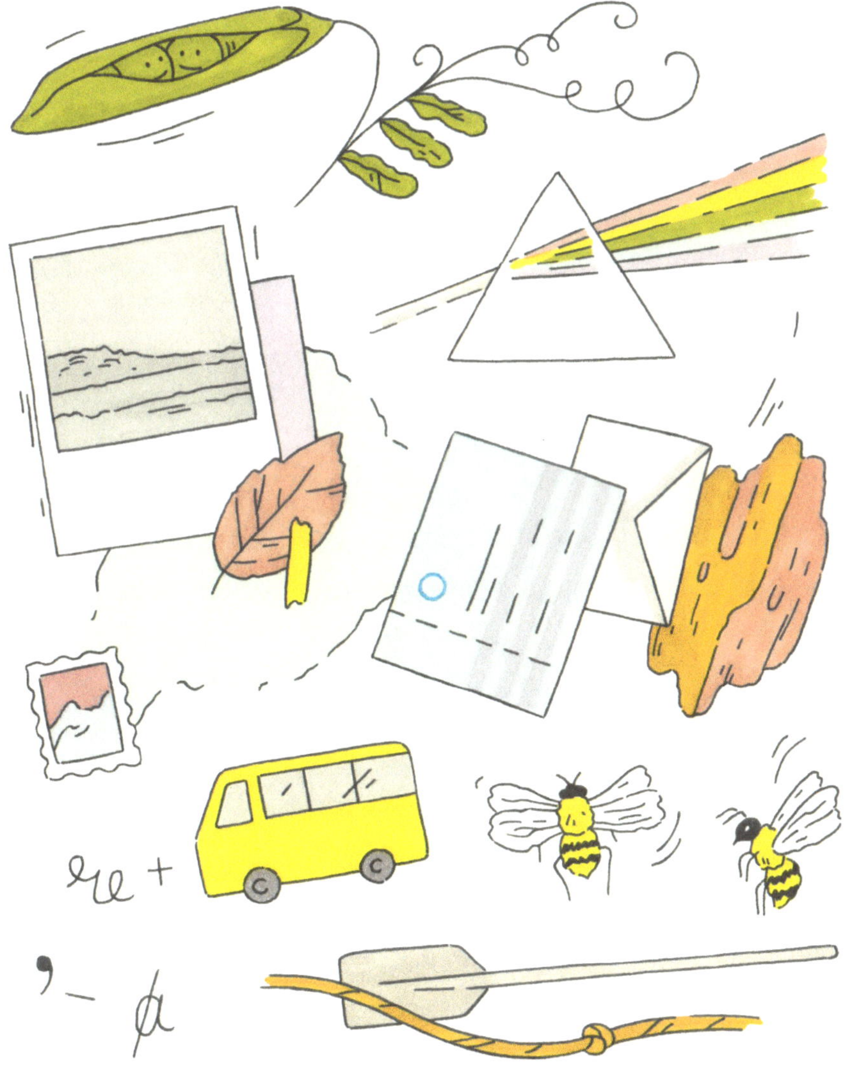

Here are a few ways I discovered to make a Drawing Journal diverse and interesting to explore for you and others.

Metaphors

A metaphor is a figure of speech that compares an object or action with something dissimilar that represents an idea or comparison. The greatest thing about a metaphor is that it links new with familiar.

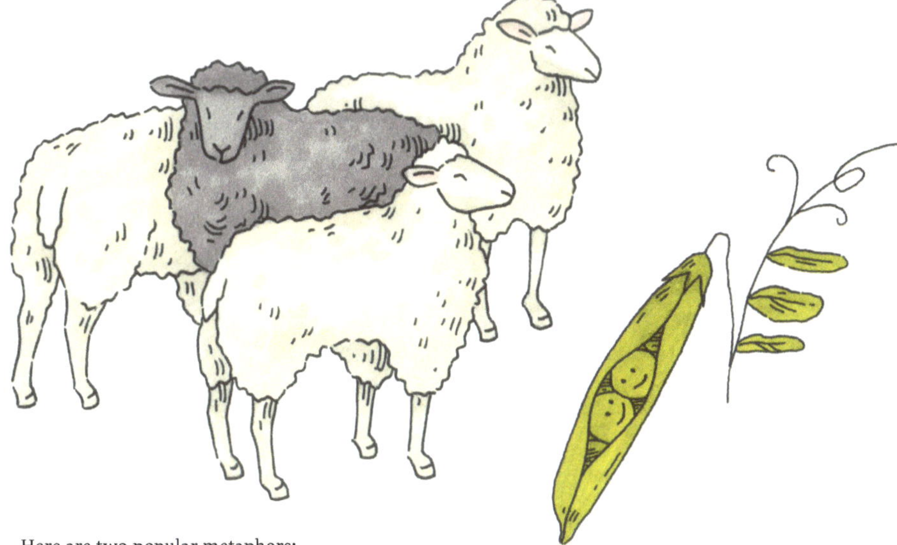

Here are two popular metaphors:
"A black sheep" and "Like two peas in a pod"

What is fascinating about drawing is that you can depict whatever you imagine, not only the things you see in real life. Keeping a Drawing Journal doesn't mean that you should draw every object you see as precisely as possible. On the contrary, it helps to express your unique style and your associations with an object.

It can be a personal observation or a common expression suitable for the situation. Once, when my mom and I were in Saint Petersburg, I depicted us as two cabbages. There is a Russian expression "to be dressed like a cabbage" which means that a person is wearing so many layers of clothes that they resemble a cabbage with its layers of leaves. It was May 3rd and the day was so unexpectedly cold that we were wearing basically everything we took on this trip.

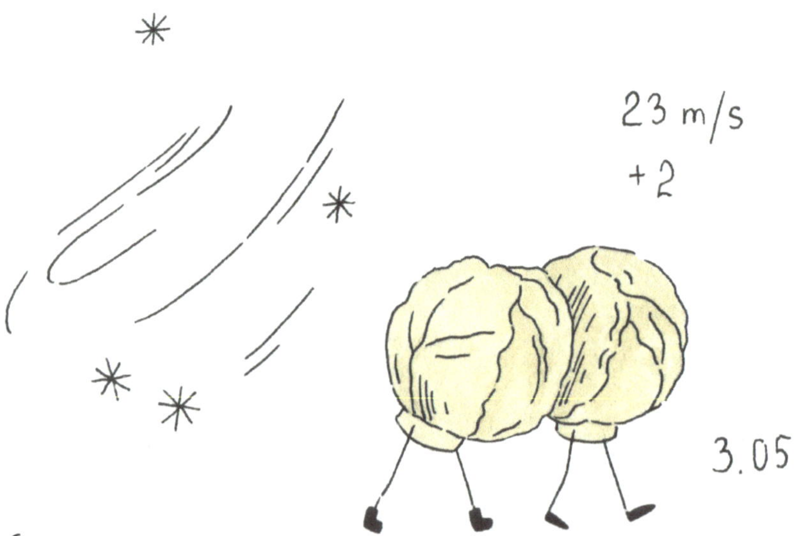

EXERCISE IX

Practicing metaphors

In my Drawing Journal, I strive to complement drawings with metaphors to make my routine more dynamic. Here are memories I captured with metaphors. Illustrate them your way and then look at my interpretations on the next page.

1. Nasal congestion
2. Visiting a dentist
3. Traffic jam in the subway

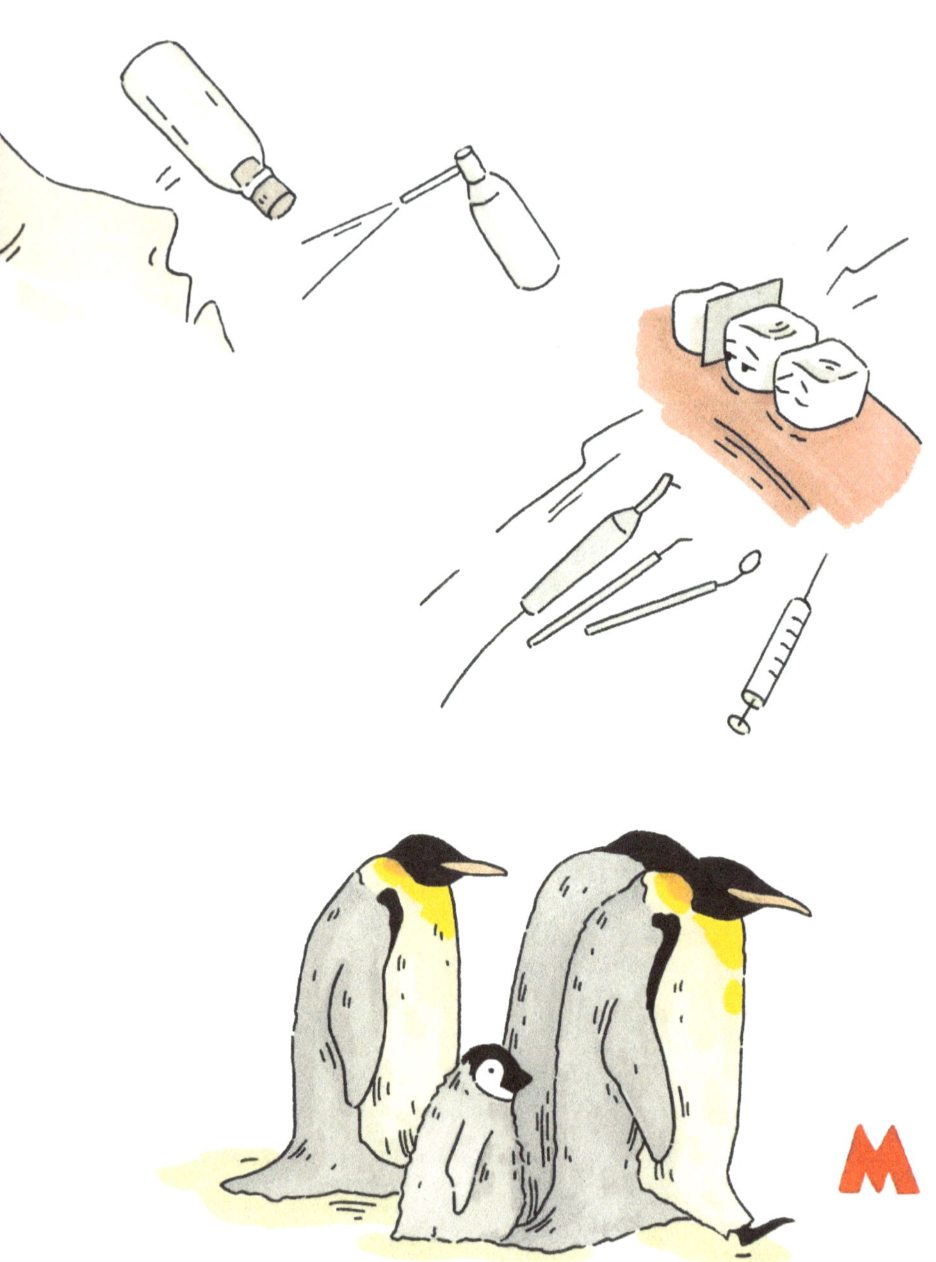

M

1. Nasal congestion. I was suffering from a protracted cold and was dreaming about getting better fast.

2. Visiting a dentist. Each time I go to the dentist I feel like my teeth are independent beings who suffer from this uninvited interruption into their lives.

3. Traffic jam in the subway. There are always a lot of people in the Moscow subway. On December 4th I got into an intense crowd of people on the way to an escalator, and it was moving drearily slowly.

Collages

A collage is an artwork made by sticking various different materials such as photographs, leaves, and pieces of paper or fabric on to a backing. In a Drawing Journal, this technique can be used for saving objects that bring up memories, inspire you, or just bring joy. Collages are a great way to start if you feel anxious about drawing everything at first. You may even enjoy them so much that you will continue using them as the main medium in your Drawing Journal.

You can use collages separately from your drawn days or combine collage elements with drawings. It looks interesting to combine different types of materials and put them into a chaotic composition. An interesting option is to continue patterns, photos or illustrations on collage elements with your drawing, so it could be a part of your art.

I like to complement drawings with elements I collected on some events and to fix them between pages with drawings. This way they complete my memories of past moments and don't interfere in the drawings scale and composition.

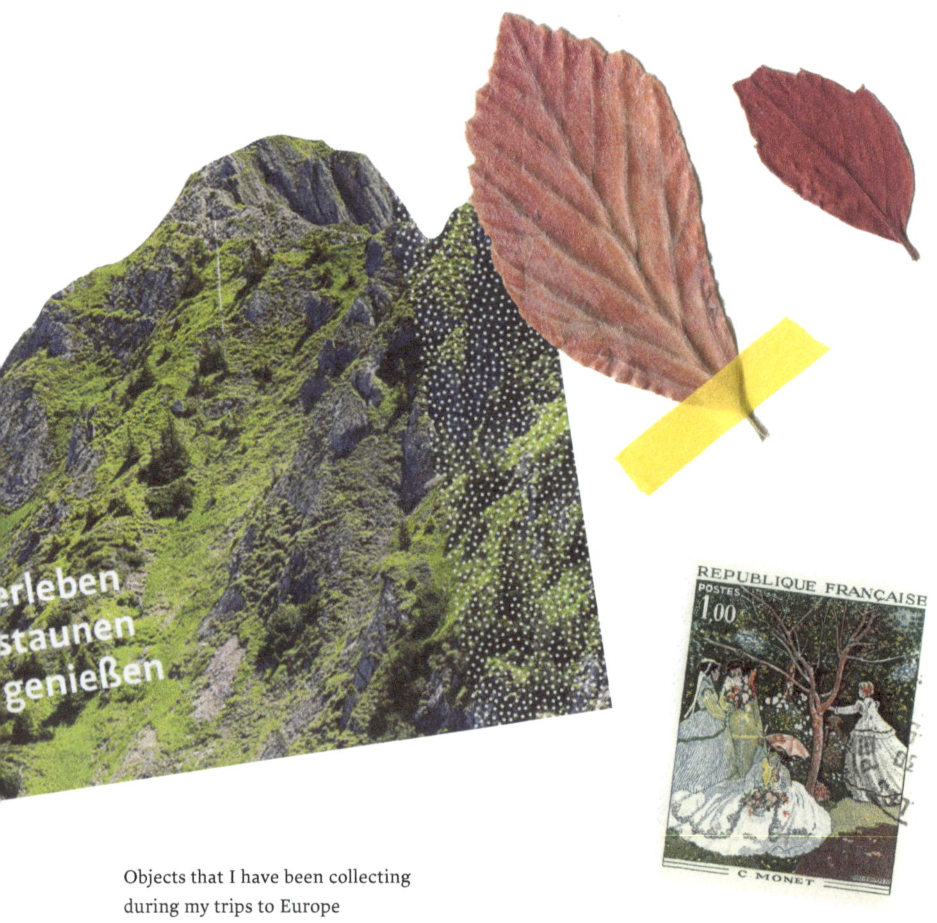

Objects that I have been collecting during my trips to Europe

You can glue into your sketchbook whatever you want as long as it's thin enough, so you can close it. Here are things that can remind past events and bring visual pleasure:

Tickets from trips and cultural events like museums, movies, excursions and so on. These elements are a great reminder of events you visited and can also have interesting designs.

Herbaria. It's my favorite option. Dried plants can be a great visual reminder of past travels. You can use any plants, leaves and flowers as long as they are flat enough for your sketchbook and small enough to fit on one page.

Before you use anything natural in your sketchbook, make sure to let the plants dry first. Once you collected a plant, put it into an envelope or between sketchbook pages and let it dry completely. If there are a lot of plants, put pieces of paper between them. Pressing a plant will help it dry faster so it won't break. Depending on the plant it will take appropriately up to 2 weeks for it to dry.

Packaging and other branding materials like business cards, stickers, and leaflets. It can be whole pieces and some parts of materials, for example, only with a logo, interesting graphics, an illustration or information.

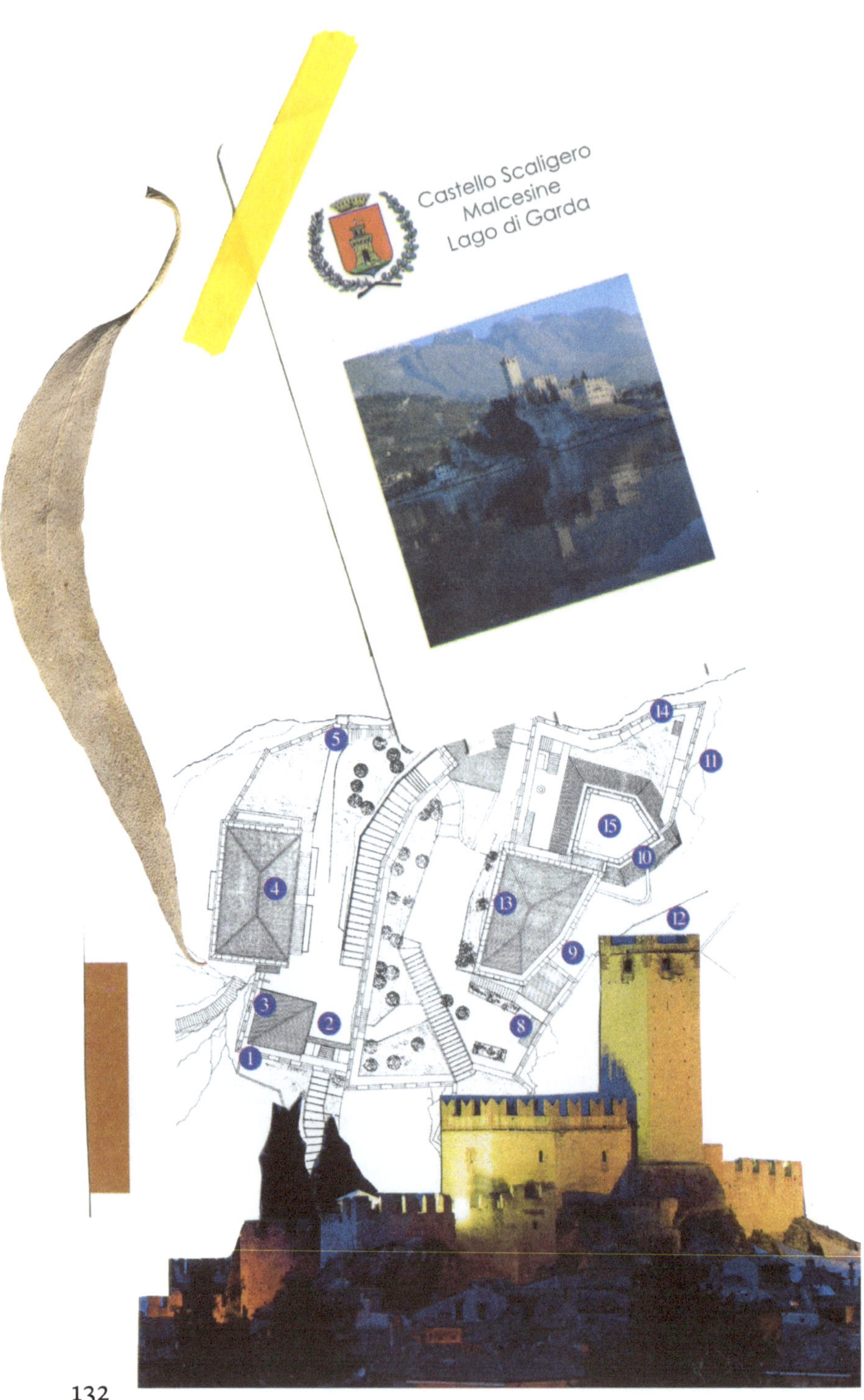
Castello Scaligero
Malcesine
Lago di Garda
1
2
3
4
5
8
9
10
11
12
13
14
15

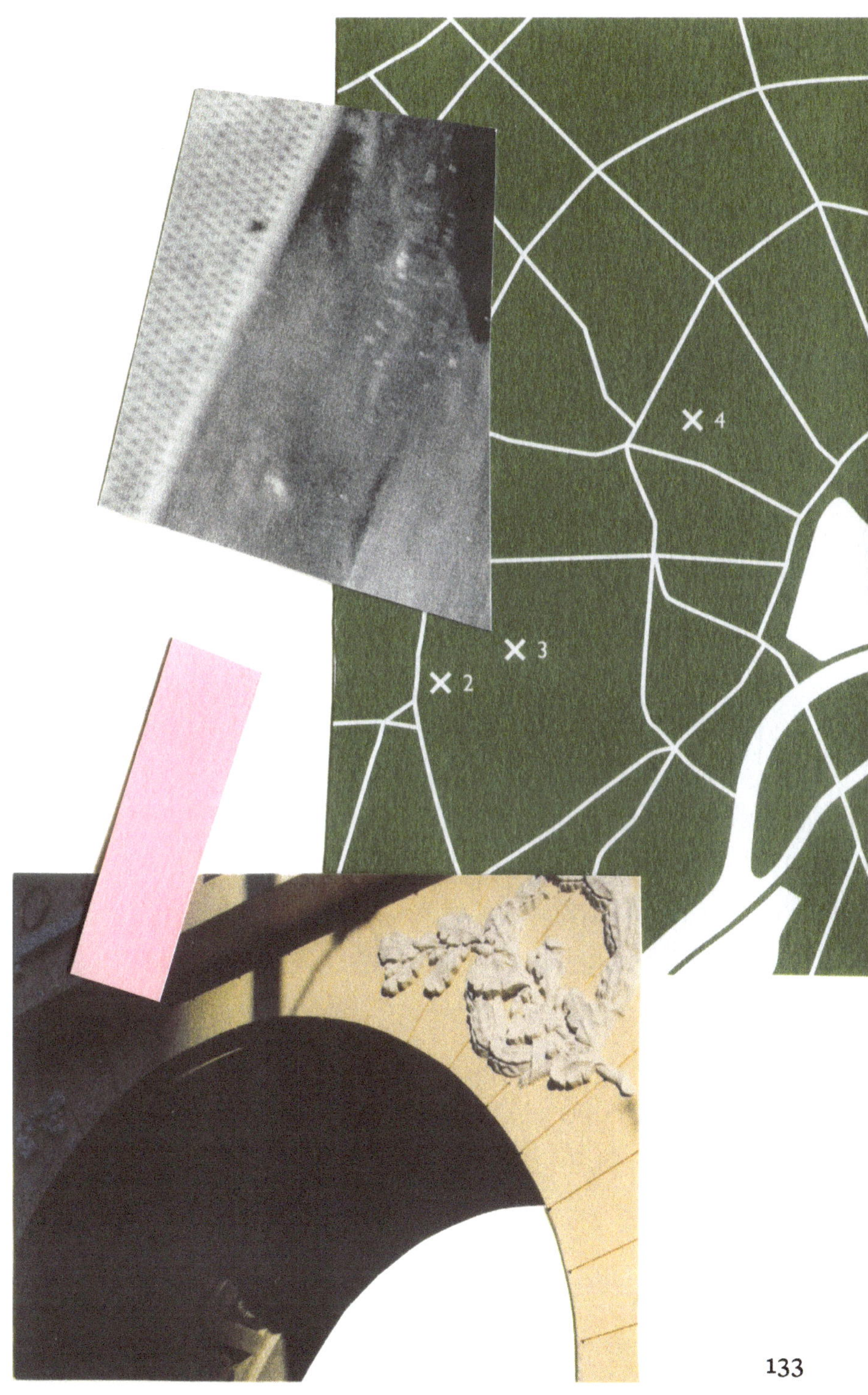
× 4
× 3
× 2

Postcards and stamps. They often can be found in gift shops, vintage and bookstores.

Photographs made with a Polaroid, photo booth, or printed from your camera or phone.

Other options. Gift-wrapping paper, fabrics, threads, paper drink coasters, menus, maps. Pieces from newspapers, magazines, posters and basically anything printed on paper.

Additional materials for creating a collage

To work with a collage you'll need: scissors, glue, paper tape, and an envelope to collect elements for collaging.

Glue. I suggest using a glue pen, it's compact, not messy and won't wet the paper like a liquid glue. When gluing elements, don't cover the entire element's surface with it, just angles and a few spots closer to the center.

Paper tape. It's a good option for making a collage on the run. Decorative taps can pin elements but also adorn your collages. Don't get carried away though, you don't want the tape to overwhelm the composition. I like to combine glued elements with taped elements. It prevents visual overload of a collage with only tape and it's just more interesting than gluing everything.

An envelope. Keeping an envelope is handy for collecting your collage elements. It's much more convenient than storing objects between pages that risk falling out.

Some sketchbooks, like Moleskine, have an expandable inner pocket in the back which can be used for this purpose. If your sketchbook doesn't have this, try glueing an envelope on the back cover inside.

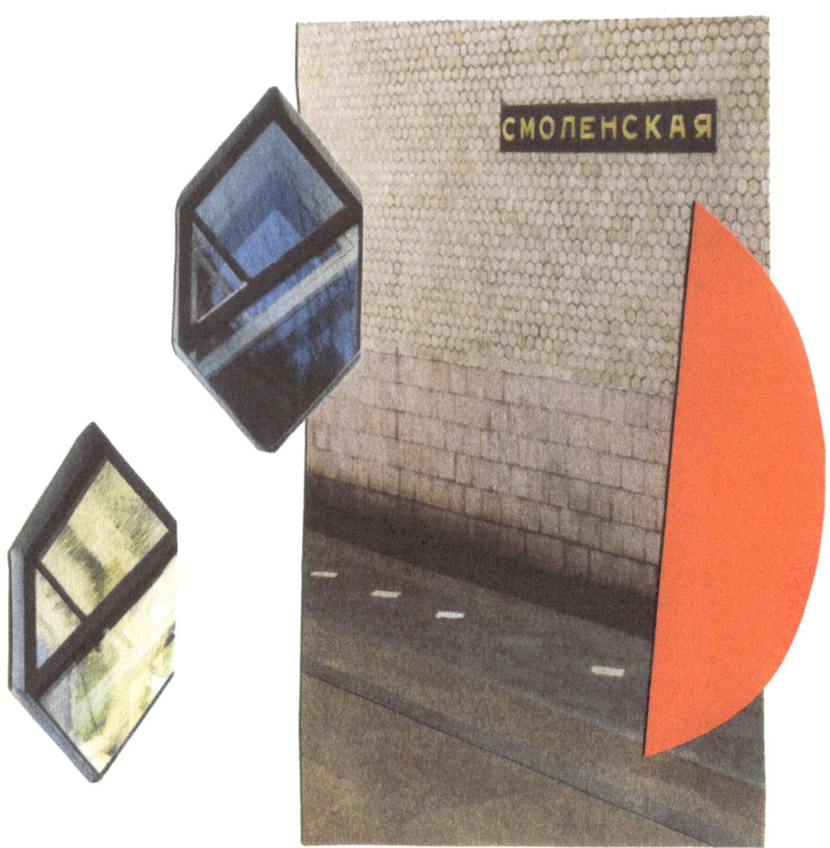

EXERCISE X

Creating a collage

During an active weekend, a day off, or a small trip collect things that interest you visually, emotionally, and represent memories from your day. Combine these elements together and don't forget about the basic rules of composition.

Rebuses

A rebus is a pictogram puzzle with pictures, symbols and letters which cryptically represents a word or a phrase. In some ways, a Drawing Journal already is a long rebus for its viewers, because it's often not obvious what was captured by an artist on its pages.

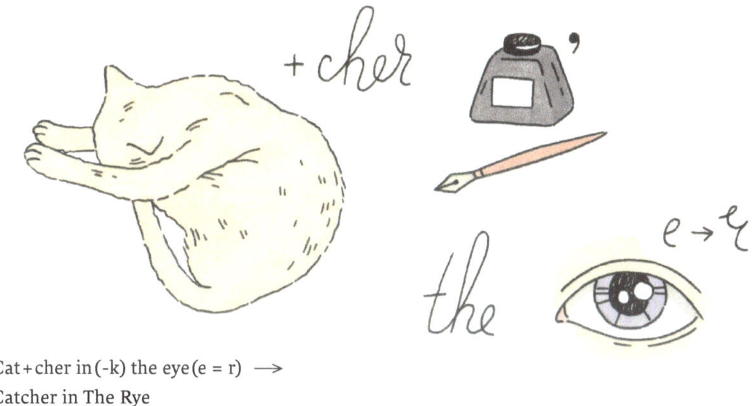

Cat + cher in (-k) the eye (e = r) ⟶
Catcher in The Rye

My interest in solving rebuses came from my early childhood. My mom bought magazines with puzzles and I loved solving them. When I started my Drawing Journal, this old passion helped me add a little mystery to my drawings.

Rebuses will exercise your mind and imagination skills. It's fun and challenging to create them and amusing for viewers to guess what answers you've hidden in them. Rebuses diversify drawings and make them more intriguing.

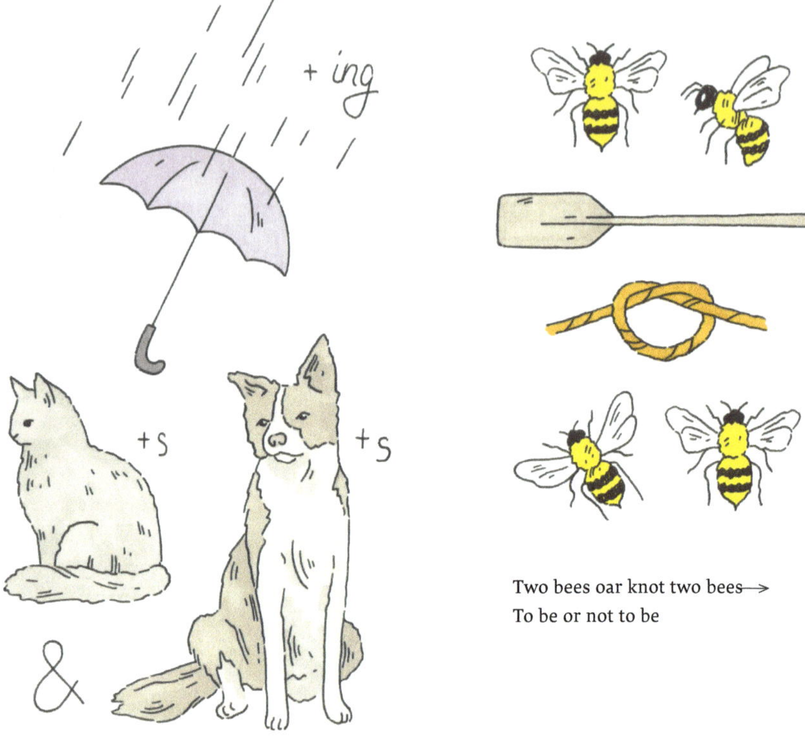

Two bees oar knot two bees →
To be or not to be

Rain + ing cat + s & dog + s →
Raining cats & dogs

Using rebuses can also be helpful when you have difficulty depicting an object in other ways. This tip often helps me when I have such troubles but still want to draw an element. I will caution you though, don't overuse them, otherwise you may make your drawings too hard even for you to understand.

Here are some simple ways to include rebuses in your Drawing Journal.

Using pictures

1. A picture used in a rebus represents the name of an object.

2. The plus sign "+" between pictures means that words hidden in the pictures must be joined to create a new one.

3. An object drawn upside down means that the word must be read backward.

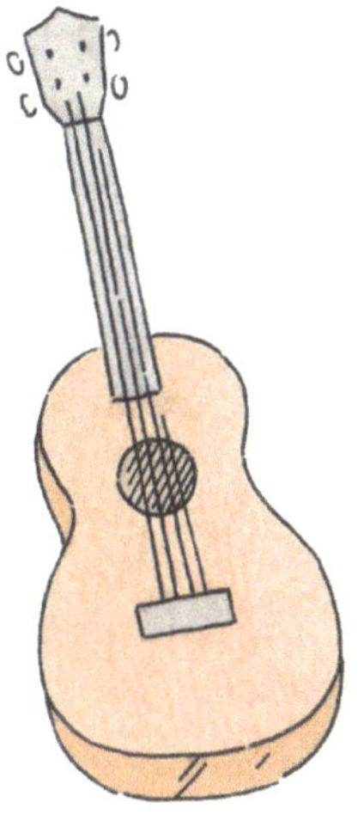

1. Guitar

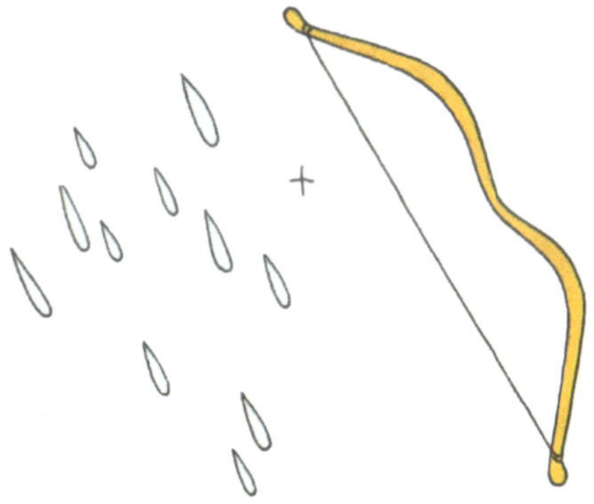

2. Rain + bow ⟶ Rainbow

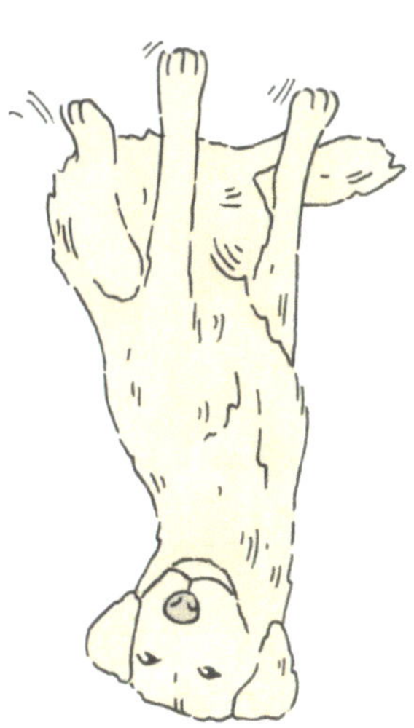

3. Inverted "Dog" ⟶ God

Using letters

Letters and signs standing beside a picture can be used for replacing, adding or removing letters from a word hidden in this picture.

Adding letters

1. Letters standing on the left or the right side of a picture mean that they must be added at the beginning or at the end of a word.

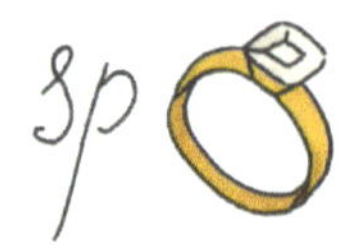

1. Sp + ring ⟶ Spring

2. The plus sign "+" can be added between letters and a picture for better understanding.

Removing letters

3. Commas are used to delete letters from the beginning or the end of a hidden word. One comma – one letter.

4. A crossed-out letter placed near a picture means that it should be removed from a hidden word.

5. An unwanted letter can also be written with the "–" sign on its left.

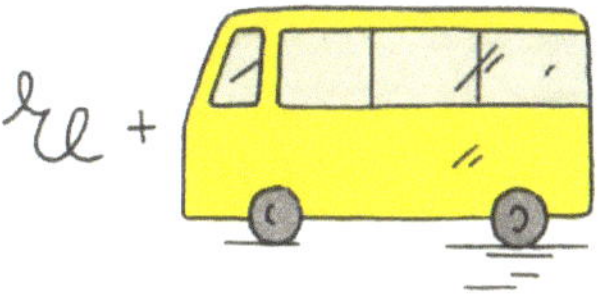

2. Re + bus ⟶ Rebus

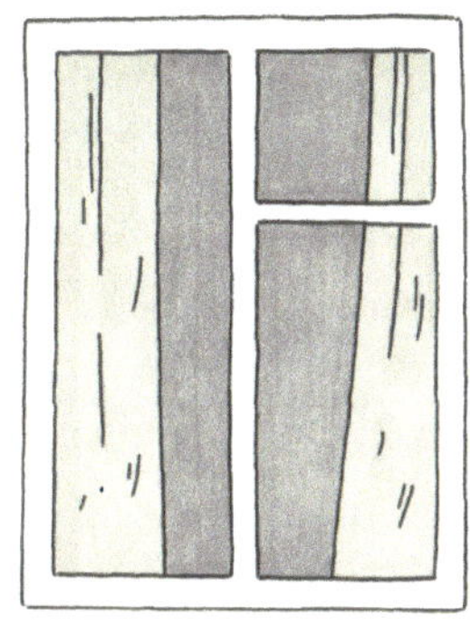

3. Window – ow ⟶ Wind

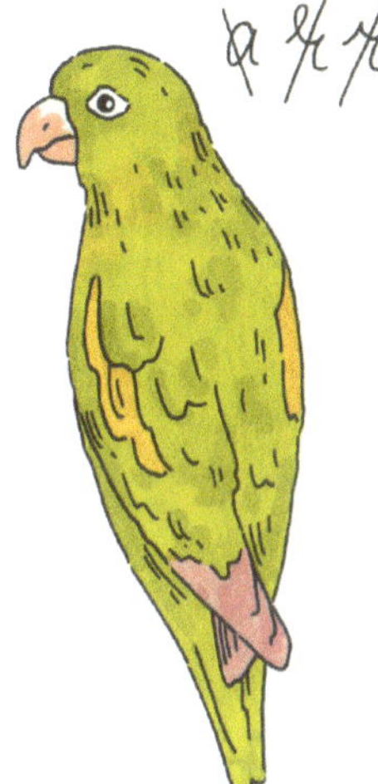

4. Parrot – arr ⟶ Pot

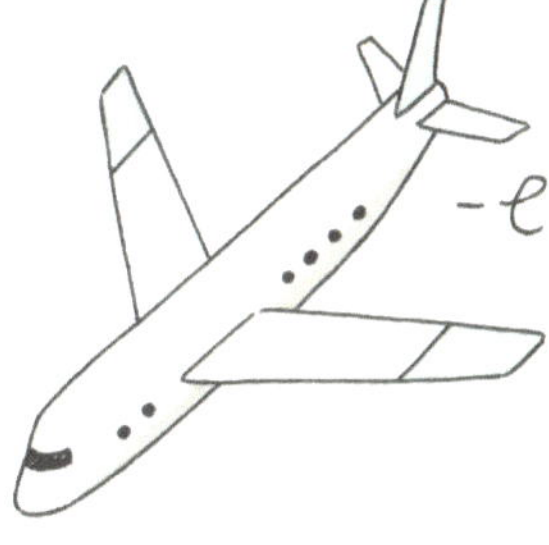

5. Plane – e ⟶ Plan

Replacing letters

6. The signs "=" or "⟶" between two letters mean that the first letter should be replaced with the second one.

7. A letter that should be replaced can also be crossed out.

8. The sign "⇆" between two letters means that they should be interchanged.

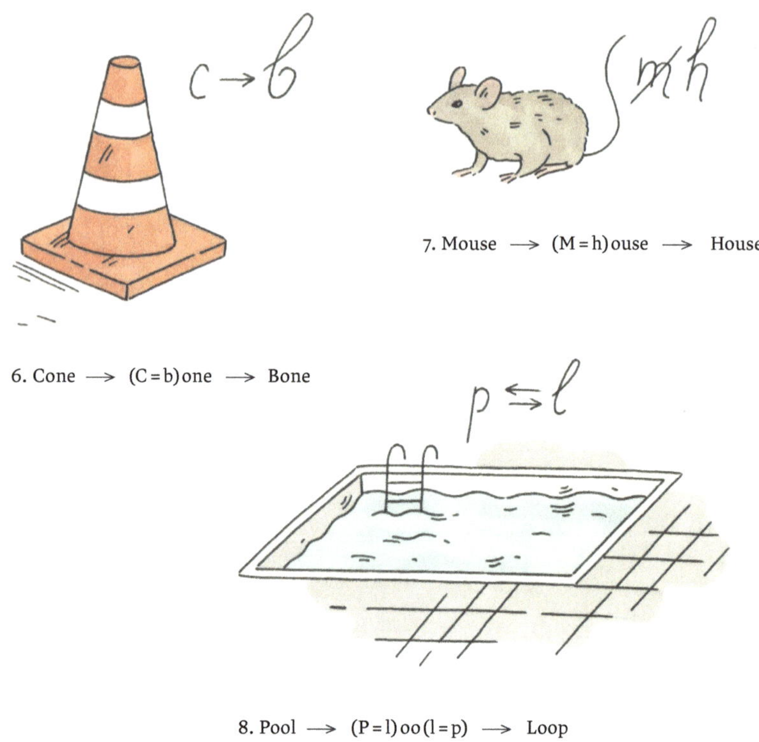

6. Cone ⟶ (C = b) one ⟶ Bone

7. Mouse ⟶ (M = h) ouse ⟶ House

8. Pool ⟶ (P = l) oo (l = p) ⟶ Loop

Using numbers

1. Comma-separated numbers beside a picture show an order in which letters of a hidden word must be read.

2. At the same time with interchanging letters, some letters can be removed from a word if necessary.

3. Numbers crossed out near a picture mean that letters under these numbers should be removed from a hidden word.

4. Numbers with the sign "⇆" between them mean that letters under these numbers must be interchanged in a hidden word.

5. A single number written on the left or the right side of a picture can be read as a word and summarised with a word hidden in a picture. The sign "+" can also be added for better understanding.

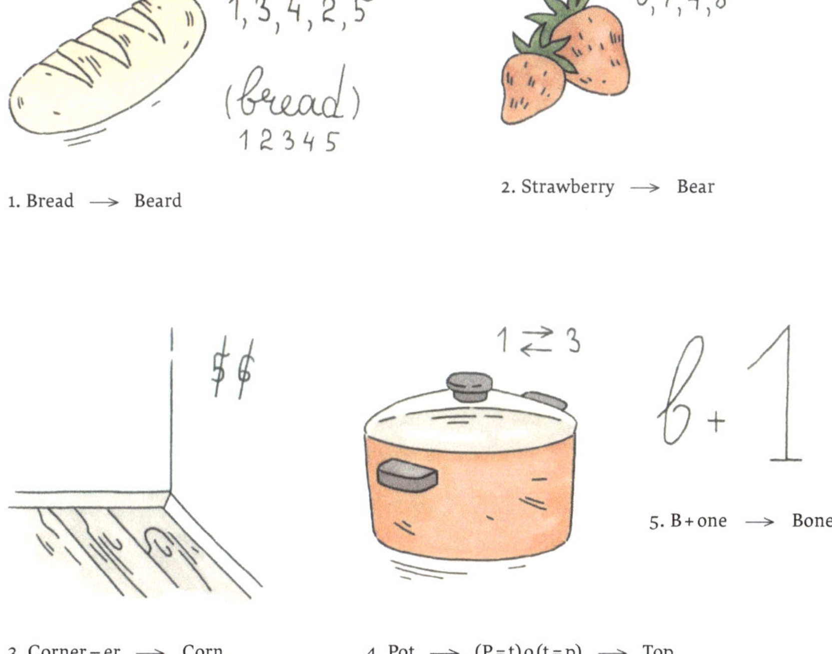

1. Bread ⟶ Beard

2. Strawberry ⟶ Bear

3. Corner – er ⟶ Corn

4. Pot ⟶ (P = t) o (t = p) ⟶ Top

5. B + one ⟶ Bone

You can create simple one-word rebuses or make rebuses more complex by adding a few rebuses together with the "+" sign in order to make a bigger word from a few small ones.

EXERCISE XI

Drawing rebuses

1. During one day write down the names of 3 things you have found interesting. Choose simple words so it will be easier to make your first rebus.

2. Look at your list and think of words that could be suitable for the rebus format. To find such words, look at each word closely. Read syllables separately. Try to delete, swap letters or to add new ones. Try applying numbers or to read a word backward.

3. Choose 3 or more rebuses and draw them here. Try different methods of encryption so you can work on remembering them all.

CHAPTER VII

Share your work with the world

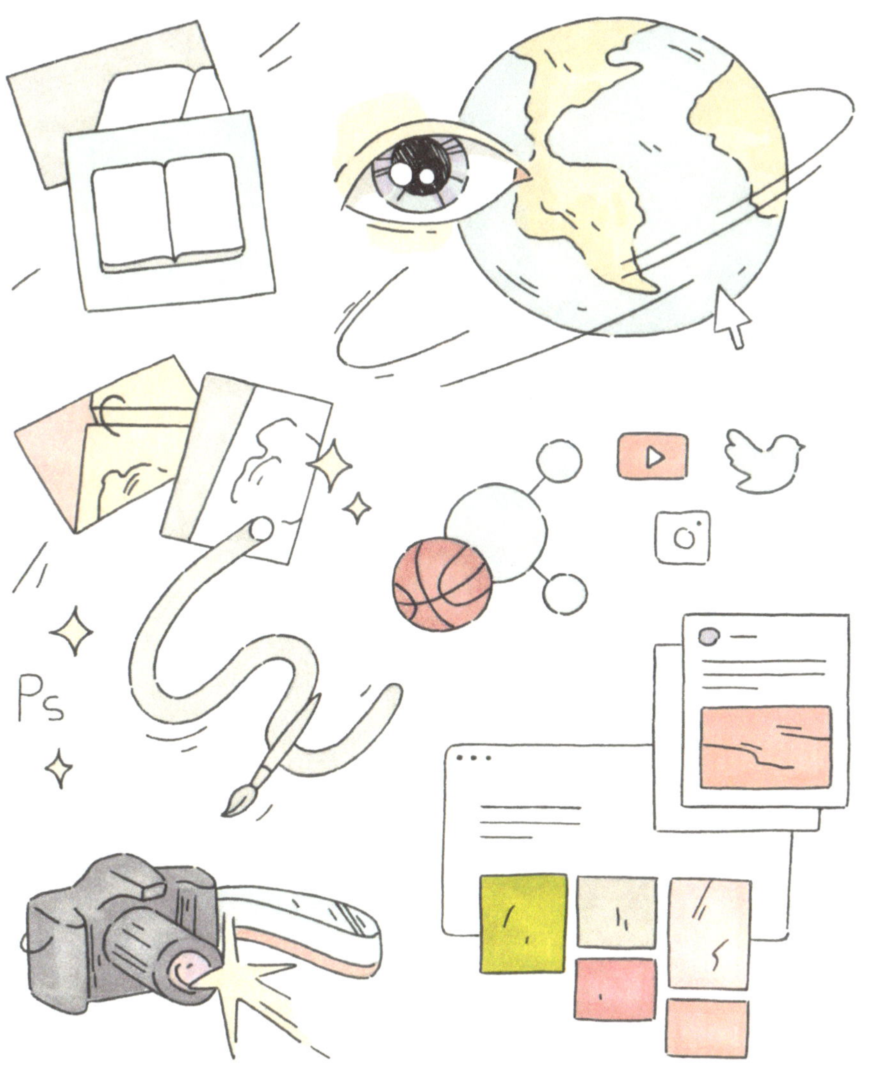

You have a choice to share your Drawing Journal or keep it private. For some people, showing their personal life with others can be uncomfortable and that's perfectly normal.

You are starting this project for yourself and if you decided not to share it with anyone, that's OK. If you keep it private, explore how you can truly make it something personal. If you are certain that you want to share your Drawing Journal, that's great. Projects like this can grow a loyal audience interested in your art and personality. You can share your project on social networks, a personal blog or a website. Here are some ideas to get started.

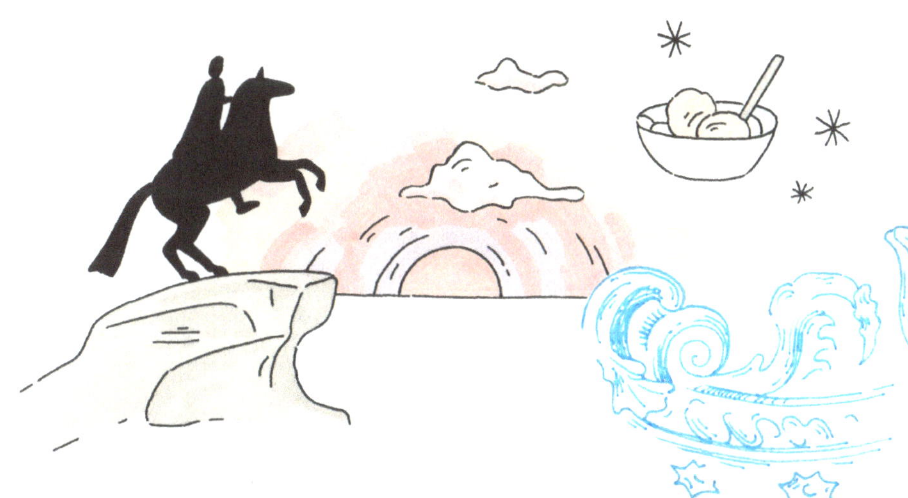

Get inspired by other creative people

At first, it might be difficult to understand where to start and how to share your drawings. It's always helpful to research and see how other artists share their work. Find websites, blogs and accounts of people with similar projects and pay attention to what they post. Look for some tips you could apply to your own project.

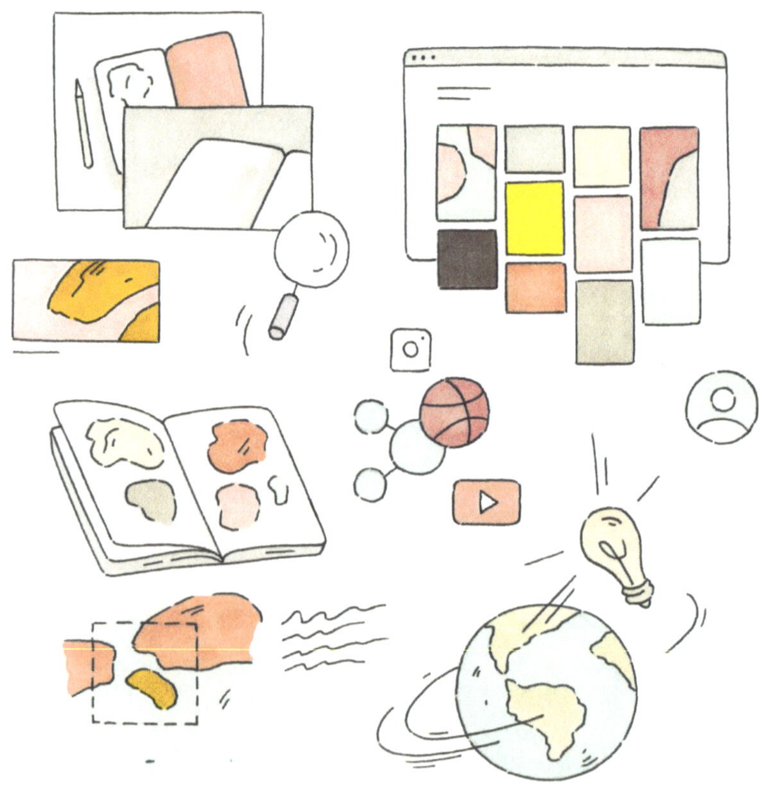

In social networks, decide if you want to follow a specific pattern or have a randomness in your posts. Tell your story the way you want to tell it. Will you show full pages with tons of details? Or will you post videos with your process and informative posts with your insight? The options are endless and completely up to you.

Make your drawings digital

Consider scanning your sketchbooks or photographing the pages. Don't worry if you don't have professional equipment, it's enough to use your phone. Make sure that the photos are well-lit and your drawings can be seen clearly.

Experiment to find a perfect and comfortable method to show your drawings to the world. For social media, I take a picture of my sketchbook on a windowsill. I then edit it in Photoshop to lighten the image, cut the sketchbook from the background, and put it on a plain gray background. This way I make all my posts look alike and neat next to each other. I know that this is probably too complex and unnecessary but I just enjoy the result.

If you want to post extensively about your project, get professional help if you have the opportunity. For the first edition of "365 Days of Daily Drawing" I rented a professional

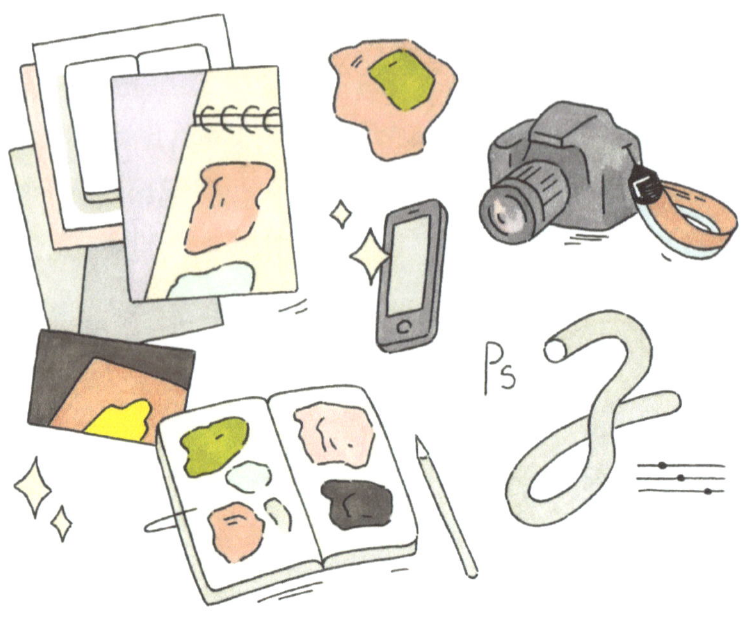

camera and took the photos myself. The photos could have been better, and I spent a decent amount of time editing them to make up for my inexperience. So for the second part of the project, I asked a photographer to help me. He took much better photos than I could have ever done myself. Don't be afraid to use these opportunities to save time and make something high quality.

Tell your story

A story is important because it brings a context — you become a real person in the eyes of a viewer. If they feel like they know you, they will spend more time with your work and be more engaged. Tell people how you started, what you have learned, and how it helped you. What difficulties you have had on your way, how you managed to deal with them and finish your project?

Make descriptions of your drawings to help people understand what you've drawn.

Share your Drawing Journal

The simplest way to share your Drawing Journal is on social networks like Instagram, Twitter and Facebook.

If you prefer something more custom, try creating a personal blog or website. Even though it may be more complicated, it will open up customization possibilities not possible anywhere else. With a blog you can post regular updates or hold office until the very end where you show off the entire project.

Either route, keep the design simple and minimal so you don't distract from your drawings and work. I suggest sharing regular updates so you can share your journey and make consistent progress.

Remember that a finished good project is better than an unfinished perfect one. You can strive to make something better for a long time and eventually get so tired of it you don't publish it at all. I still struggle with this but I try to be more prudent.

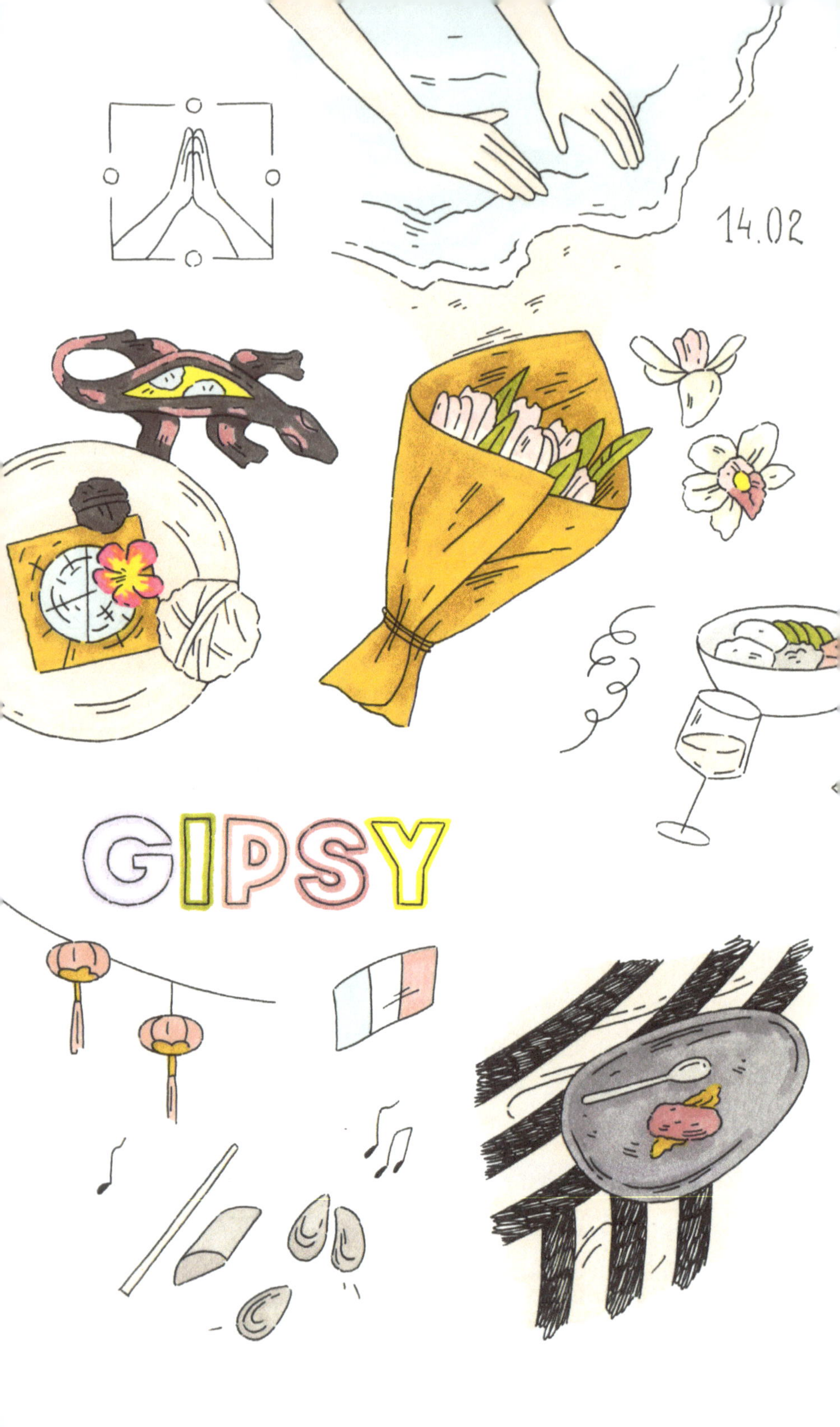
14.02
GIPSY

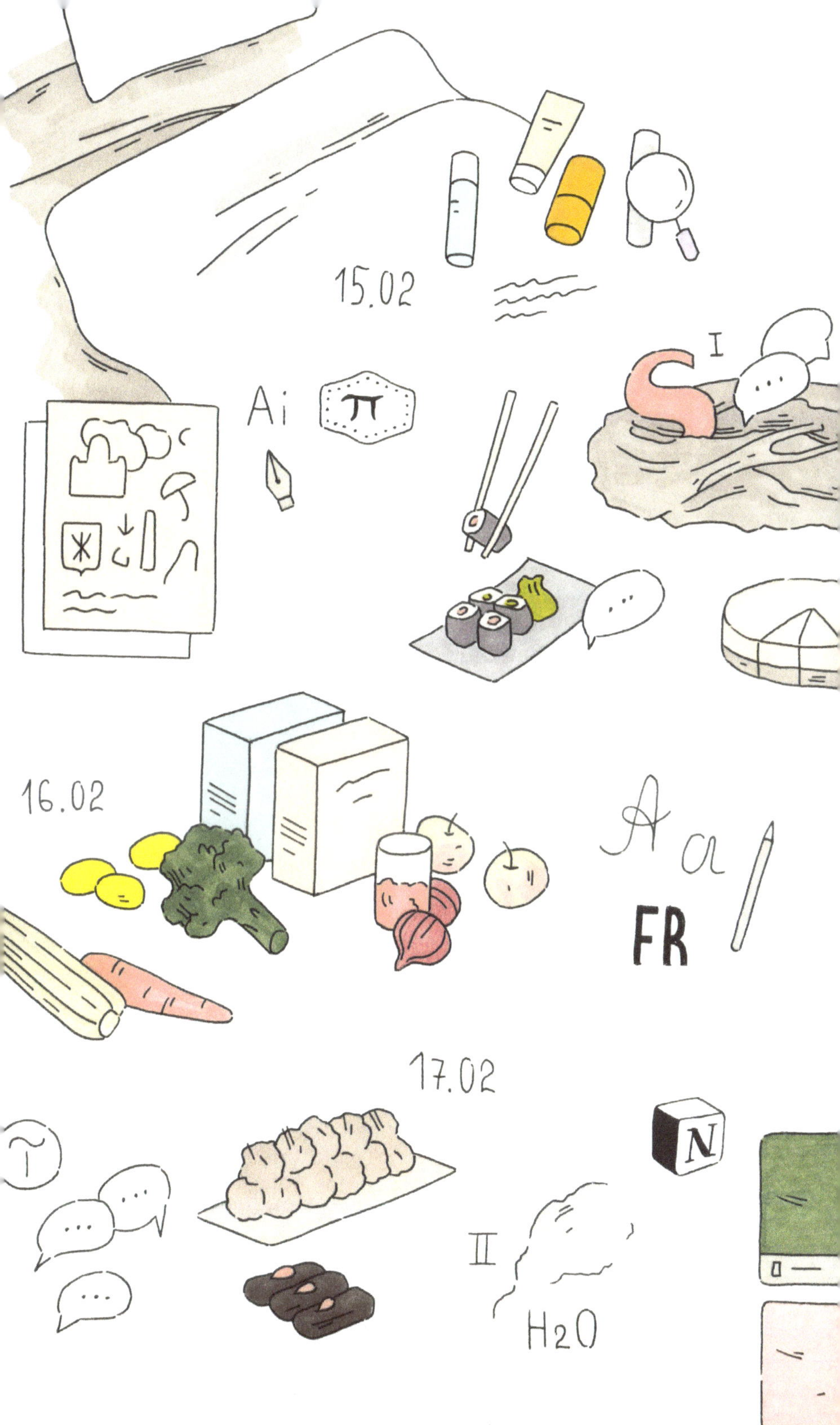
15.02
Ai
π
I
...
...
16.02
Aa
FR
17.02
...
...
...
N
II
H_2O

I post my Drawing Journal on Instagram and my personal website. On my website, I decided to publish my one-year project all at once because I wanted it to be a full story. You can see it on JuliaZass.com which I made with Tilda Website Builder (tilda.cc).

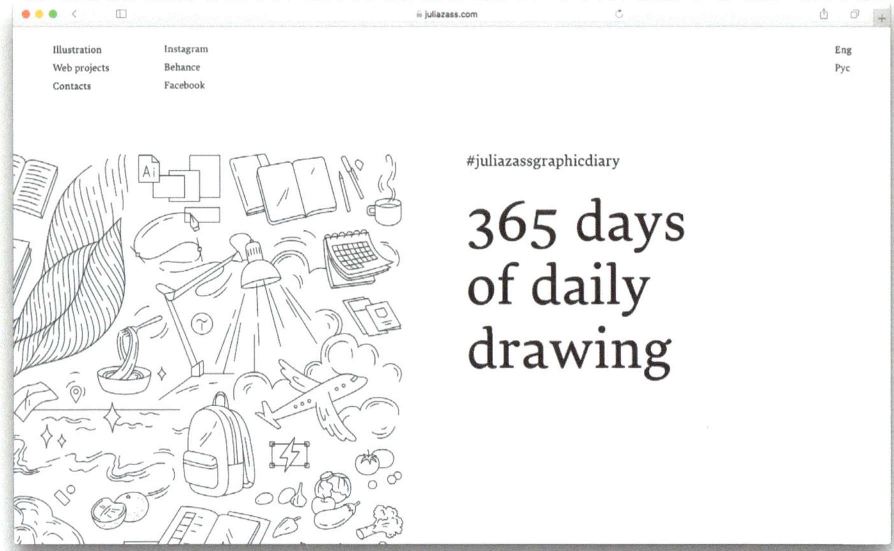

One-year drawing project on my website
juliazass.com/365_days_diary

Promote your project

Promoting your work as important as publishing it, it can bring you a new audience and unexpectedly great projects and collaborations.

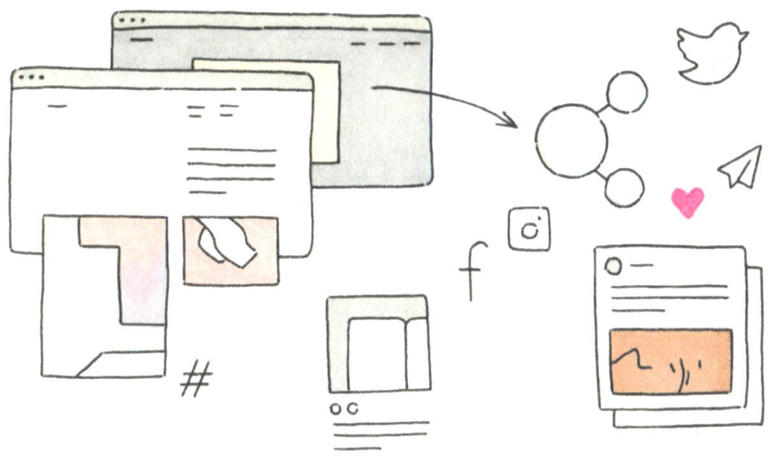

After starting your website or blog, first, add its address on your social networks and make a post about it to attract first viewers. Each time when you make an update, share it on all social networks. Second, research different creative communities and inspirational websites and share it there too.

When I finished my "365 Days of Daily Drawing" project I submitted it on some inspirational web design resources. A few of them published the project and that's how I first met my publisher who suggested I create this book.

Don’t feel pressured

Don’t feel pressured to share your Drawing Journal immediately. It is OK to observe for some time and understand how open your drawings will be and then decide if you want to share them or not.

It’s important to become comfortable with your pace, style, and the project itself. I probably don’t post my drawings as often as I should but I don’t push myself to. I share when I see an opportunity for something special. This project is about pleasure and positive emotions.

CHAPTER VIII

Common difficulties and how to deal with them

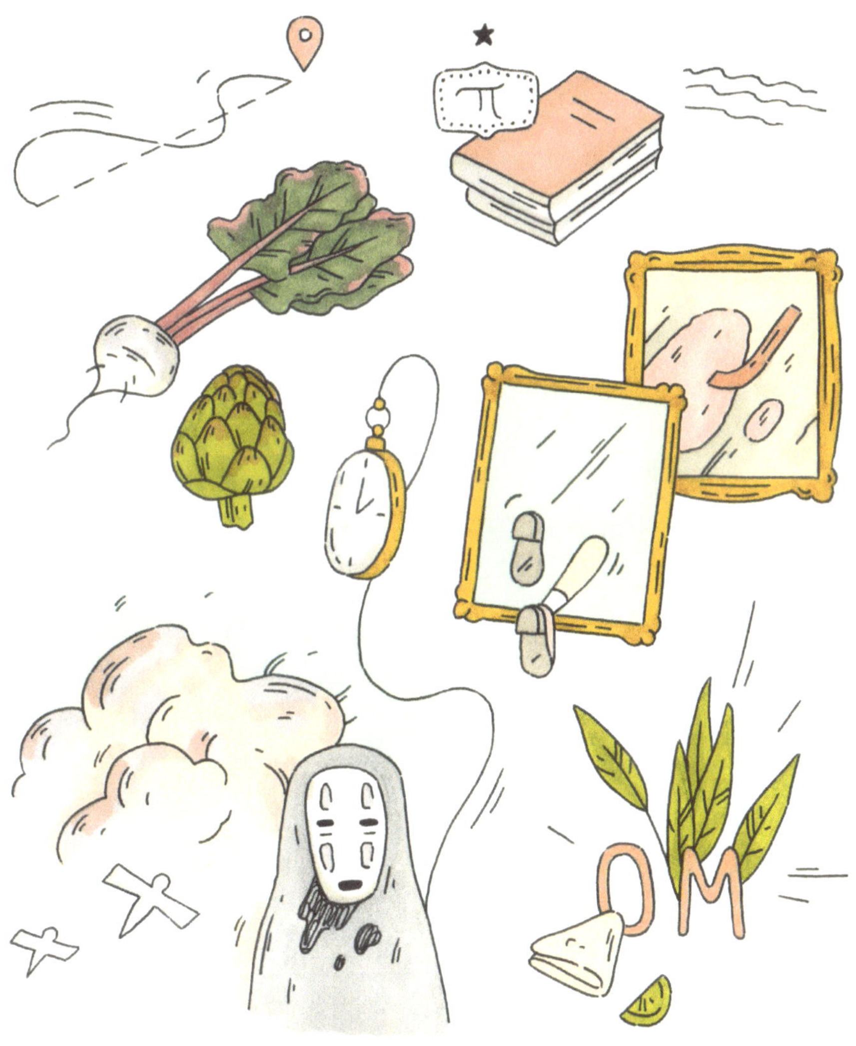

It can be not easy to discipline oneself to draw every day, be inspired, or find time and energy to draw. During my daily drawing practice, I faced all these troubles, and eventually have found some solutions that help me to draw every day.

How to draw a routine

We all have days that can be boring. You may ask yourself, “Where do I find the desire and inspiration to draw when there is nothing going on outside of my daily routine?” From time to time I have this problem and I’ve found a few ways to deal with it.

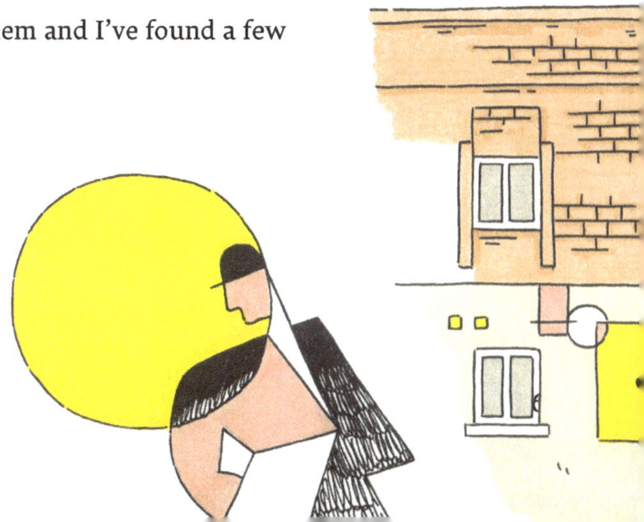

Change your habits

This is where the fun starts. After I had been drawing for a couple of months I realized that desperately seeking for things to draw is not enough when I have monotonous days. This project helped me understand that I wanted to see more interesting things, meet interesting people and be more inspired. This realization drove me to be more purposeful and do this outside of my usual habits and comfort zone.

Start with small modifications, they don't have to be dramatic and life-changing. Let's look at a few options to start with.

Take new routes

Change your daily route once in a while, it may take longer, but it will definitely give you new views and impressions. Take a walk instead of using transport. Skip your usual subway station and walk to the next one, so you could discover new buildings, streets and neighborhoods. If you have a subway route with transfer to other lines try to change it if possible so you could see new subway stations with their different design and architecture.

Using a bike is the easiest way to try new routes but be careful while looking around and, of course, don't take pictures while you are moving.

Luckily for me, I work in the city center and have a few subway stations to choose from. From time to time I skip the closest one and I'm usually rewarded with something along the way; like talented musicians playing on a subway platform, a flock of birds flying beautifully above a city square, or new marble patterns in the station's architecture, which I always enjoy to capture.

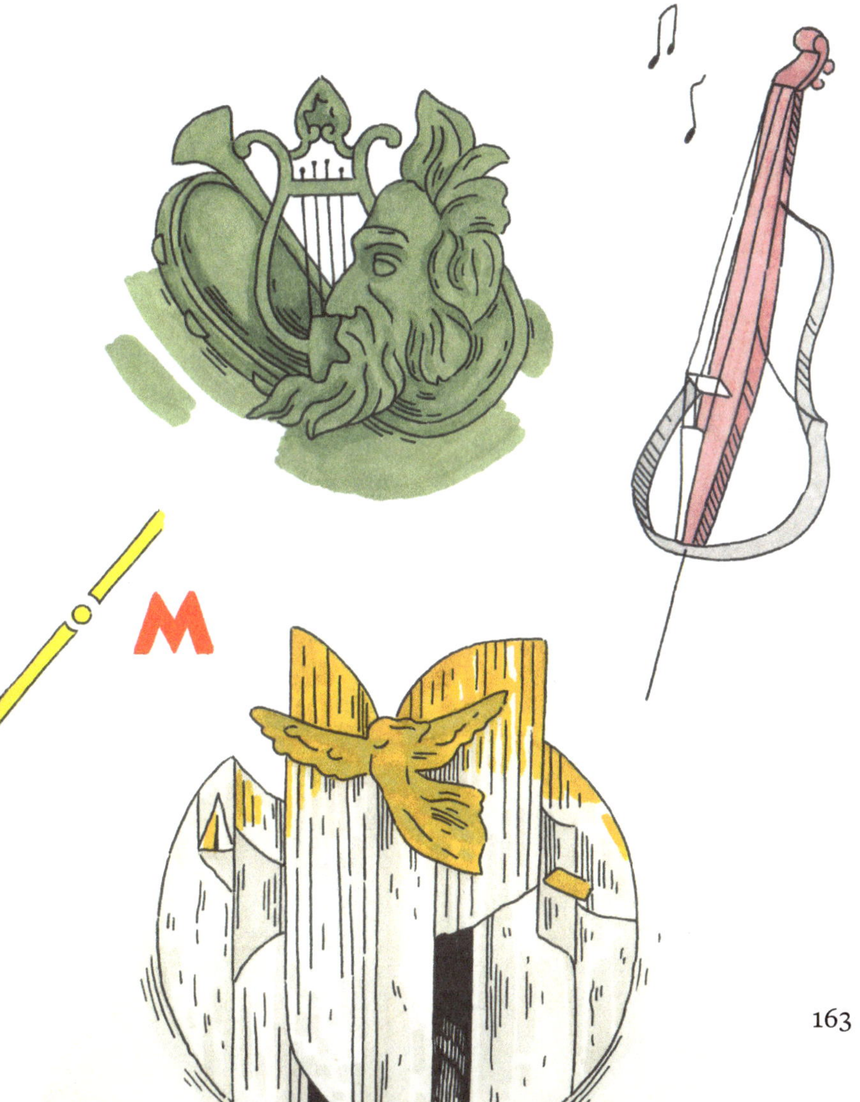

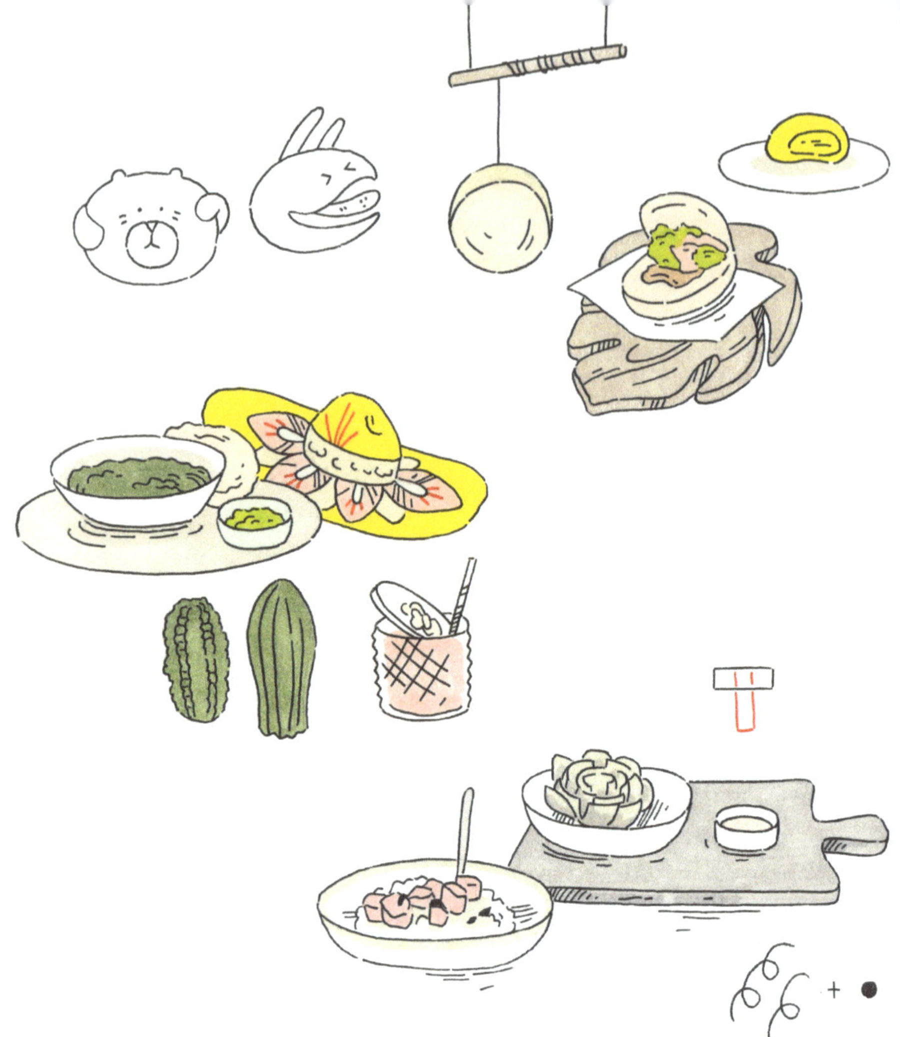

Try new food

Go to a new authentic restaurant and try some unknown cuisine. When you're there, look beyond just the food and pay attention to the interior design, serving, and even the dinnerware.

If you want to try something at home: cook new dishes, try new cheese, vegetables, or a dessert. Serve your food with creativity, pay attention to details, and enjoy it!

Take a small trip

It's not necessary to spend a lot of time and money on travel. Just go to a neighboring town a few hours away for one day or a weekend. It's often enough to break out of a stagnant routine and get inspiration from new architecture, museums, cafes and people.

When I feel the need to recharge and there is no opportunity to travel far, I go to Saint Petersburg for a weekend. It's only a few hours from Moscow and I discover a different atmosphere with fresh impressions from the places I already know.

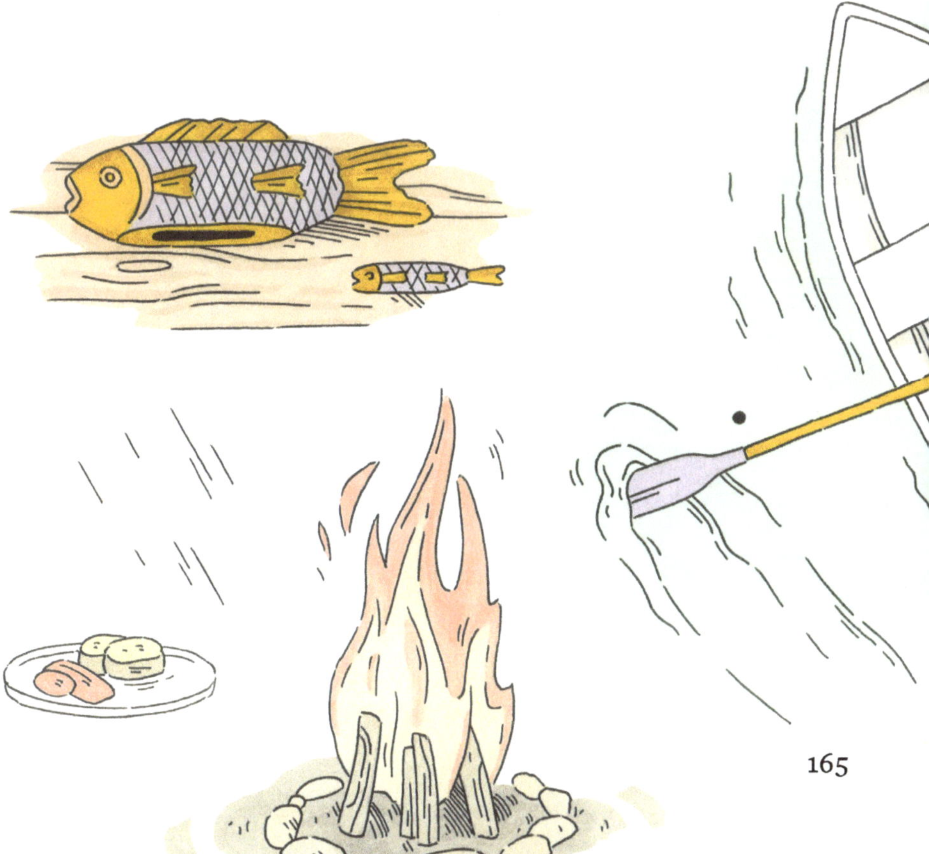

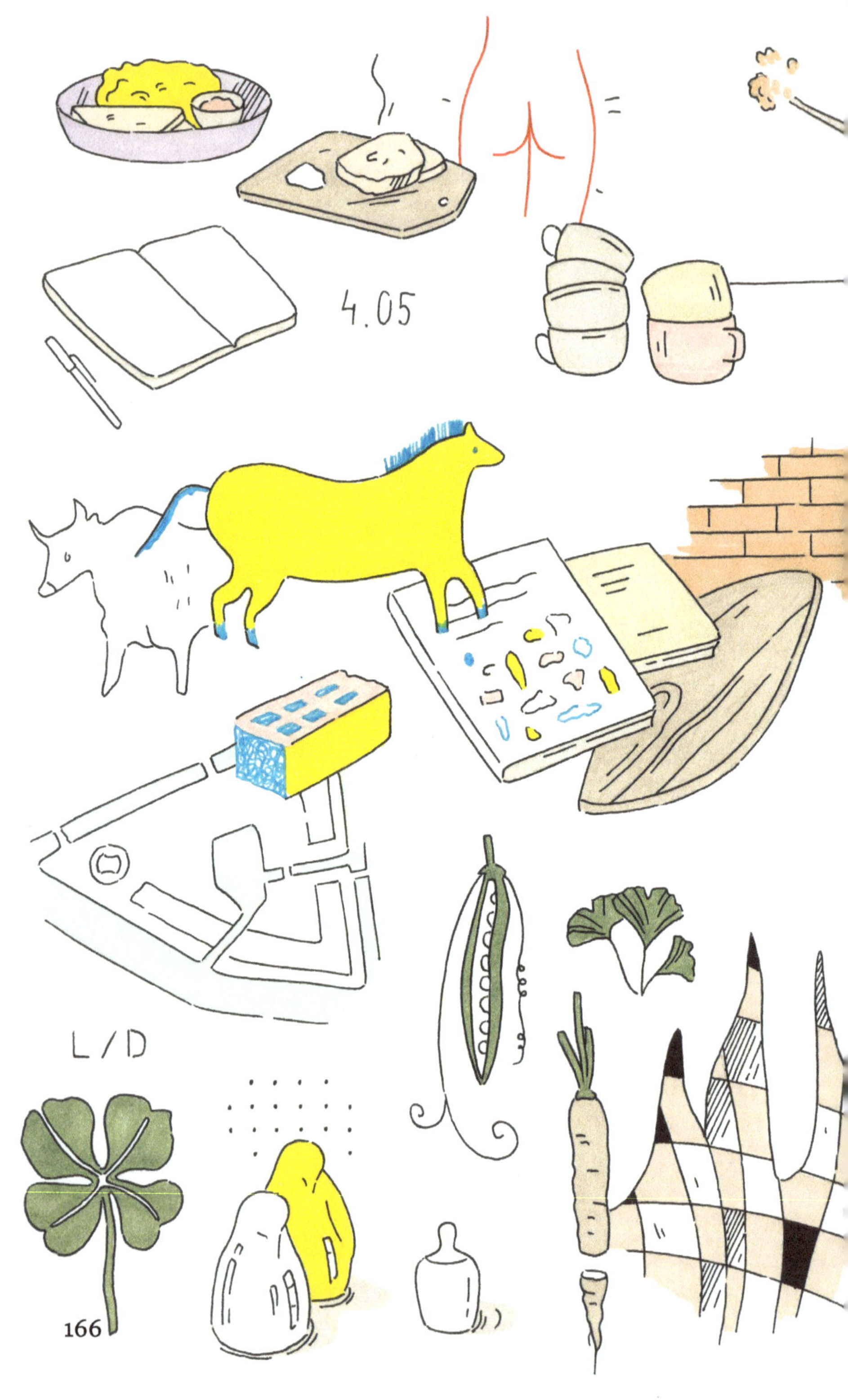
4.05
L / D

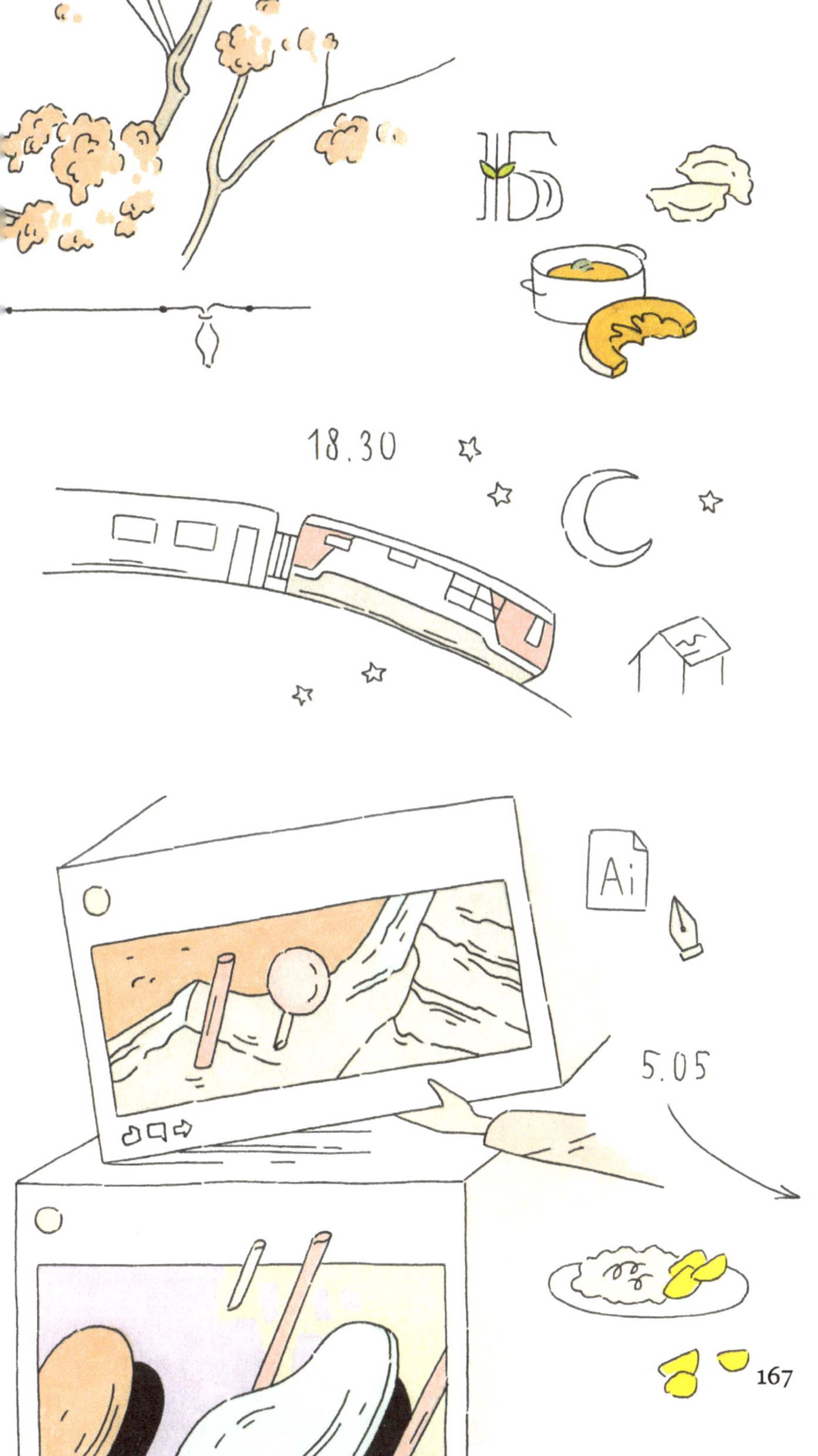
18.30
Ai
5.05

Educate yourself

Go to exhibitions, museums, lectures, libraries, local courses, online classes, or listen to educational podcasts. Learning is a great way to develop your skills and get some nutrition for your creativity.

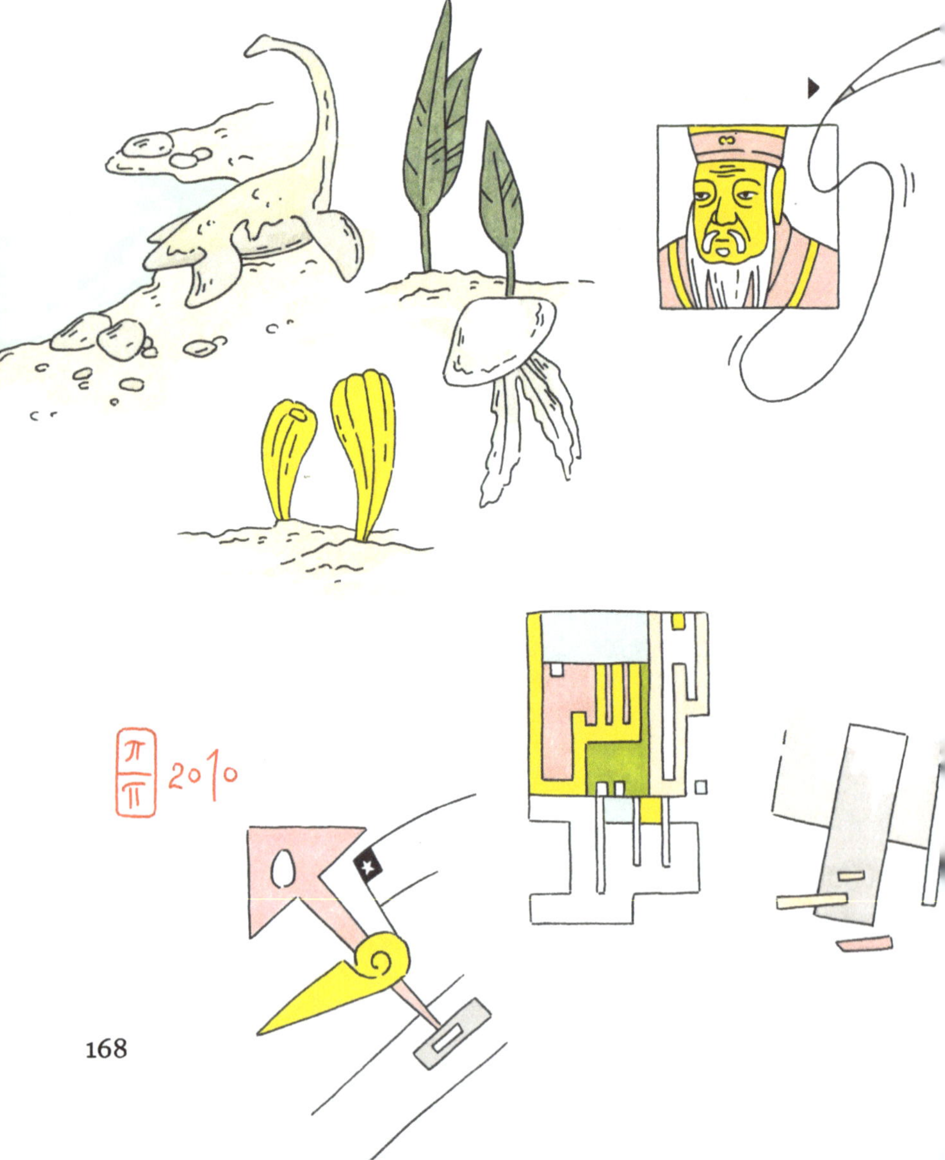

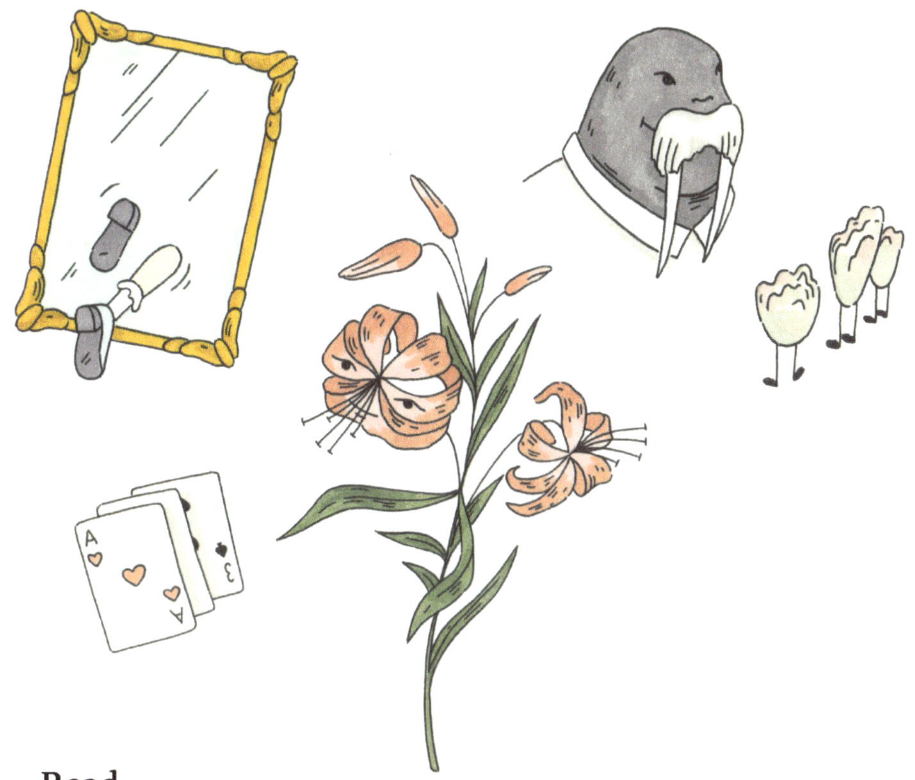

Read

This is an obvious but still necessary resource of inspiration, which helps to grow knowledge, develop imagination, and supplement your daily routine.

I vividly felt it when I was rereading "Alice in Wonderland" in the first year of keeping my Drawing Journal. It's one of the best books to expand your consciousness and imagination. It has amazing characters, scenes to draw, and shows that all boundaries are only in our heads. I strongly recommend reading it to expand opportunities for your imagination, especially at the beginning of drawing daily.

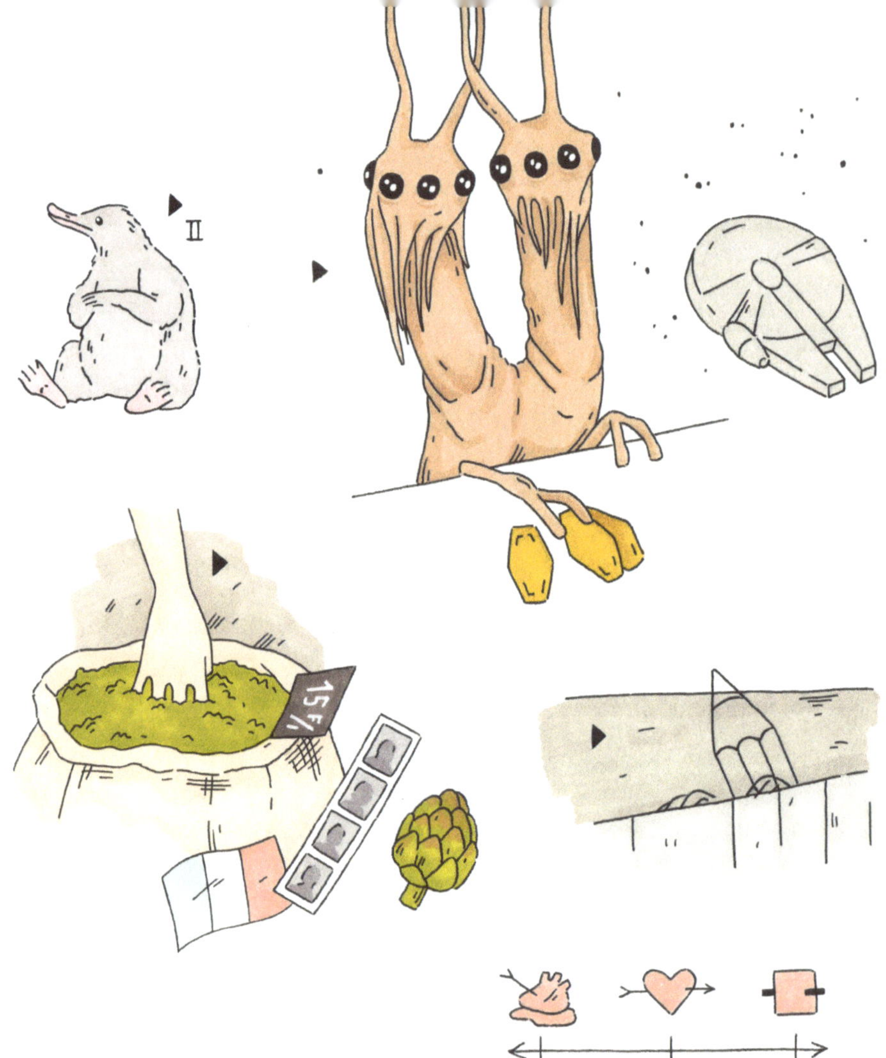

Watch sci-fi, documentary and fantasy films

It can be hard to go to events, meetups, and social events when it's cold outside or your workday sucks all your time and energy. Receiving new information through video content is an easy way to replace offline impressions once in a while.

Always choose new over the familiar

Every time you have an opportunity, try something new. It may be uncomfortable at first to go out of your comfort zone but I believe that over time it will be worth it.

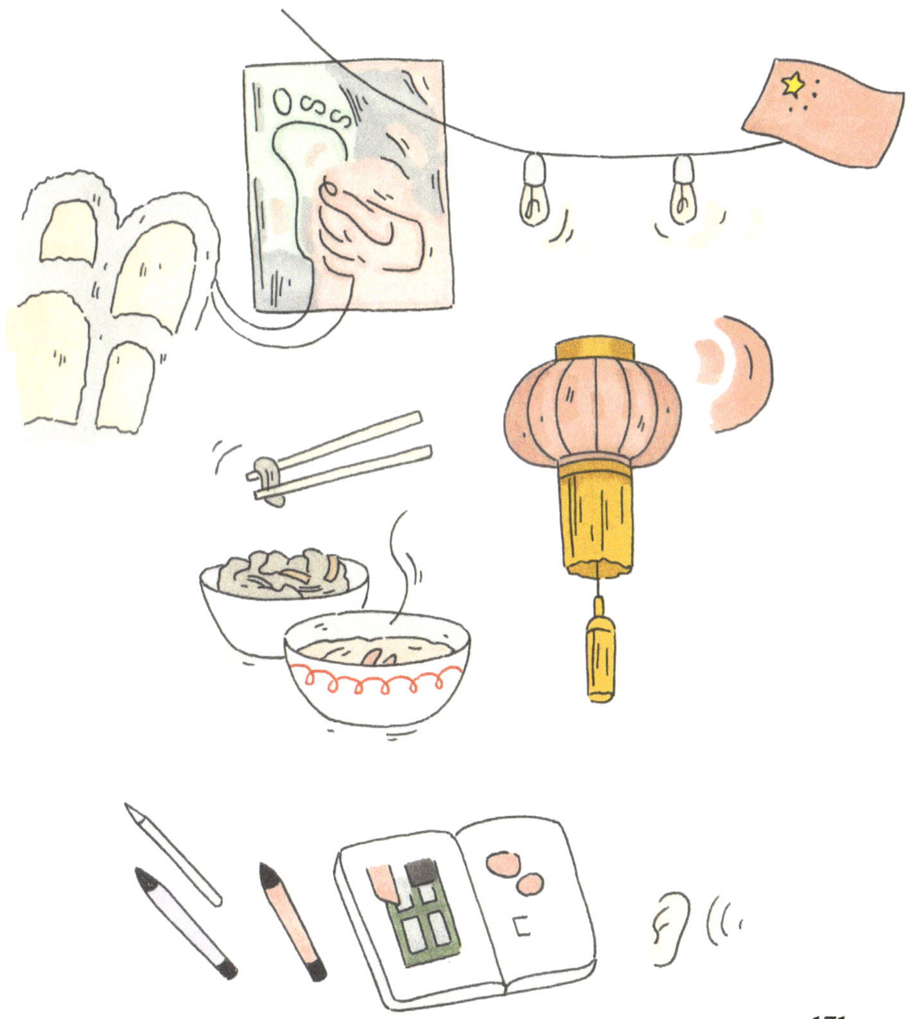

EXERCISE XII

Illustrating movies

Here is a list of good movies which you probably have seen. Illustrate them any way you feel and then look at my versions on the next pages. Try to capture the movies by depicting the main characters, objects which impact the story, or memories you may have from watching them.

1. “Interstellar” (2014) by Christopher Nolan
2. “Spirited away” (2001) by Hayao Miyazaki
3. “Star Wars: Episode IV — A New Hope” (1977) by George Lucas
4. “Back to the Future” (1985) by Robert Zemeckis
5. “WALL·E” (2008) by Andrew Stanton
6. “The Grand Budapest Hotel” (2014) by Wes Anderson

Some of these movies I watched while keeping my Drawing Journal, some I drew especially for this exercise. If you haven’t seen something from this list, you can replace it with one of your favorite movies or you can watch them and then draw your impressions. Here is a space on the next three pages for your drawings.

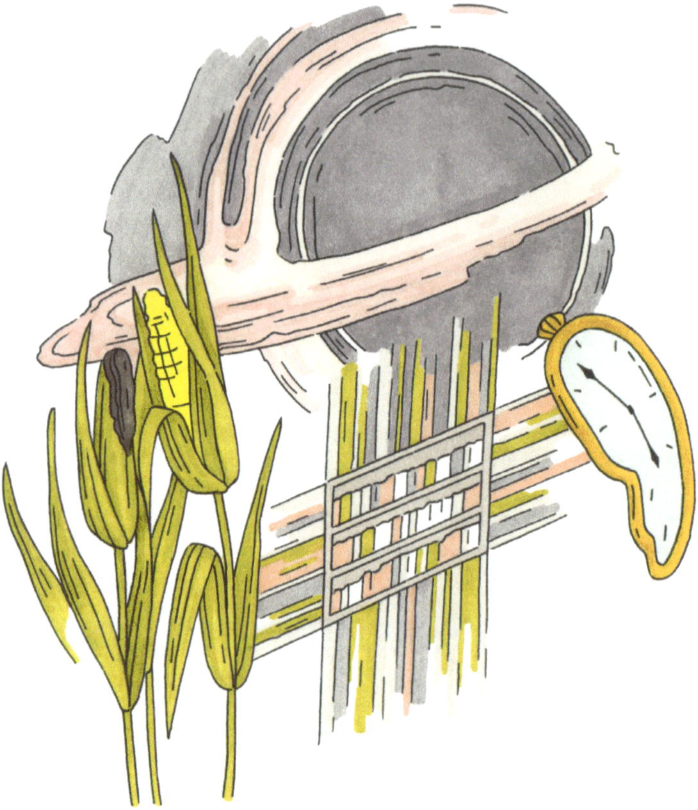

“Interstellar” (2014)
by Christopher Nolan

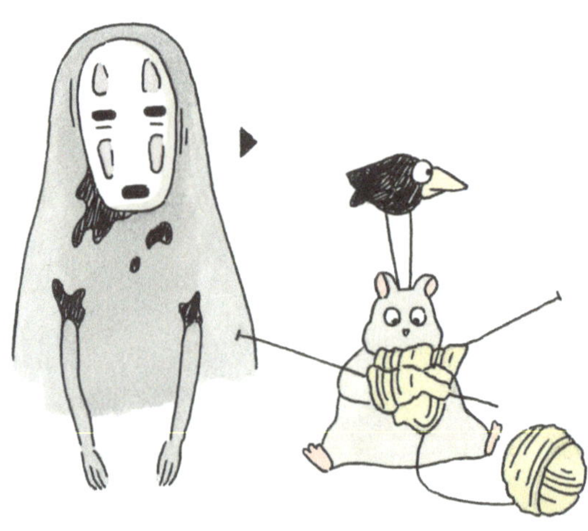

“Spirited away” (2001)
by Hayao Miyazaki

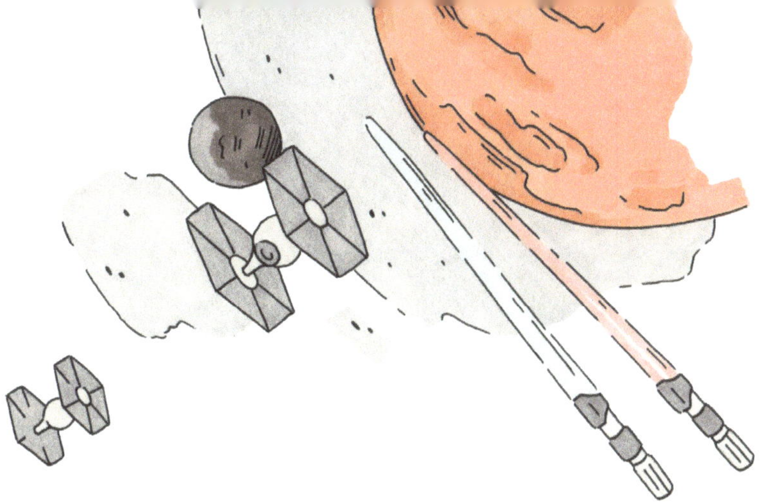

“Star Wars: Episode IV — A New Hope” (1977)
by George Lucas

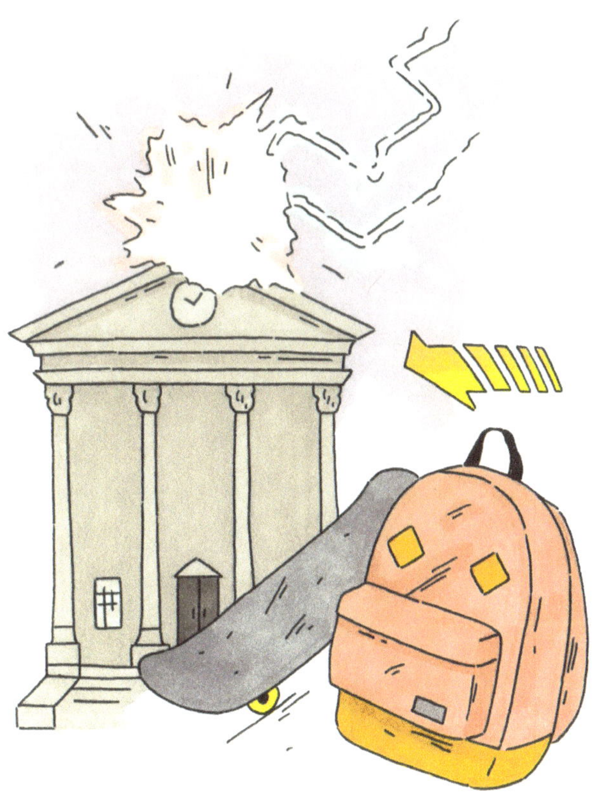

“Back to the Future” (1985)
by Robert Zemeckis

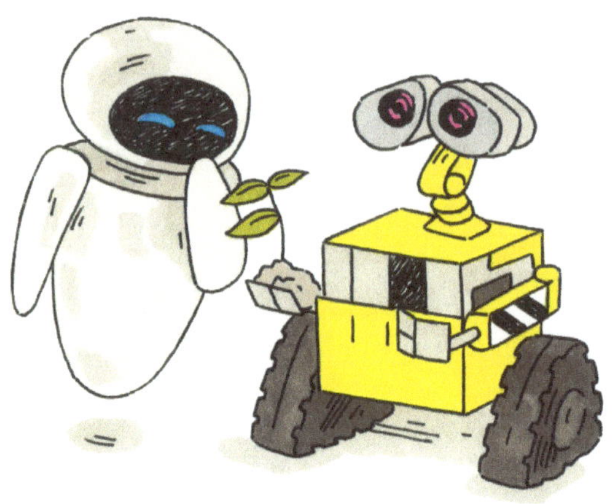

"WALL·E" (2008)
by Andrew Stanton

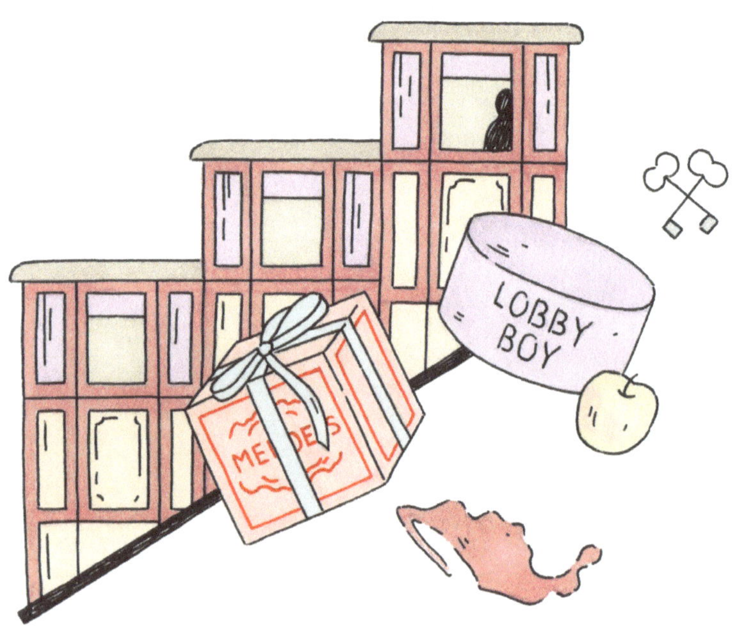

"The Grand Budapest Hotel" (2014)
by Wes Anderson

Draw the same object different ways

If you're having a hard time finding a diverse set of elements and events, try drawing your routine objects in a different way each time.

For example, I often have lunch at the same Indian place.
If I drew my lunches the same way every day it would become way too boring. So I came up with a few versions of it. This cafe has beautiful food serving and an atmospheric corner with plants and a beautiful statue of Ganesha. I combined these objects in my journal so my lunches won't look monotonous.

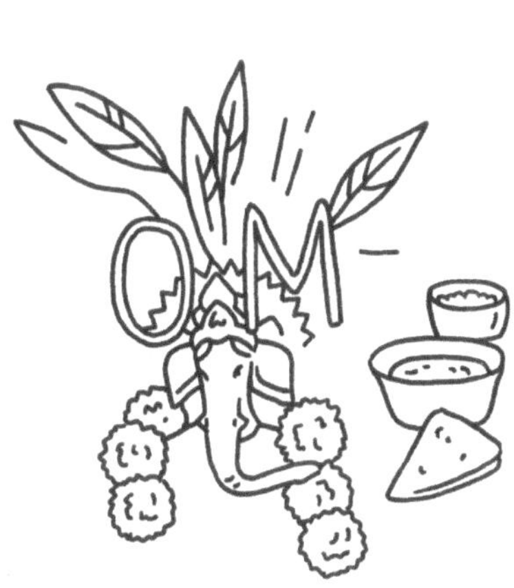

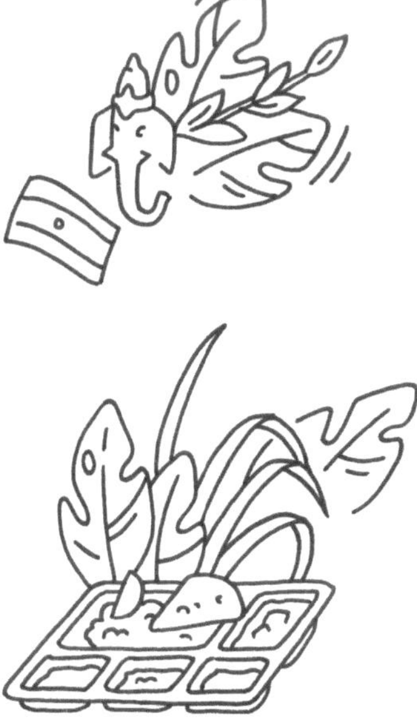

Various interpretations of having a lunch in the same Indian place from the first year of my daily drawing practice

EXERCISE XIII

Drawing a few interpretations of one object

Choose an object or an event you encounter daily. Create 3 versions of it and draw them here.

What to do with mistakes

Artists, illustrators and other creative people can stereotypically be perfectionists. We tend to focus on little details and mistakes few people will notice, instead of thinking about the main goal of our project.

Train yourself to not focus on your mistakes and get upset if something goes wrong. You have started a Drawing Journal to inspire yourself, it's normal that in the beginning, you may have difficulties with your drawings. Be patient, take a breath, and relax. These tiny details really mean nothing compared to the big project you are working towards now.

Move on and focus on meaning, not perfection of drawing.

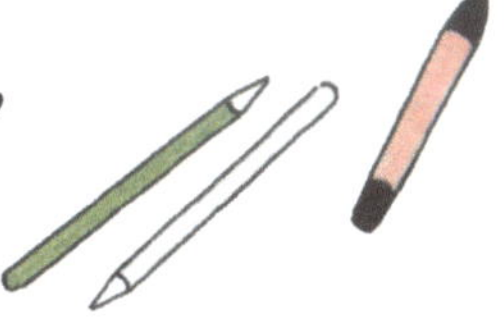

To be honest, I have had this problem in my Drawing Journal too but I've managed to work past my perfectionist tendencies. I used to spend unnecessary time attempting to fix all my mistakes, which most of the time only made the situation worse. Sometimes I'd even redraw everything on a page, which was absolutely not worth it and didn't bring me any joy. Remember, struggle is not what a Drawing Journal is all about. Just keep drawing.

If it's impossible to ignore, there are a few ways to fix a mistake easily. Try covering a mistake with a dark color in the shape of something relevant to the context. It can be an abstract shape, circle or square. If that doesn't work try covering a mistake with a collage.

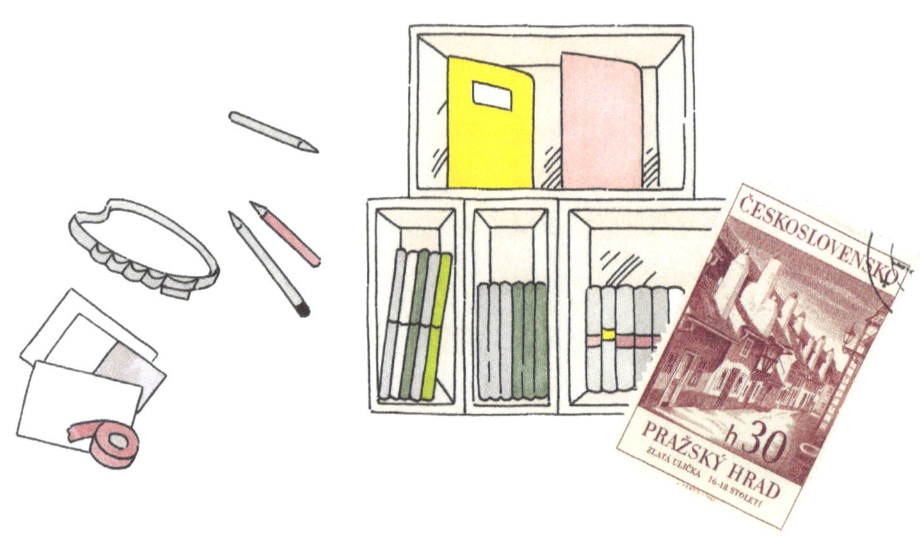

How to find time to draw

People often ask me how I manage to draw every day while having a full-time job and freelance projects. I admit that it's not always easy, but with practice and patience, it's possible.

I often draw my day in the evening, right after dinner. This is a perfect time for me because the events of the day are still fresh in my mind, I can reflect on the day, and I can think about what I would like to do tomorrow. We all have a couple of hours during which we just rest, watch TV, or hang out with family and friends. I just added my daily drawing ritual to this time of the day.

The time I spend on drawing usually varies from 20 minutes to a few hours a day. It always depends on the number of events during a day and how often I'm distracted.

Practice

Practicing is the key to becoming better at any skill. A Drawing Journal is no different. When you draw every day, it will become easier for you to recall what happened during the day and draw it. Within a few months, you'll be quicker, more decisive, and in tune with the process. You just need time to get used to it. Be patient and continue on.

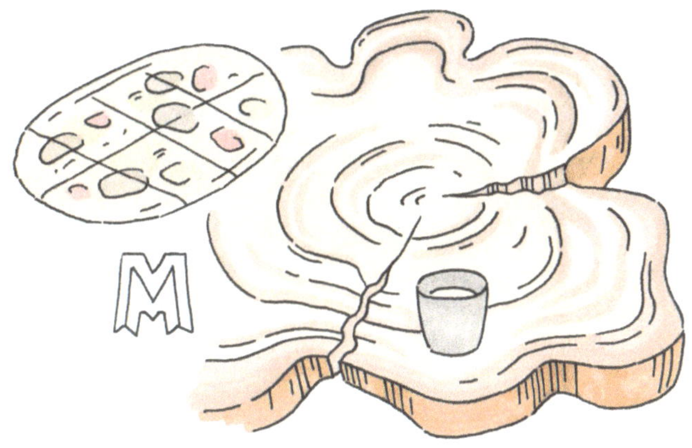

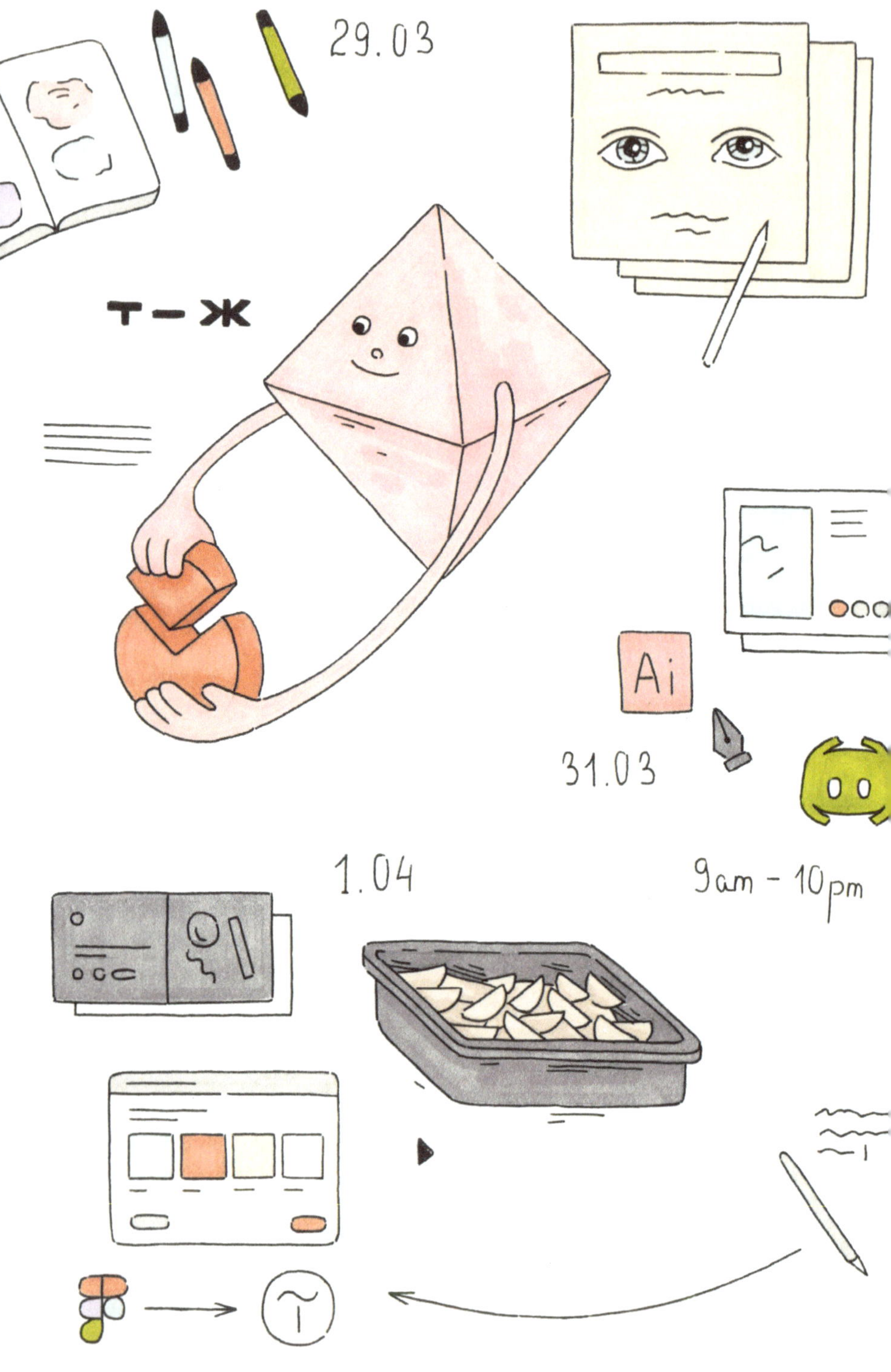
29.03
Т–Ж
Ai
31.03
1.04
9am - 10pm

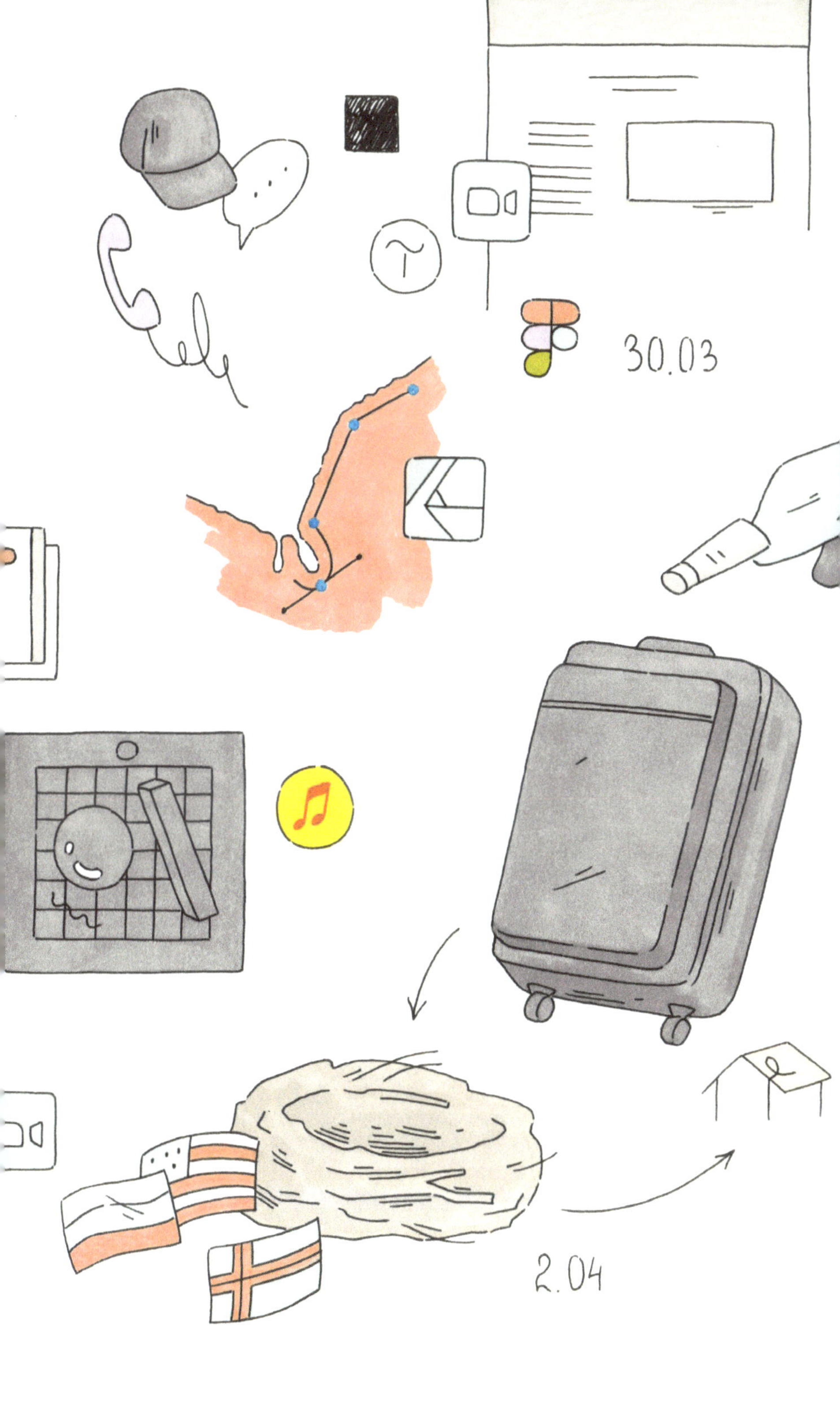
30.03
2.04

Don't complicate drawings

The more complex your drawings — the more time you will need to spend on them. For a Drawing Journal it's important to use a drawing style and materials that have a reasonable balance between being informative, beautiful and fast. Choose easy-to-use materials and don't overload your drawings with details, shading, hatching, or an excess of colors.

The most important thing is to express your memories and enjoy the process of drawing, rather than being stressed trying to complete beautiful but complex drawings.

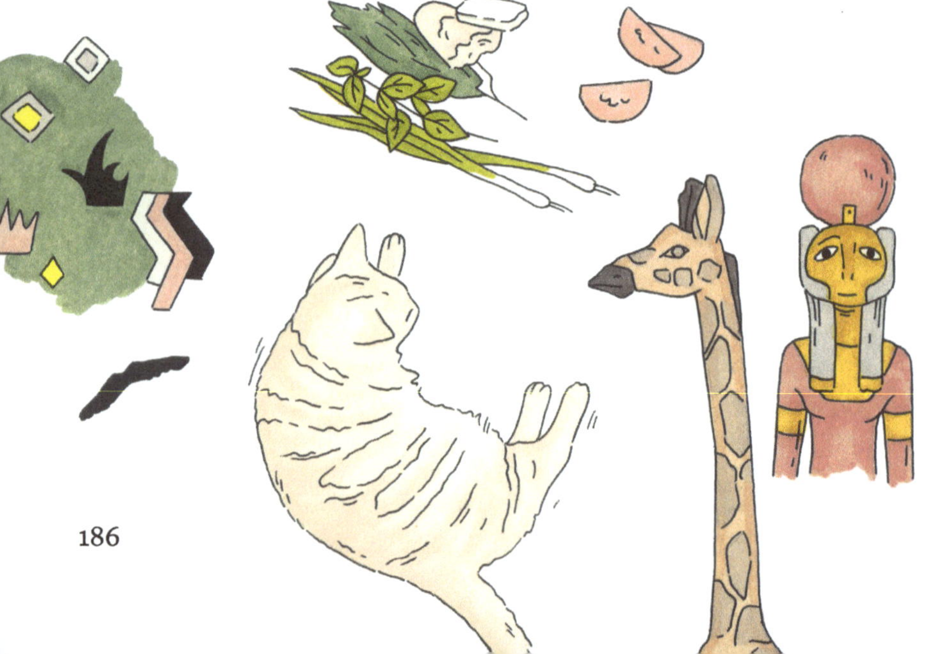

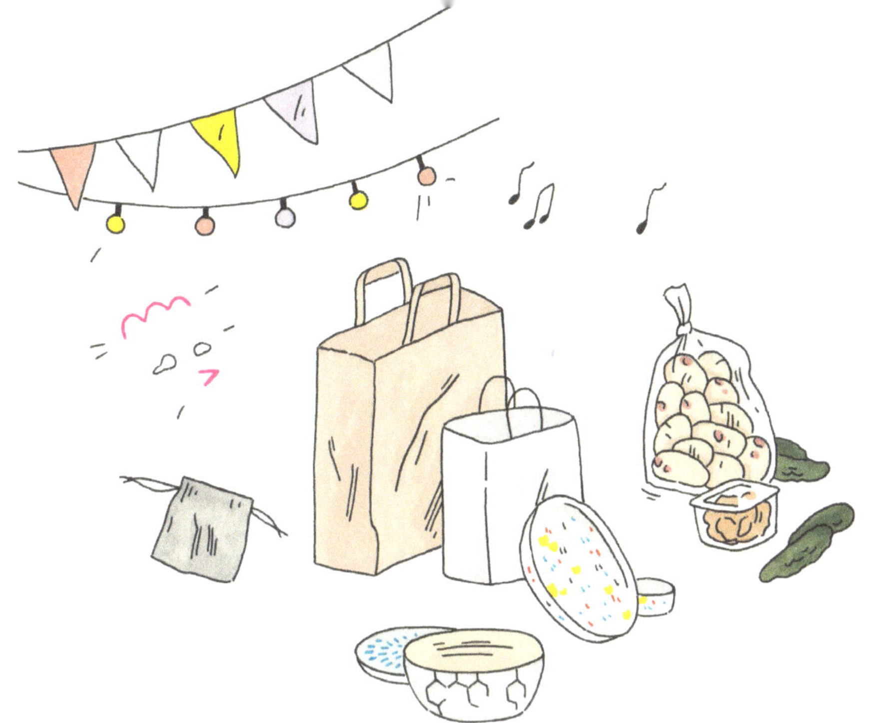

Combine drawing with other activities

The easiest way to find time for regular drawing in a busy schedule is to combine this activity with your other daily businesses and routines that you already have.

Draw during meals, while on the subway or bus, while spending time with friends and family, while watching TV, while listening to podcasts or while waiting for someone or something.

Over time my drawings have become quite complex. First I draw with a pencil then I add color with markers and finish it with a black pen. I enjoy it but when there are a lot of things going on, it's hard to complete drawings right away. I recently started a new routine to help me overcome this. I delay drawing with a pen to save time in the evening. At the end of a day, I draw with pencil and color markers and during lunch at the office the next day I complete it with a pen. It saves me time and gives me an opportunity to pleasantly break up the workday.

Draw little by little during a day

Sometimes during the day, you may have 5-10 minutes breaks. This time can be spent on depicting interesting moments right away or, at least, making sketches of what you are going to draw later.

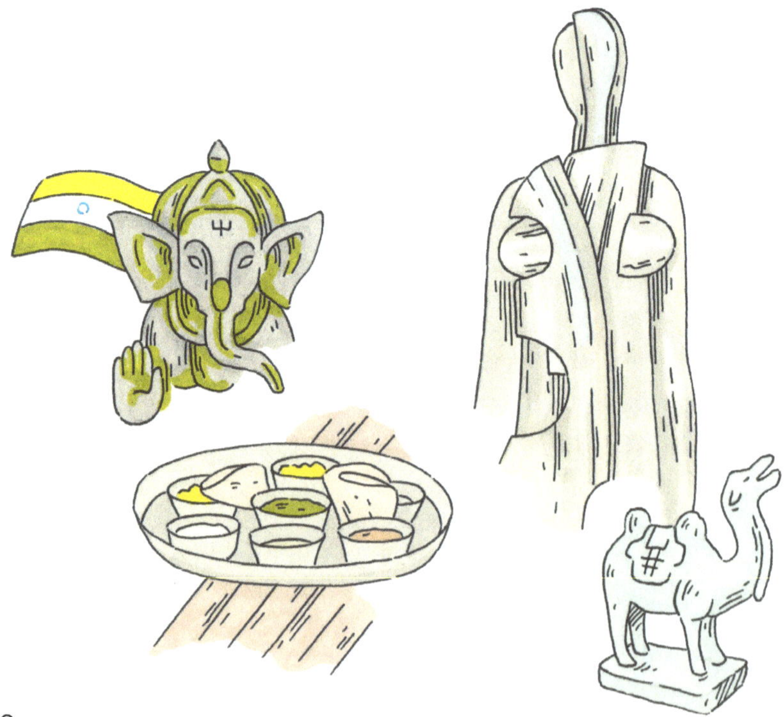

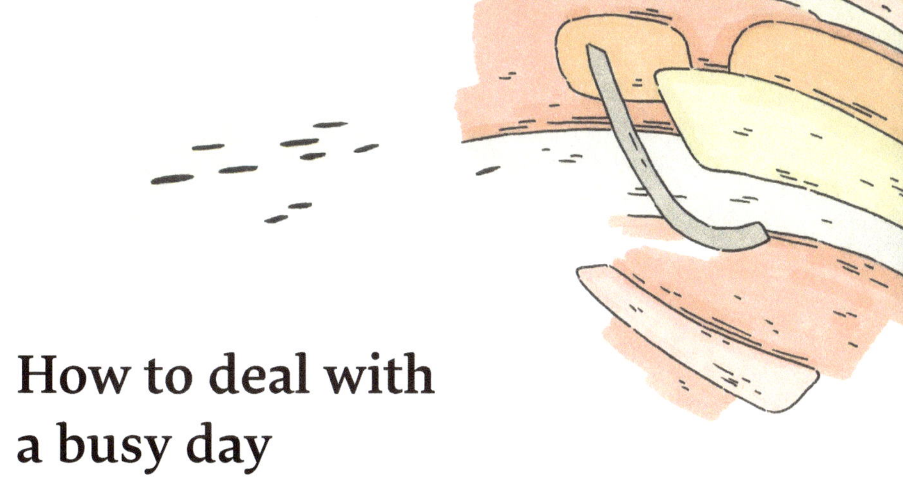

How to deal with a busy day

Sometimes you may not have an opportunity or energy to draw. You may have had a tense day or maybe there have just been so many moments that you'd like to draw you don't have the time to create them all. I came up with a few scenarios to help you in these situations.

Draw it on the next day

If you are too tired or don't have time in the evening, postpone drawing until the next morning. Go to bed and try to wake up a little bit earlier and have a nice cozy morning with drawing and contemplation. Sometimes this option is even better because you are fresh and full of energy.

Lately, especially during weekends, I intentionally postpone my drawing to the next morning when I feel more relaxed and able to enjoy the process. I believe these feelings show themselves through the quality of my drawings.

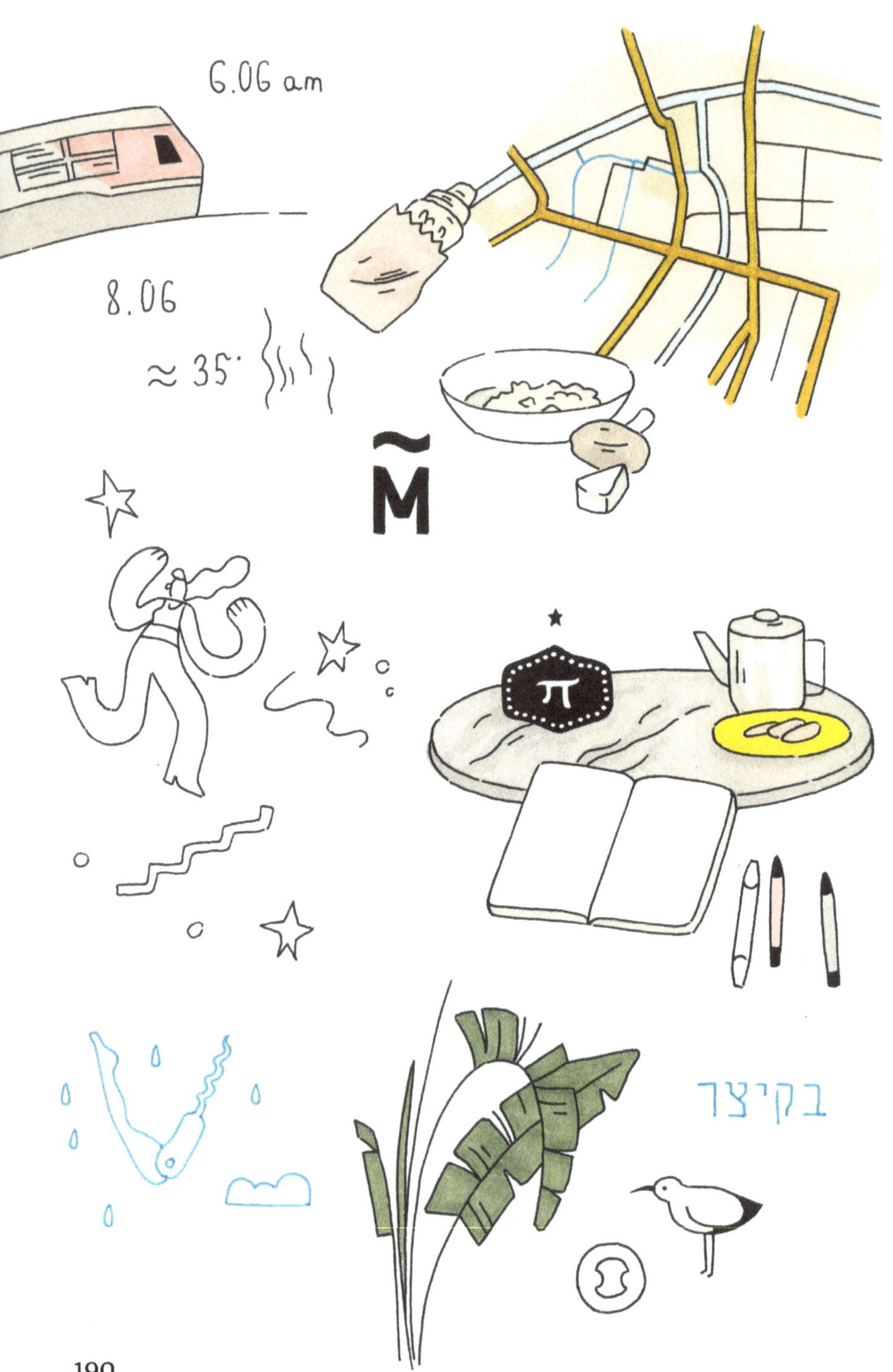
6.06 am
8.06
≈ 35°
M̃
π
בקיצר

Be brief

It's OK to cut moments of your day if you don't have enough time and energy to draw them all. Just draw a few or even one key memory of a day so it would help you to remember the complete day later.

Take quick notes and photos

Taking notes is useful not only at the start of the project but also when you feel like you have no time to actually do the project. I find that it's not a problem to remember the events of one day but if you have a lot going on or you're afraid you'll forget something, just take quick notes and photos of what you want to draw later.

Skip a day

You shouldn't feel that skipping a day is a disaster that ruins the whole project. There is no pleasure in forcing yourself to do something. Just take a break and draw the next day with newfound vigor.

How to deal with a few busy days

It is inevitable that there will be a period when you feel overwhelmed, and it will be difficult to give proper attention to your Drawing Journal. I find this happens when I'm very busy at work or am on a long trip.

If I wouldn't have been taking photos of my impressions during my trip across Europe I wouldn't be able to capture everything I want. For example, like this small house I saw in Memmingen, Germany.

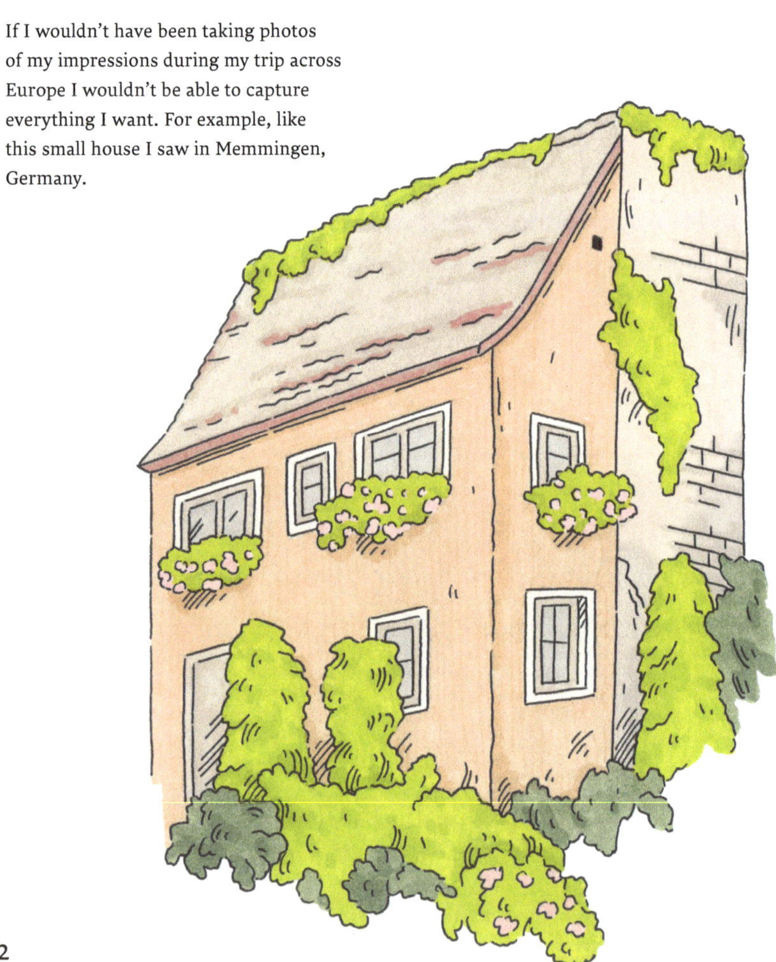

In these situations, you can use all tips from the previous section but if you have a strong desire not to skip days, it's vital to make more notes and photos than you might normally. Otherwise, in a few days, you won't be able to remember all the important events and details.

What if you miss a day?

If you don't have the opportunity to take notes or photos, or you simply don't have the desire, just skip it. Don't think of skipping a day as the end of the project, move on and try again tomorrow. Nobody is going to have a perfect record, especially when you are building a new habit. Why should you let one misstep destroy all the progress you've made?

During my years of keeping a daily Drawing Journal, I've had many moments where I've had to skip a day. During one especially stressful month, I couldn't draw at all for ten days in a row. To make matters worse, I had filled every page of my last sketchbook and I didn't have the opportunity to buy a new one. So even if I had wanted to start up again, I couldn't (This is when I learned to buy a few sketchbooks ahead of time for future use).

I had to sit back and accept that I was having a rough time. I took a little rest, bought missing supplies and returned to my project with new energy and excitement. This is when

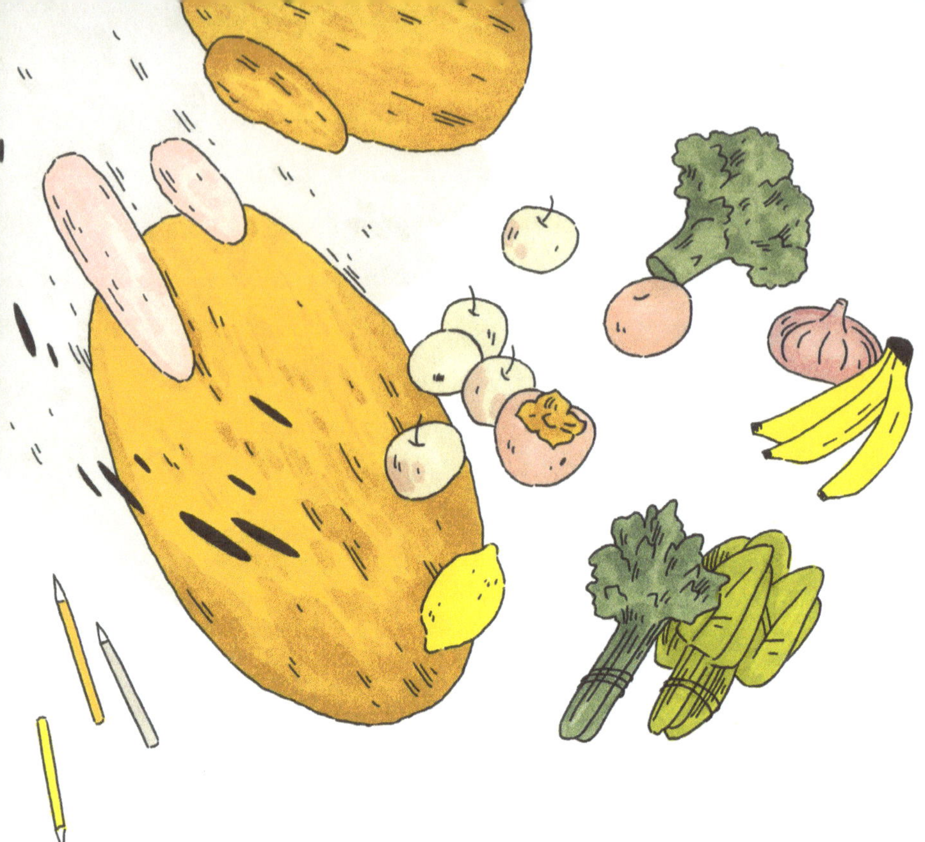

I refreshed the style of my drawings by adding color and making the composition more spacious. The lesson here is that, in the end, this pause helped me to grow and improve my project.

How not abandon your Drawing Journal

Repeating the same routine every day can be exhausting, and drawing can start to weigh you down. Here are a few tips which help me to keep engaged every day.

Make it diverse

Don't be afraid to experiment. If you start becoming annoyed, change your drawing style, technique or approach.

After you have been drawing daily for a while, your drawing skills will improve and you can confidently go to the next level and make your drawings more complex. Speaking from experience, my drawing style has changed a few times already. It has developed from crowded line drawings to spacious colored ones with details and shadows. I like that I don't know what the next stage will be — new ideas come unexpectedly and sometimes a style changes unintentionally by itself.

When you experiment, remember that it's often better to develop a style and technique that will be taking a small amount of time to use it to draw your day completely. Otherwise, you will not be able to draw every day at a comfortable pace.

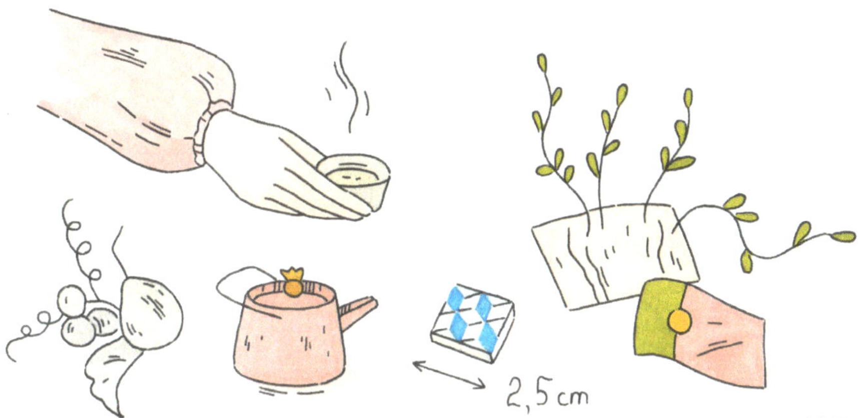

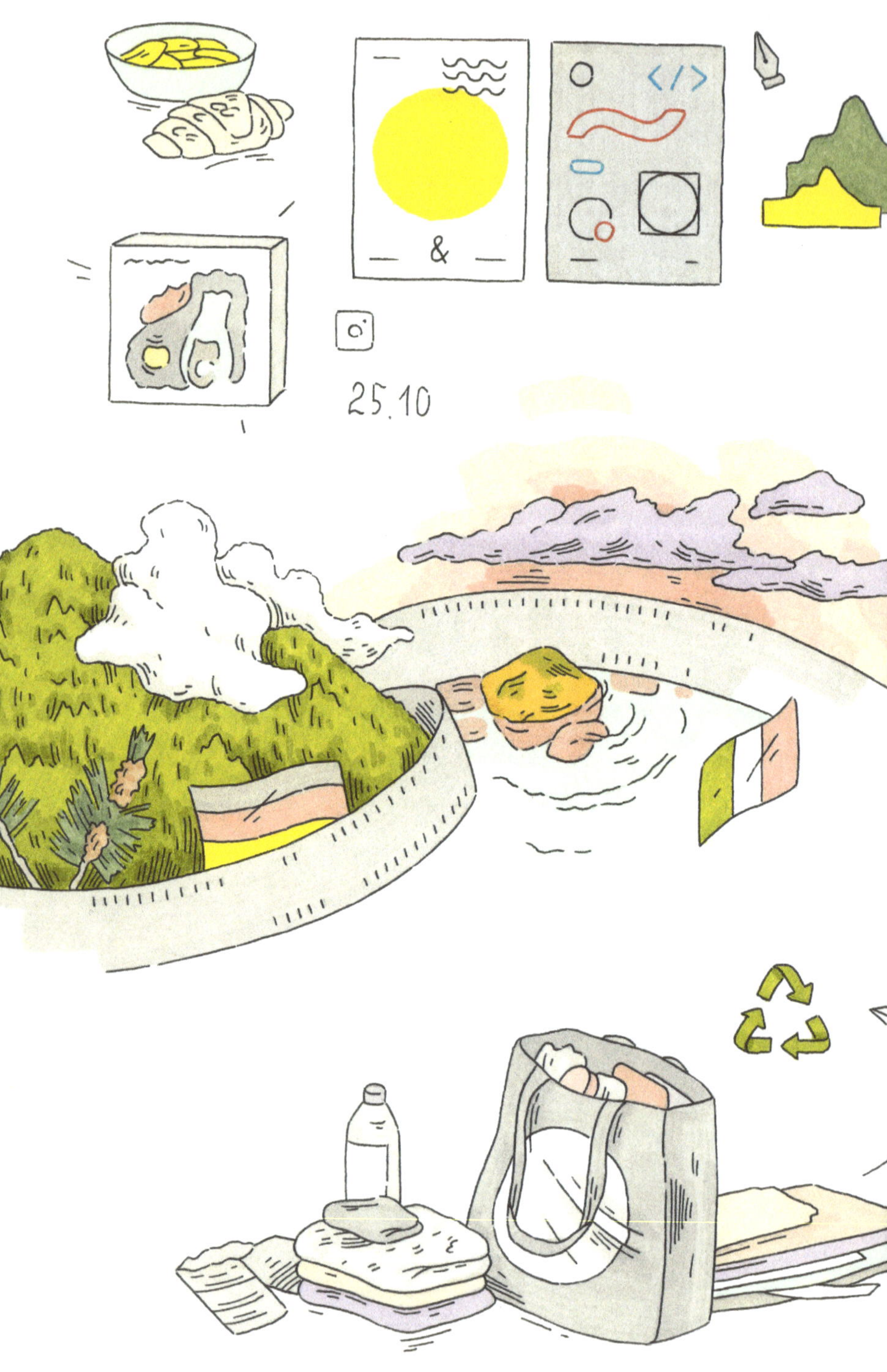
&
</>
25.10

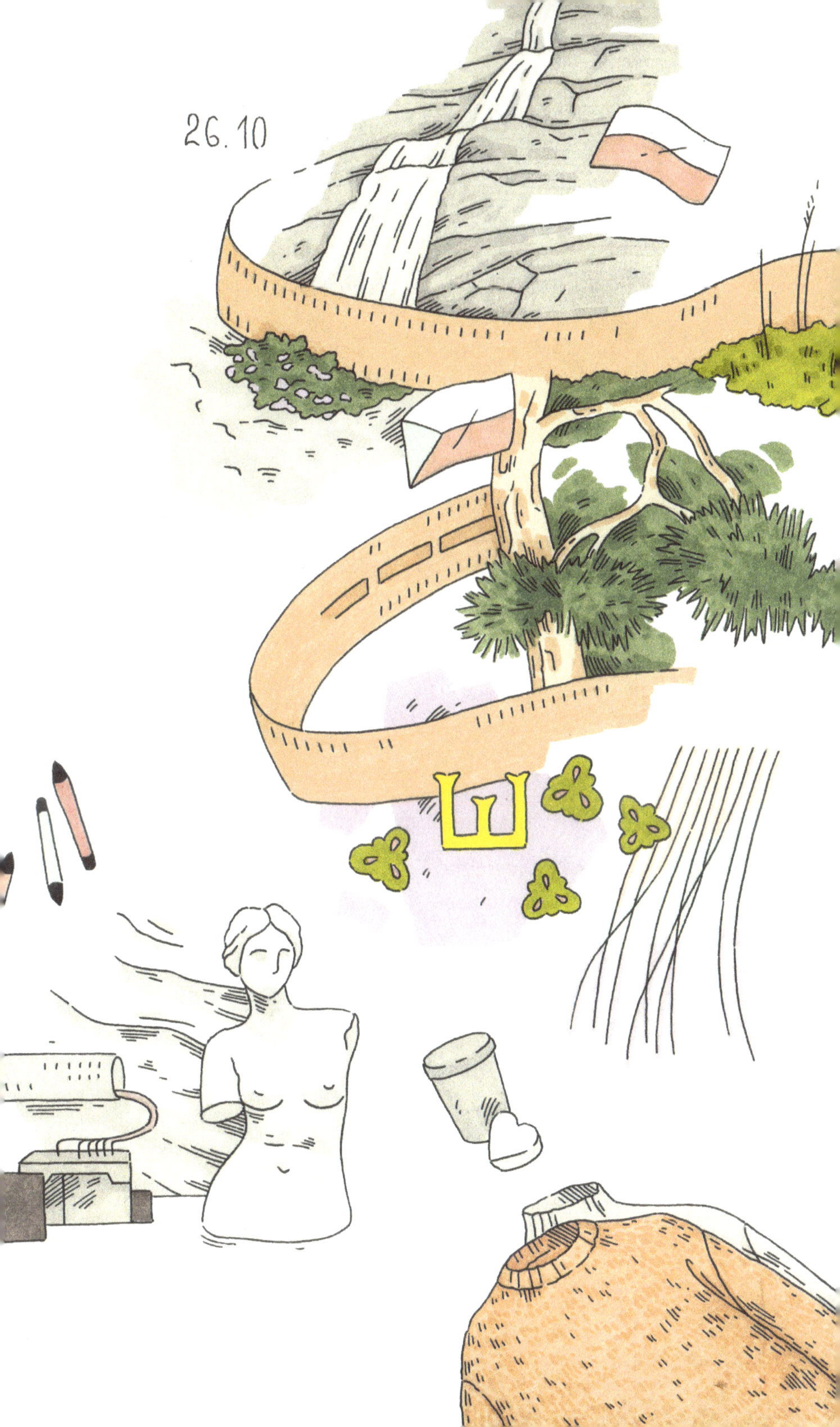
26.10
Ш

Change your drawing materials

Choose a different sketchbook format or start to draw with different drawing instruments. If you were using a pencil — try a pen, ink or something else. Add color pencils or markers if you had only black and white drawings. Add collage elements to your drawings.

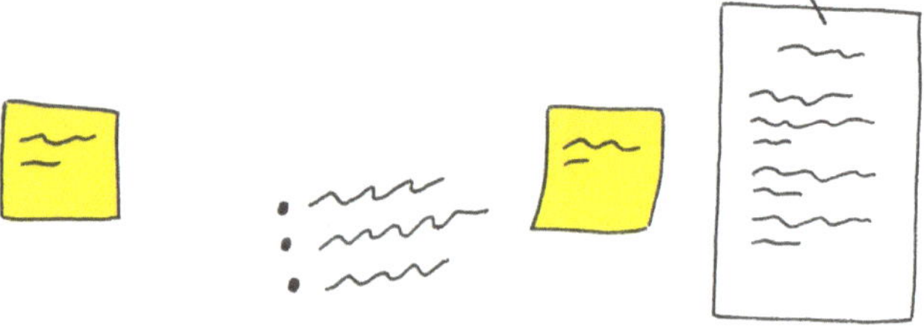

Remind yourself why you started

When you started this project there must have been a few reasons which inspired you to try it. Think of them and the sense of accomplishment you will feel after you've keep your Drawing Journal for a significant period of time.

You can write these reasons down in your sketchbook or pin them above your working table so you look at them regularly.

For myself, I can't say that I have specific reasons to draw my life every day, I just feel that this practice makes my life better, it's as simple as that.

Reward yourself

You have been doing such a great job already with disciplining yourself to draw every day and accomplishing your goals. Make yourself little gifts when you cross significant drawing daily dates — the first week, month, 3 months and so on. It will encourage you to keep going and it will be clearer that you are making progress.

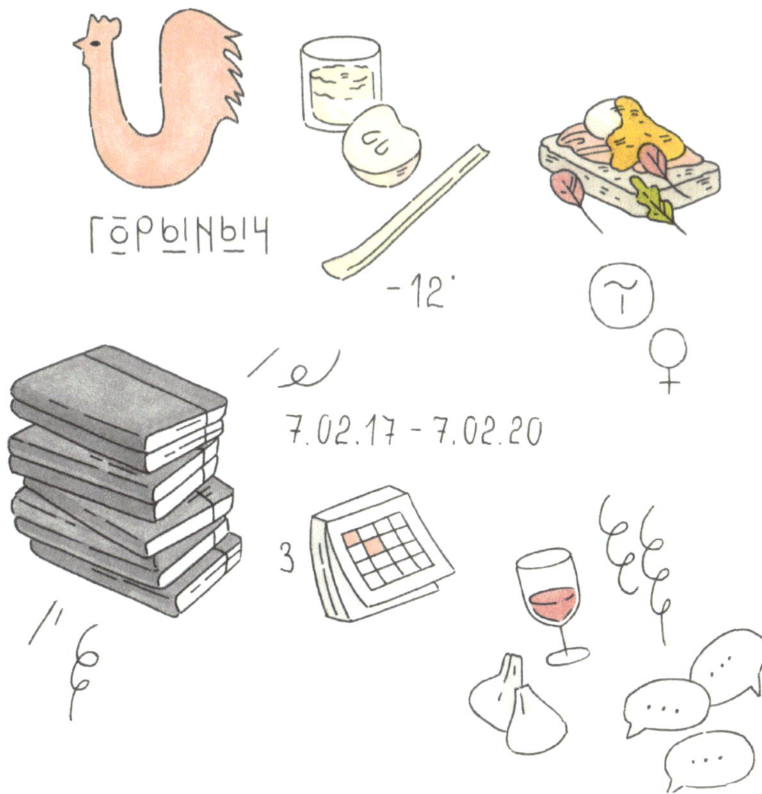

The illustration of the day when I was selebrating 3 years of daily drawing. In the morning I've had a nice breakfast with my colleagues, and after work I've spent the wonderful evening with my friends.

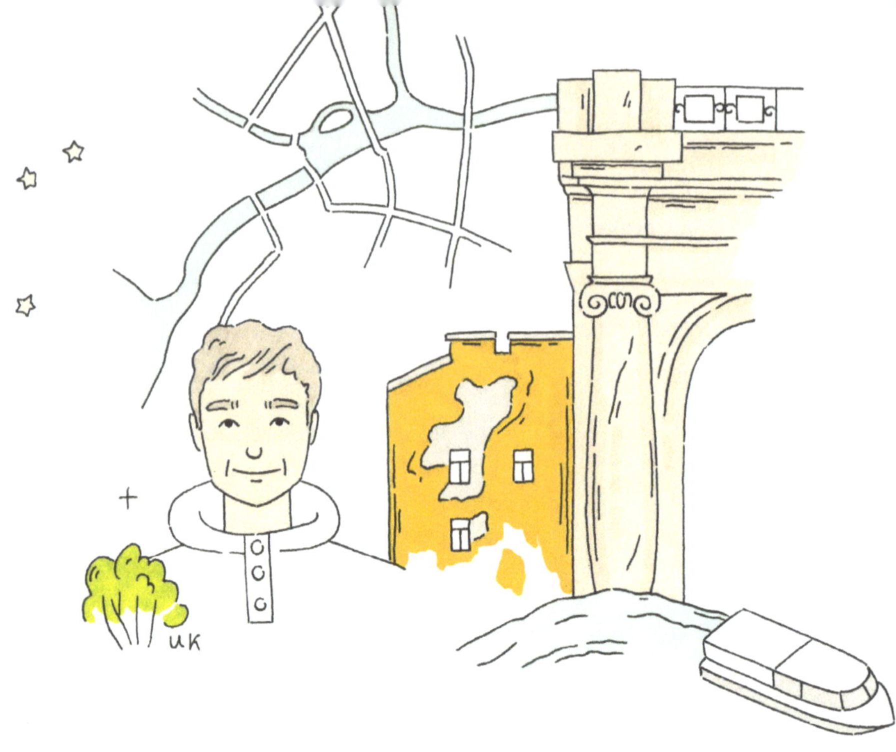

Create a habit-tracker

For some people, it might be motivational to keep a habit-tracker. A habit-tracker is a checklist that helps to build a regular habit by checking off the days you've kept on track. It can be a good way to see how many days you have already kept your new habit and how many days are left to reach the next milestone.

Check each day you draw off in your habit tracker. This will help you to stay motivated as it becomes an ingrained habit.

Here is a habit-tracker for 365 days which you can use to develop your new habit of drawing daily. Don't forget to celebrate each accomplishment!

The habit-tracker for 365 days

1 ○ ○ ○ ○ ○ ○ ○
2 ○ ○ ○ ○ ○ ○ ○
3 ○ ○ ○ ○ ○ ○ ○
4 ○ ○ ○ ○ ○ ○ ○
5 ○ ○ ○ ○ ○ ○ ○
6 ○ ○ ○ ○ ○ ○ ○
7 ○ ○ ○ ○ ○ ○ ○
8 ○ ○ ○ ○ ○ ○ ○
9 ○ ○ ○ ○ ○ ○ ○
10 ○ ○ ○ ○ ○ ○ ○
11 ○ ○ ○ ○ ○ ○ ○
12 ○ ○ ○ ○ ○ ○ ○
13 ○ ○ ○ ○ ○ ○ ○

14 ○ ○ ○ ○ ○ ○ ○
15 ○ ○ ○ ○ ○ ○ ○
16 ○ ○ ○ ○ ○ ○ ○
17 ○ ○ ○ ○ ○ ○ ○
18 ○ ○ ○ ○ ○ ○ ○
19 ○ ○ ○ ○ ○ ○ ○
20 ○ ○ ○ ○ ○ ○ ○
21 ○ ○ ○ ○ ○ ○ ○
22 ○ ○ ○ ○ ○ ○ ○
23 ○ ○ ○ ○ ○ ○ ○
24 ○ ○ ○ ○ ○ ○ ○
25 ○ ○ ○ ○ ○ ○ ○
26 ○ ○ ○ ○ ○ ○ ○

27 ○ ○ ○ ○ ○ ○ ○
28 ○ ○ ○ ○ ○ ○ ○
29 ○ ○ ○ ○ ○ ○ ○
30 ○ ○ ○ ○ ○ ○ ○
31 ○ ○ ○ ○ ○ ○ ○
32 ○ ○ ○ ○ ○ ○ ○
33 ○ ○ ○ ○ ○ ○ ○
34 ○ ○ ○ ○ ○ ○ ○
35 ○ ○ ○ ○ ○ ○ ○
36 ○ ○ ○ ○ ○ ○ ○
37 ○ ○ ○ ○ ○ ○ ○
38 ○ ○ ○ ○ ○ ○ ○
39 ○ ○ ○ ○ ○ ○ ○

40 ○ ○ ○ ○ ○ ○ ○
41 ○ ○ ○ ○ ○ ○ ○
42 ○ ○ ○ ○ ○ ○ ○
43 ○ ○ ○ ○ ○ ○ ○
44 ○ ○ ○ ○ ○ ○ ○
45 ○ ○ ○ ○ ○ ○ ○
46 ○ ○ ○ ○ ○ ○ ○
47 ○ ○ ○ ○ ○ ○ ○
48 ○ ○ ○ ○ ○ ○ ○
49 ○ ○ ○ ○ ○ ○ ○
50 ○ ○ ○ ○ ○ ○ ○
51 ○ ○ ○ ○ ○ ○ ○
52 ○ ○ ○ ○ ○ ○ ○ ○

Take a break from your Drawing Journal

If, despite all these tactics, you still feel tired of this project and don't want to continue, take a break from daily drawing. It's important to balance the necessity and joy of drawing. If you stop enjoying this process, it will be the end of your project. You can return to it whenever you feel ready or even not return at all. It's possible that the Drawing Journal gave you everything it could and it's time to move on and develop your creativity in another way.

CHAPTER IX

Conclusion

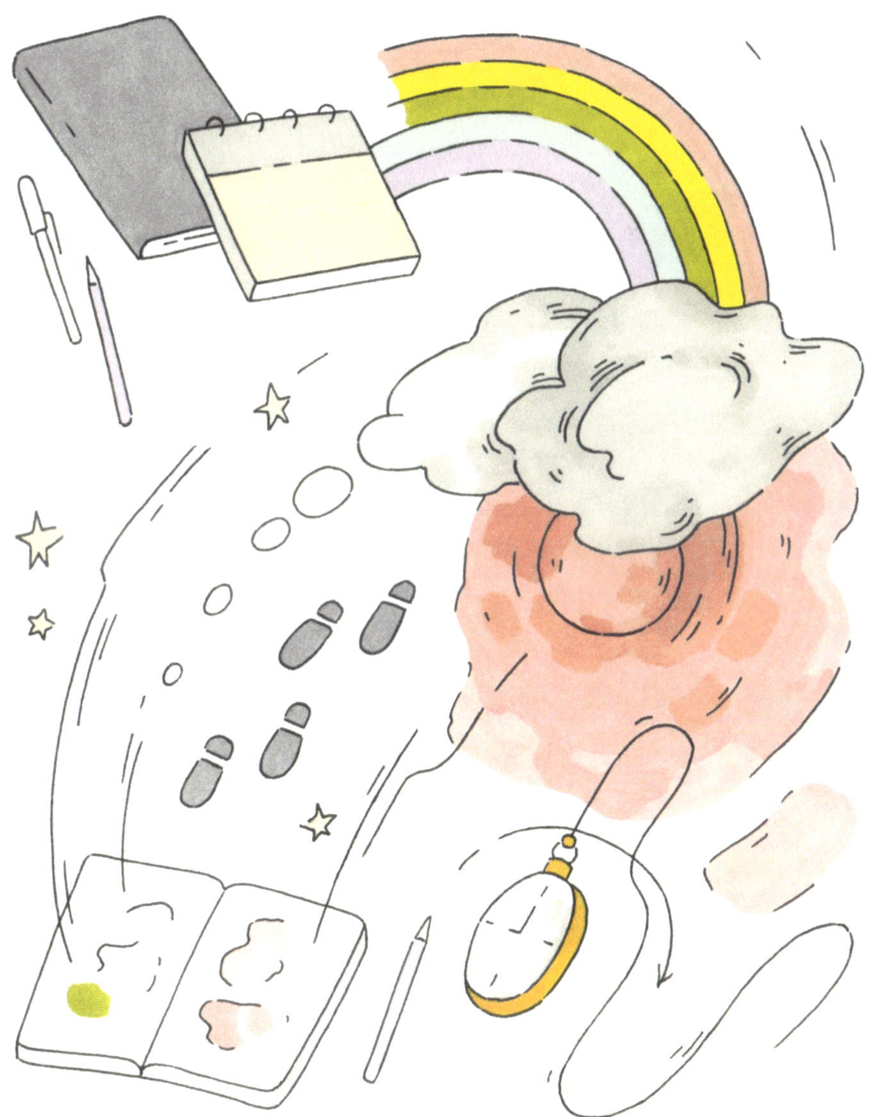

The beauty of a Drawing Journal is in its vast opportunities and ways to capture your impressions. It's not expecting high drawing skills and masterpieces. It doesn't require a lot of time and energy. It just gives you exactly what you need, and only in your way.

Don't downplay your capabilities and don't think that you might fail. You can always change the regularity, format or style of your Drawing Journal. Just start capturing your impressions and see how it works for you.

A Drawing Journal is a beautiful journey for your mind and soul. And I sincerely hope that it will illuminate your life, give a lot of food for contemplation and will open unexpected wonders of daily drawing.

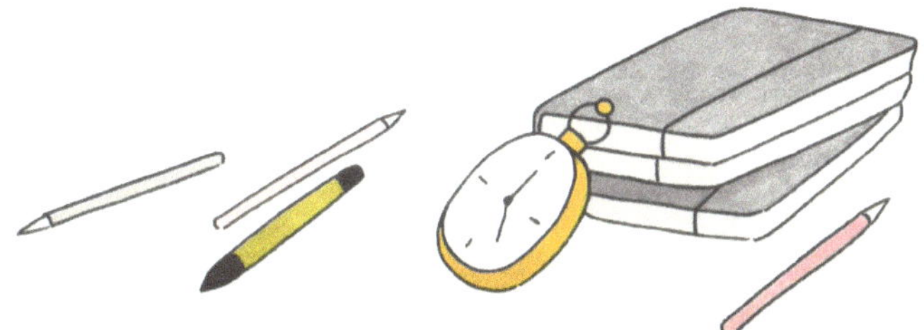

Thank you page

This book would have never been born if not for my family and friends who helped and inspired me during this path.

I want to thank my parents Lidiia Fedorova, Sergey Zass, and my stepdad Konstantin Krasikov who were always supporting me and nurturing my artistic skills.

I thank my friends Kristine Rusakova, Tanya Orlova, Yana Plustcheva, and Masha Belaya for being next to me, inspiring me to keep drawing and pushing me to finish the book.

I want to thank my friends Dmitriy Orlov, Liza Kazantseva, Anya Mochalova, Tanya Skornyakova, Aziza Kireyeva, Masha Kuzmina, Grisha Egorov, Sergey Orlov, and Alexandr Orlov. They read the draft of the book and gave me valuable advice on how to make it better.

I thank my publisher Joshua Sanabria who supported me through the whole process of creating the book and made this all happen. He has patiently waited for me to correct every tiny detail and finish the book beyond all the deadlines we anticipated.

Lightning Source UK Ltd.
Milton Keynes UK
UKHW050419161221
395685UK00001B/14
* 9 7 8 1 7 3 2 9 4 5 1 9 7 *